'At Togakushi' (Nagano Prefecture).

LONDON SCHOOL OF ECONOMICS
MONOGRAPHS ON SOCIAL ANTHROPOLOGY
No. 32

KINSHIP
AND ECONOMIC
ORGANIZATION IN
RURAL JAPAN

BY

CHIE NAKANE

UNIVERSITY OF LONDON
THE ATHLONE PRESS
NEW YORK: HUMANITIES PRESS INC.
1967

Published by
THE ATHLONE PRESS
UNIVERSITY OF LONDON
at 2 Gower Street London WC1
Distributed by Constable & Co Ltd
12 *Orange Street London* WC2

Canada
Oxford University Press
Toronto

© *Chie Nakane,* 1967

Library of Congress Catalog Card No. 66-10915

Printed in Great Britain by
ROBERT CUNNINGHAM AND SONS LTD
ALVA

PREFACE

In this essay I present the principles of one important sector of social organization in Japan, and establish its framework.

Japan is a difficult setting for anthropological study because of the enormous diversity and complex integration of the social factors involved. Japanese kinship structure, with its multiple historical and local factors, and unlike that of the Chinese or of the Hindus, does not belong to the category of unilineal systems, nor to any kind of descent pattern found in the published literature of social anthropology. Social anthropology, developed by micro-synchronic studies of simpler societies, and with its major analysis devoted to descent systems, has to face in Japan a critical methodological test. In this essay, I, as a social anthropologist, want to overcome these drawbacks of anthropological method, and to demonstrate one of the new approaches by which an anthropologist can cope with the data from a sophisticated society. I also wish to show how social anthropology can contribute to a field normally dealt with by sociologists, historians and economists.

The materials on which this discussion is based come from a vast amount of data covering various rural areas in Japan as well as more than three centuries of time (from the beginning of the Tokugawa period to the present day). These data partly arise from micro-sociological studies carried out by Japanese scholars during the last fifty years. There are a number of interesting studies of Japanese rural society carried out by American anthropologists, including the important pioneering work of the late J. F. Embree (see Bibliography III). However, my concern here is with the Japanese literature, written in the vernacular by Japanese sociologists, economic historians and other social scientists, and containing a wealth of material not yet fully analysed by western scholars. The examination of this material in the light of modern methods of social anthropology is my chief concern. (In order to avoid confusion, I do not discuss the differing views and the disputes exhibited by these works, because many are not only irrelevant to issues in current social anthropology, but also cannot be understood without explanation of the Japanese academic climate. Also I discuss rather than present the data, a detailed bibliography of which is given at the end of this book—Bibliography II.) Most of this literature, however, is concerned either with the description of particular ethnographic data, or with ideological interpretations of *the* Japanese family or village structure. Again, many recent works concerned with Japanese kinship use a typological approach, being interested in local varieties of custom in which kinship is taken as one of the cultural elements. None of them has attempted systematic theoretical generalization on the basis of a structural analysis of the data concerned with Japanese kinship, which is the major subject of this essay.

I have supplemented the literary materials by a small set of data derived from field observation of my own in several villages in different areas, including two villages where I have been continuing intensive studies: Gorohei-shinden village in Nagano prefecture and Koshiozu village in Aichi prefecture. I take the view that the value of the findings from an individual's own field work is extremely restricted for the purpose of generalization in a society such as that of Japan, whatever may be the intrinsic importance of the data. Hence my own work is integrated with an immensely greater bulk of research published by others. What I am most concerned with in this study is to interpret different, sometimes apparently contradictory, ethnographic data from various areas, and synthesize them for generalization. I think Japan presents a fortunate field for such a study by an anthropologist, because research by historians and economists is available at the local as well as at the state level. I have used these studies, not as a simple addition to anthropological data, but to give more sophistication to my anthropological method, and as an aid to my interpretation of data. I particularly want to call the attention of anthropologists to this since they have tended to interpret Japanese data within a synchronic context only and with comparatively shallow time depth. Indeed, to some extent the results of my analysis contradict conclusions arrived at by recent field anthropologists who have dealt with Japanese social organization.

I focus upon a couple of major problems which are in my view the most significant, rather than describe the full configuration of elements. Since the social organization constantly changes, any descriptive picture of a given situation cannot present *the* Japanese social structure. Also, for comparative purposes in a wider historical and geographical context, a certain reduction and selection of elements which comprise a micro-society should be made. Hence, a total descriptive picture of a micro-society is neither the starting point of my discussion nor the model image of Japanese society.

I approach the central problems intentionally through the *household* and *local corporate group* of the rural community, whose economy is based on irrigated rice cultivation. In Japan for centuries past the greater part of the population has lived by this traditional pattern of agriculture. The reason I use *household* and *local corporate group* instead of family and descent group, in the conventional anthropological manner, is that the data from Japan have dictated this. By this approach I expect to uncover problems which those social anthropologists who have concentrated their interest on kinship study have tended to overlook. Theoretically these corporate groups are not kin groups, and though they involve kinship elements, economic factors and local political power-relations are more important. That is why the title of this book is '*Kinship and Economic Organization in Rural Japan*', instead of simply *kinship organization*.

The discussion will deal in detail with one form of local corporate group known as *dōzoku* in Japanese sociology. The *dōzoku* has had fairly wide geographical distribution in agricultural villages in many areas of Japan, with considerable time depth—roughly two hundred years. Research by Japanese social scientists on social organization during the last thirty years shows a fairly strong concentration of interest on the subject.

Apart from this richness of material, the reason why I have chosen this particular form of local grouping for study is that it has been found in the middle and upper strata of village populations, strata which are involved in land ownership and property transmission. This *dōzoku* is a somewhat similar institution to the lineage of China in its functional role within a total community structure. I take the view here that a structural principle closely related to kinship appears in the handling of property. Only when a set of individuals related through kinship or other ties is faced with the allotment or transmission of available economic resources does each given society seem to produce regularities by which to react to the situation. In each given society the alternatives for choice are fairly limited within the available range. This kind of regularity has produced a local corporate group in the form of *dōzoku* in Japan, and of lineage organization in China. The difference in the structure of such institutions seems to be due to the underlying kinship principles, and to economic factors.

The reason I have chosen a broad historical range of more than three hundred years is as follows. First, considerable data from this period are available for analysis by the techniques of social anthropology. Secondly, this period shows economic changes at the national level so pervasive that no single village community escaped their influence: the introduction of a commercial economy and of industrialization. Politically also Japanese society in this period was transformed: from the feudal to the modern system of government. Thus it can be observed how the original structure reacted to economic change, and in what way it produced new organizations to adjust to such change. It can be seen also which elements were discarded, which were modified and which were retained unaltered. Japanese social organization can be understood only by the examination of such dynamic processes.

The framework of this study was formed, and the major part of the manuscript was written in 1960–61, when I held a lectureship in the Department of Cultural Anthropology, School of Oriental and African Studies, and was also associated with the Department of Anthropology, London School of Economics and Political Science, University of London. My profound acknowledgements go to my colleagues and students at these institutions, and also to the seminar members in social anthropology at the University of Cambridge and the University of Manchester, with whom I had many stimulating discussions on this subject.

Above all I owe a great deal to Professor C. von Fürer-Haimendorf who kindly gave me all the facilities to do this work while I was in London; and to Professor Raymond Firth, my teacher, whose stimulating suggestions and detailed comments encouraged me to complete this work, and who kindly suggested its publication.

Also I am greatly indebted to Japanese colleagues in different disciplines: particularly to Dr S. Oishi, economic historian, with whom I had the opportunity to conduct field work in the same village, and with whom I have had many stimulating discussions; to Professor K. Ariga, sociologist, who kindly helped me by presenting his unpublished data for my scrutiny; and to Professor M. Fukushima, legal sociologist, and Professor T. Ouchi, agricultural economist, for their kind guidance. My thanks go also to the Institute of Oriental Culture, the University of Tokyo, through whose generous understanding I have had every facility to pursue this work.

My thanks are also due to Professor Ronald Dore, who made useful suggestions and criticisms on the final stages of the manuscript; to Professor Maurice Freedman and Mr Anthony Forge, who were kind enough to check the final typescript; to Mrs D. H. Alfandary for her help with the manuscript.

Finally, a special acknowledgement must be made to Mr Junkichi Mukai, the well-known contemporary Japanese artist, for his most generous help in drawing 'At Togakushi' especially for the frontispiece of this book. It exquisitely captures the atmosphere of a Japanese village.

Tokyo, September 1965   C. N.

CONTENTS

I. BASIC STRUCTURE OF HOUSEHOLD AND
   KINSHIP   I

2. BASIC VILLAGE ORGANIZATION IN HISTORICAL
   PERSPECTIVE   41
   Setting of Rural Japan   41
   Internal Structure of the Village   58

3. ANALYSIS OF LOCAL CORPORATE GROUPS
   WITHIN A VILLAGE   82
   A. *Dōzoku*   82
   B. *Oyako-kankei*   123
   C. *Kumi*   133

4. THE FUNCTION OF MARRIAGE RELATIONS   150

   CONCLUSION   167

   BIBLIOGRAPHY   173

   INDEX   199

CONTENTS

PLATES

'At Togakushi'   *frontispiece*

1. Irrigated paddy fields just after the transplantation
2*a*. Irrigation at Gorohei-shinden village
 b. Thrashing paddy after harvest   *between pages*
3*a*. A farmer's house   *74 and 75*
 b. A young couple working in a greenhouse
4. Transplantation in the Togukawa period

5. Urushi Buraku in Kagoshima prefecture
6. At a gathering of *tanokami-kō* in Urushi *buraku*
7. Record books of the *kō* association of Koshiozu   *between pages*
8*a*. Hiyoshi-jinja, the village shrine of Koshiozu   *138 and 139*
 b. Wedding ceremony at Hii Buraku

MAP

Map of Japan with prefectures   *facing page* 1

FIGURES

1. Plan of a Farmer's House   3
2. Establishment of *shinrui* relations   27
3. Category of kin normally included in *shinrui*   28
4. *Shinrui* in terms of household category   29
5. Japanese kinship terminology   34
6. Major scheme of *Five Categories of Shinzoku*   39
7. Basic scheme of irrigation in Gorohei   78
8. Relations of households of a *dōzoku*   87
9. Basic scheme of relations between households of the *dōzoku*   89
10. Genealogical relations of household heads of Saito *dōzoku*   99
11. Graveyard of Saito *dōzoku*   100
12. Variations of household relations in Saito *dōzoku*   104
13. Household relations in Nishimura *koochi* in Asao   132
14. Marriage relations among four households centred on
    Furukawa household in Koshiozu   165

TABLES

1. Increase and decrease of agricultural population   52
2. Rate of distribution of the yield from tenant wet rice land   55
3. The number of agricultural households by tenure   57
4. Distribution of lands by households of *honbyakushō* and *kakaebyakushō* in Gorohei in 1713   62
5. Number of *kakaebyakushō* grouped by *honbyakushō* in Gorohei in 1758   68
6. Distribution of *kakaebyakushō* grouped by a *honbyakushō* with indication of temple affiliation, in Gorohei in 1758   69
7. Composition of Gorohei village in 1667   70
8. Changing process of the holdings by each household in Saraike during the period between 1644 and 1702   72
9. Distribution of holders by *koku* in Shimo-daiichi in the period 1685–1871   73
10. Distribution of plots by owners, with the number of tenants, in Gorohei in 1771   75
11. Distribution of plots and cultivators according to the water flow in Gorohei in 1771   76
12. Distribution of households in terms of *kumi*, *koochi* and *maki* in Asao   130
13. The basic scheme of the *kō* proceedings in Koshiozu   147

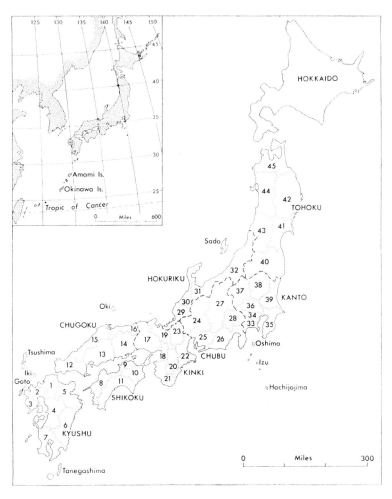

1. Fukuoka	13. Hiroshima	25. Aichi	37. Gunma
2. Saga	14. Okayama	26. Shizuoka	38. Tochigi
3. Nagasaki	15. Shimane	27. Nagano	39. Ibaragi
4. Kumamoto	16. Tottori	28. Yamanashi	40. Fukushima
5. Oita	17. Hyogo	29. Fukui	41. Miyagi
6. Miyazaki	18. Osaka	30. Ishikawa	42. Iwate
7. Kagoshima	19. Kyoto	31. Toyama	43. Yamagata
8. Ehime	20. Nara	32. Niigata	44. Akita
9. Kagawa	21. Wakayama	33. Kanagawa	45. Aomori
10. Tokushima	22. Mie	34. Tokyo	
11. Kochi	23. Shiga	35. Chiba	
12. Yamaguchi	24. Gifu	36. Saitama	

I

Basic Structure of Household and Kinship

CONCEPT OF IE (HOUSEHOLD)

The primary unit of social organization in Japan is the household. In an agrarian community a household has particularly important functions as a distinct body for economic management. A household is normally formed by, or around, the nucleus of an elementary family, and may include relatives and non-relatives other than these immediate family members. Its composition varies according to the specific situation, such as the stage in the cycle of the domestic family, and the economic situation of the household. However, its sociological importance is such that a household of any kind of composition is regarded as one distinct unit in society, represented externally by its head, and internally organized under his leadership. Once established a household is expected to remain intact in spite of changes of generations. In a village community it is the household, not family or kin group, that forms the basis of social organization.

This co-residential group forms an independent property group, the members of which alone have exclusive rights of inheritance. The members of the household, sharing the common economy, are considered as the closest social entities to ego, more important than any other, even close kin, who are not members of the household. This strong consciousness of the residential domestic group is symbolically phrased in terms such as 'under the same roof', or 'the relationship in which one shares the meals cooked in the same pot'.

This basic sociological unit of co-residential members of a house is called *ie* in Japanese.[1] The term *ie* is often used in socio-

[1] *Ie* is pronounced as two syllables: *e* in the Japanese romanization is always pronounced as *é* in French. The romanization in this book is according to the Hepburn system.

I

logical literature as an equivalent of family, but the English term *household* is closer to the conception since it includes all co-residents and is not necessarily restricted only to the members of a family. Strictly speaking, *ie* is a unit which is primarily defined by the criterion of local residence, while family involves primarily kinship and affinity. In Japanese etymology *ie* itself indicates residential criteria, signifying 'hearth' (*he*). (*I* is a prefix: the combination of *i* and *he* becomes *ie*.) The house building itself is also called *ie*. Further, the *ie* is not simply a contemporary household as its English counterpart suggests, but is conceptualized in the time continuum from past to future, including not only the actual residential members but also dead members, with some projection also towards those yet unborn. The *ie* is always conceived as persisting through time by the succession of the members. Hence succession to the headship is of great functional importance, and the line of succession is the axis of the structure of *ie*, while the house gives the material and social frame of *ie*. The members of a household normally correspond to a family, but the shape and composition of a family are always subject to the structure of *ie*; at the same time the *ie* has the capacity to include persons other than immediate members of the family.

Once established, the house building itself becomes an indivisible spatial unit, forming a basic social unit in a community. An individual must first be a member of a household; it is a fairly widespread custom that a house has a house-name by which individual members are addressed. The organization of a community in rural Japan is built only on the basis of the household, not on the individual of the family, or on the descent group. Thus the *ie* is the most important structural element in the analysis of kinship and economic organization in rural Japan.

PRINCIPLES OF HOUSEHOLD SUCCESSION

The head of the household, a position normally occupied by the father of a family, manages its farming, controls its property, and represents the household externally. The property and other various kinds of rights which are of vital importance for agriculturists are attached to the household—theoretically at least not to the individual or to any kind of descent group. These rights, in their operation, are held by the head exclusively, and he should be succeeded by one of his sons, who has the right to share in the

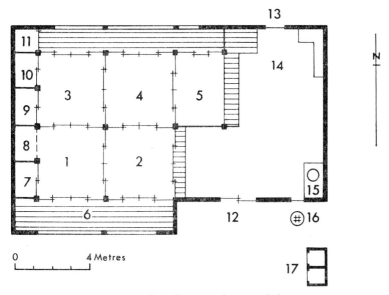

FIGURE I. Plan of a Farmer's House (*Ie*)

1. Guest room: facing the garden; where guests are entertained formally. 2. Living room: also used for greeting guests. 3. Shrine room: this room is used for prayers, but otherwise is hardly used in daily life. 4. Bedroom: other rooms can also be used as bedrooms. 5. Dining room: an open hearth (*irori* or *he*) about 1 metre square is commonly placed near the entrance of this room, except in warmer areas such as Koshiozu. This room opens on to the kitchen (ground level) and together with it serves as a general living room. These five rooms are divided by sliding doors (seen in Plate 8*b*), so that it is possible to open up a larger space on special occasions; their floors are about 70 cm above ground level, and are covered with thick straw mats. 6. Corridors run along both sides of the house, with wooden sliding doors along their outer edges which can be closed at night. At the entrances of rooms 2 and 5, the floor projects as small platforms into the kitchen. 7, 10 and 11. Closets. 8. *Tokonama* (alcove): the honourable centre of the house, ornamented by a picture and arranged flowers, as seen in Plate 8*b*. 9. Shrine; an image of Buddha and ancester tablets etc. are placed for daily Buddhistic service. 12. Main Entrance. 13. Back-door. 14. Kitchen: the rest of this large space at ground level is used as a workroom. 15. Bathroom. 16. Well. 17. Lavatory.

This plan, with four raised rooms and a ground level kitchen at the side, is the basic pattern of the traditional peasant house. (This particular plan is taken from a house in Koshiozu village.) The plan can be enlarged, either by adding rooms to the west or north, or by adding a second floor (as seen in Plate 3*a*).

RJ B

management of the property on the ground of his being a co-residential member making a considerable contribution of labour to the economy, and a man on whom the head can depend in his old age. In rural Japan it is common for the transmission of the headship to take place during the father's lifetime.

There are two important rules of succession to the headship common throughout Japan. One is that *the head should be succeeded by the 'son', not by any other kind of kinsman.* However, the successor is not necessarily the real son; any male (whether he be kin to the head or not) can be 'the son' provided that the necessary legal procedure has taken place for him to become a member of the household (*ie*) by the relationship commonly expressed as 'adopted son' or 'adopted son-in-law'.

The adopted son is taken when the head has no real child. The adopted son-in-law is taken when the head has no son but a daughter. When the daughter's husband becomes the successor of his father-in-law, as well as the inheritor of the father-in-law's household property, he is called an adopted son-in-law. An adopted son-in-law may also be taken when the head has no child, in the following manner: the head may adopt a daughter first and later by her marriage obtains an adopted son-in-law. Or, without any child, he may adopt a young married couple as son-in-law and daughter-in-law. An adopted son or adopted son-in-law may become the successor even when the head has a real son, though such cases are rare; when the head considers his real son is not fit to be his successor, such action may be taken.

By the adoption of son or son-in-law, the 'father' and 'son' relationship is firmly established, as expressed by the fact that an adopted son or son-in-law takes the surname or the same personal name as the head.[1] This he assumes as if he were the real son, being cut off legally from his real father and the members of his natal household.

This adopted son may be taken from among the kinsmen of the head, such as his younger brother, cousin, or more remote relatives (including his wife's). But a man who has no kinship relation at all to the head is often taken. In some cases a servant or a collaborator of the head may become an adopted son, or son-in-law.

---

[1] Before the Meiji period, commoners were not allowed to have surnames. There was, however, a widespread usage by which the successor took his predecessor's personal name.

Normally the adoption takes place between households of fairly equal status, as in the case of a marriage arrangement, which I describe later (pp. 152, 158).

Adoption has been very common among Japanese. This is because every household, once established, needs a successor to the head. An adopted son or adopted son-in-law has exactly the same rights in succession and inheritance as the real son. This is closely related to the rule that rights of succession and inheritance in the *ie* only go along the line of 'father' to 'son', and not through any other consanguineal descent line.[1] For the continuation of the *ie*, one must have a son to whom the headship and property can be transmitted. If a man has not established a relation of 'son' to the head, he has no right of succession, and though he may get a share of the property when he becomes independent from the household, which implies a kind of analogy to the father-son relation, he is clearly differentiated from the 'son'. (The details will be discussed in Chapter 3.)

Through this 'father-son' relationship (whether by initial kinship or by adoption) inescapable economic and moral ties are established between the two statuses: the son, being given the economic advantage, has an obligation to feed his predecessor in his old age, and the latter's dependants. Among an agricultural population the household is thus a distinctive enterprise with insurance for old members, rather than simply the residence of a family. Thereby it entails the strong desire to ensure its continuance: to get a successor is the great concern of the household head.

Another important rule of succession to headship of the household is that *it should be by one son only; never by two or more sons jointly*. Whatever the composition of a household may be, its basic structure is always in terms of this principle. Hence in Japan, theoretically there has been no joint family structure like that of the Chinese or the Hindus. If a household is occupied by two brothers with their wives and children, there is a sharp functional and status distinction between the two—between the successor and the non-successor. The family of the non-successor is considered as comprising 'extra members', not 'full members'

[1] In the absence of a grown-up son (real or adopted), the wife or daughter (or other members of the household) of the deceased head may act as the head, but in such cases their role appears to be only temporary.

of the household. In fact it is very rare for two married brothers to reside in the same household for a long time, though sometimes such cases do occur, possibly because of the economic situation. Even in such a case the brother of the head never becomes the successor unless he becomes an adopted 'son' of the latter. The principle of father-son succession is combined with the principle of the one-son-succession, and produces a residential pattern in which married siblings are expected to have separate households. Non-successors are supposed to leave the father's household on marriage, whether or not they may be given a share of the property. Once they have established their own independent households, each forms a distinctive property unit, in which again the same principle operates.

This process entails status differentiation among the brothers: successor and non-successor. In actual working, inheritance tends to be influenced by the principle of succession; the successor always gets the father's house and tends to have the lion's share of the father's property. This distinction becomes more obvious when the household possesses considerable property, and has high social prestige in the community. Even if the land is divided equally among the brothers, the successor gets the father's household with various rights and advantages, including the prestige of having an older house to which the ancestor cult is attached. Thus a non-successor is at a disadvantage through his inferior social and economic situation. Further it is a frequent phenomenon that an outstandingly wealthy household in a community tends to maintain an especially sharp discrimination between successor and non-successor, because it desires to keep its social and economic status intact.

This situation may appear also among the less wealthy, among households with little land to be divided among sons. In such a case it is a very common arrangement in rural Japan for the successor to take the property intact, while his brothers leave the household without receiving any share, and seek their fortune somewhere else. However, the household would give the departing brothers shelter until they could establish themselves. It is interesting to observe that today, though the 1947 post-war Civil Code gives equal inheritance rights in the father's property to all sons and daughters, among agriculturalists non-successors hardly ever demand this right. It is still very common for them to leave the house and land intact to their brother who succeeds. In return, they are given only education, the degree of which depends on the household economy and the personal inclination of the head. In fact, if farmers today had to divide their property among all brothers and sisters, it would become impossible to live on most farms. Agricultural life in present-day Japan seems to be carried on largely by means of the renunciation of their inheritance-right by non-successors. This situation also applied to the majority of farmers before the war. However, the life of those who left for the cities was not necessarily poorer than that of the successors to land. Many of the urban dwellers succeeded in establishing themselves satisfactorily, and some of them even preferred to do so freed from obligations. Particularly today, when the availability of well-paid employment is great, the majority of sons prefer to leave for urban areas rather than to 'succeed' by farming. The degree of discrimination between successor and non-successor is minimized among those who have no property worth inheriting, and whose economy depends on individual earnings, rather than on productive utilization of the household property.

In the above discussion it is clear that there are two kinds of households in terms of sociological history: one is that of a successor, and the other is that of a non-successor. The former includes the successor's elementary family and his parents (or parents-in-law) with their unmarried sons and daughters, while the latter is formed normally by one elementary family. However, in the next generation this small household also will grow into a larger one, and may again produce a new household by its extra members. The genealogical relationship between the households has by itself no sociological importance, as it has in the case of a lineage or ramage, unless a set of such households is involved in a common economic and political relationship (see Chapter 3).

This is also in accordance with the weak relationship of siblings as compared with the strong functional relationship of father and successor son. Social organization in rural Japan is indeed structured by this outstanding principle, which regards the vertical line as of supreme importance against the collateral line. The well-known Japanese proverb, 'The sibling is the beginning of the stranger' may well reflect this structural process.

VARIATIONS IN WAYS OF TRANSMISSION OF THE HEADSHIP

Based on the principles of the succession rule just described, there are various forms of transmission of the headship according to individual household and locality. It is generally understood in Japan that when the head has male offspring, succession to him in the household goes to the *eldest son*. This had been the pre-dominant social pattern, and also the legal pattern enforced by the old Civil Code till 1947, when the new post-war Civil Code came into force.[1] In pre-war Japan, it was a well-observed fact in many households which followed primogeniture that the parents reared their eldest son with so much care and expectation that he tended to develop quite a different personality from his brothers. However, data collected from various parts of Japan and with considerable time depth reveal that there have been great variations in succession patterns not only according to locality, but also according to individual cases. The following major ways of choosing the successor provide a wide range of alternatives.[2]

According to the reports of *Minji-kanrei-ruishū* and *Zenkoku-minji-kanrei-ruishū*,[3] and the reports of field observers over the last fifty years, an eldest son succession pattern, in which there is a strong tendency to secure the succession as early as possible, is shown by data from Yamagata, Iwate, Akita, Miyagi, Ibaragi

[1] In this discussion the old Civil Code refers to the Civil Code (Min-pō) Book IV *Shinzoku* (Relatives: including regulations on family and kinship relations) and Book V *Sōzoku* (Inheritance) promulgated and enforced in 1898 (Meiji 31). (Books I, II and III came into force in 1896. The first Civil Code in Japan was promulgated in 1890, but it did not come into operation at once.) The post-war Civil Code (Shin-min-pō), in which Books IV and V of the old Code suffered drastic change, was promulgated and came into effect in 1947 (Shōwa 22). Hereafter the 'old Civil Code' refers to the former, and the 'new Civil Code' to the latter.

[2] The legal and social implications of succession and inheritance patterns are best presented in Nakagawa, 1938.

[3] The Department of Justice in the early Meiji era carried out a survey of local customs throughout Japan in order to obtain reference materials for establishing the Civil Code. A report was published in 1877 under the title *Minji-kanrei-ruishū*. It included also some usages of the later Tokugawa period. In 1880 further materials which had been compiled were combined with the earlier report and the completed findings of the survey were published under the title *Zenkoku-minji-kanrei-ruishū*. The data from these books are quoted in various studies of the Japanese family system and local customs. With particular reference to household succession, data are conveniently arranged in *Ōmachi*, 1958.

IOWA STATE
UNIVERSITY
BOOK STORE

THANK YOU FROM UBS

maile@ia.freei.net

Pw: xuan

57

~~472~~ ~~4522~~

572 - 4522

50010 - 515

1383
1403
‾‾‾‾‾‾‾‾‾
2

1390⁰

and Shizuoka prefectures, which geographically show some concentration in the north-eastern parts of Japan. Among them the following variant rules are found, both of which have been explained as 'in order to share the labour'.

A. According to the sex of the first-born child. When it is a son, this real son is chosen as the successor; if it is a daughter, her husband becomes the successor, regardless of whether a real son is born afterwards. In the latter case the adopted son-in-law has the right of succession over the real son.

B. Only the eldest son is chosen as successor. When this son is too young to succeed, the head will take an adopted son-in-law (the husband of the eldest daughter), to whom he temporarily transmits his headship, placing his real small son as a quasi-adopted son of the latter. In this manner the adopted son-in-law occupies the headship till the real son is fit to occupy it. Hence the son of the daughter whose husband is the temporary head, has no right to become the successor.

This pattern includes also such a case as when the successor has died leaving a small son; then the adopted son-in-law (the husband of an elder sister of the deceased) assumes his position temporarily. During this period the real son of the late successor is placed in the position of quasi-adopted son of the temporary successor.

In contrast to the above cases, there are those of ultimogeniture, youngest son succession. The parents remain with the youngest son, while elder sons leave the household at marriage. This category emerges from the data from Nagano, Aichi, Kochi, Miyazaki and Nagasaki prefectures, whose geographical distribution is in the middle and south-western parts of Japan. Further, there is another pattern in which the parents choose one of their sons as the successor, regardless of birth order. The distribution of this pattern is similar to that of the youngest son succession.

It seems that according to the locality one of the above patterns is dominant. However, detailed and closer micro-surveys reveal that actual succession cases show considerable variety among individual households in the same locality. The variation in succession patterns seems to be not simply a matter of local custom, but involves to a great extent economic factors both internal and external to the household. The patterns have been influenced, too, by the Civil Code. For instance, the primogeniture succession rule laid down by the old Civil Code dominated the succession pattern of the majority of the population. The new Civil Code abolished primogeniture, but the legacy is still found strongly. It is difficult in all cases to distinguish economic reasons for the difference in succession patterns from factors of local custom. Nevertheless, economic reasons can be seen at least in the following circumstances.

From the data I have examined so far, it seems to me that succession by a younger son or by one chosen son would appear where the economic situation is such that all sons can be provided with means adequate for their independence, yet at the same time the household economy can be managed by the labour force of an elementary family. In such a situation, it is a wiser arrangement in terms of distribution of labour force to let the elder sons establish independent households while the father is at work; and when the father reaches the age at which his labour is insufficiently productive, to let the younger son succeed to his household.

On the other hand, where economic competition is great owing to the shortage of capital resources and to the lack of other means of income, the primogeniture succession pattern seems likely to develop. Again, where more labour is required in farming land of low fertility, as is often the case in northern Japan, it is difficult for one man's labour to support his growing family; to add another man's labour in the peasant household therefore brings more advantageous economic management. However, to maintain more than two couples with their children seems difficult; the balance of productivity and consumption seems to lie at this point. The eldest son has the advantage of his younger brothers in coming to be a co-worker of the head, and therefore is naturally placed as successor to the headship. When they marry younger sons have to leave the household to find other means of income. At worst, as happened sometimes in the past when they had no land portion from the head, and were unable to find other economic means to support a family, they were forced to remain celibate in their natal household.

Succession by primogeniture also tends to appear in the wealthy sector of the society. The degree of institutionalization of the household becomes greater, and the line of succession through 'father-son' becomes more important. In order to keep the succession line firm, there is a tendency to earlier appointment of the successor, and thus to primogeniture.

Certainly among very poor households, whose property has no particular significance, any type of succession may take place according to individual members' convenience. This is also the case in many recent households with small land holdings: sons, including the eldest son, prefer to take jobs in industry (which are easy to get nowadays) rather than to 'succeed' to their father's household and farm, from which they can hardly expect a better income. However, in spite of such a tendency and the abolition of primogeniture by the new Civil Code, this latter seems still to be the prevailing pattern among agricultural households.

In relation to the ways of transmission of the headship attention must be drawn to the varieties of residential pattern. Various social and economic rights including that to the ancestral altar are attached to the household. Hence normally the successor's elementary family resides in the same household with his parents, while other members leave the household at their marriage. So far as the successor is concerned, his family of procreation and family of orientation are inseparable from his residence.

However, in some cases transmission of the headship accompanies a residential separation between the successor's elementary family and his retired father's family. This custom is known as *inkyo-sei* (head-retirement system), or *inkyo-bunke* (branching off of household at retirement of head). The term *inkyo* itself signifies 'the retirement of the head', but does not necessarily involve residential separation, but when the term used is *inkyo-sei* (*inkyo-system*), then it implies the custom of residential separation of the retired head, including his wife and often unmarried children too. The old couple, handing over the household to the successor, leave for a new smaller house called the *inkyo* house (built usually on land in the same house site), or for a newly built section of the original dwelling-house. According to local custom, such a residential separation may or may not be marked by separate hearths and division of property.

The *inkyo* system appears to be closely related to the change of residence of the successor's wife. In example (A), in the case of Koh village, by the marriage of the successor (the eldest son), the wife moves her residence to the successor's house: it takes some time for the old couple to change their residence to a small *inkyo* house built in the same compound—one week to several years—and this depends on the individual household arrangement. In some cases the straitened household economy will not allow an *inkyo* house to be built until a few years after the successor has married. However, it is a normal arrangement, and one to which positive moral value is attached, that the old couple and new couple do not reside in the same house for more than a few years after the successor's marriage. The old couple remain in this *inkyo* house by themselves till death, letting all their children marry out; the house made vacant by their death will again be used by the present household head and his wife when they retire. When the couple of the second generation come to retire while one or both of the first generation (parents) are still alive, another *inkyo* house is required; couples of different generations will not reside in the same house.

In example (B), from Izu-Oshima, the husband has had to visit his wife during the early part of their married life (see p. 13n.). Around the time when the first child is born, the members of the wife's house express agreement to let their daughter move to her husband's house; the husband's parents, with their unmarried sons and daughters, then hurry to move away from their house. In example (C), from Izu-Toshima, the wife moves her residence at a fairly advanced stage of her marriage; she works at her husband's house, but returns to her natal house every night with her children. Meanwhile, the brothers and sisters of her husband marry out, and this is soon followed by the husband's parents' residential change. The wife then moves her residence to that of her husband.

(D): A further variation is practised in Koshiki-jima in Kagoshima prefecture. At the successor's marriage, a new small house is built, and the successor and his wife instead of the old couple occupy this. When all his brothers and sisters have married out, the successor and his family return to the main house; in exchange, his retired parents occupy the small house. An analogous case is also found in Koshiozu village in Aichi prefecture. There, the young couple sleep in a small attached house in the earlier stage of their marriage, and later they occupy the main building by exchange with the husband's parents.

The timing of the shift of the old couple to the *inkyo* house largely depends on local custom as well as on the economic condition of the individual household. However, in a given locality, a fairly uniform system seems to be practised; different types are unlikely to be found mixed in a given locality.

Throughout these various arrangements, it is noticeable that the *inkyo* system involves the custom that one residence should not be occupied by more than one couple. As expressed overtly, the residential move of the successor's wife is the direct cause of the residential move of the successor's parents. The residential move of the successor's wife implies the establishment of her status as the mistress of the household, and it is common that the move of the old couple marks the formal transmission of the headship to the successor.[1] However, in the case of an earlier residential separation (for example, when the head-to-be-retired is still in his forties), the headship may still be held by him when he changes to the *inkyo* house. In such a case the headship and the main residence do not coincide. It seems normal practice that if the head-to-be-retired is still young, the residential move from the main house tends to be delayed. In general those who practise the *inkyo* system tend to have an earlier transmission of headship than those who are not involved in this system.

It is important to note here that though the *inkyo* system separates the members of one household into two residences, in some cases even with separate hearths, and forms separate productive units with land apportioned between them, these two houses together form one distinctive unit, a single household (*ie*) and single property unit. The major part of this unit is attached to the main house, and the old couple will be fed in their old age by the head's successor who lives in the main building in the same compound. If the retired couple are still active, they may work for themselves; otherwise they become economic dependants of the successor. The *inkyo* house together with the main house is counted as one unit in the village organization, and is represented

---

[1] One mistress in one household seems to have been an ideal arrangement even among those who did not have the *inkyo* system. There is a fairly widespread custom, though nowadays only found in remote hill villages and on small islands, that a wife who marries the successor of a household remains in her parental house after the wedding, being visited by her husband every night. (The children borne by her remain with her.) She will move to her husband's house only at his taking over the headship, i.e. when her mother-in-law leaves the position of mistress (see Yanagita, 1948).

by one head—normally the head of the main house. Thus in the local administrative organization the household structure based on the principle of succession is not distorted, in spite of such various residential and economic arrangements.

In order to practise an *inkyo* system, there must be sufficient residential space in the possession of each household in the community to allow for the *inkyo* house. It is interesting that I found that the villages where an *inkyo* system has prevailed during several generations have had some kind of labour market where extra members (non-successors) could seek a job on leaving the village. The number of households in such a village, and the distribution of the house-site land (enough to have an *inkyo* house) for each household, have been kept more or less unchanged through the generations. These conditions accord with a lack of the possibility for expanding arable land, or for employing any productive means in the village other than the traditional form of economy. For example, in Koh village, I found that the *inkyo* system has been maintained at the expense of the 'non-successors' who left the village and engaged in other jobs; if they had established their households in the village, there would have been no space for *inkyo* houses. Moreover these members could not establish their households because of the lack of extra house-sites.

Hence the maintenance of the *inkyo* system as a local custom in which the majority of the villagers are involved seems to be closely related to the internal as well as to the external economic situation of a village: a balanced situation between the number of households of a village and the limited resources; a relatively stable economy for each household; and reasonably equal economic standing as between the households of a village. Moreover every household must be able to maintain constant economic activity; and to have enough house-site land to allow an *inkyo* house. At the same time a village should have an external labour market in which extra members can seek to establish their new economic life. Otherwise an *inkyo* system can be practised only where a household can expand its house-site land and fields to accommodate extra members as well as the old couples. Where such conditions are prevalent there may occur *inkyo-bunke*. An *inkyo-bunke*, an establishment of a branch household by an *inkyo*, is practised in the following way.

At the transmission of the headship, which occurs soon after the successor's marriage, the old couple depart from the house, taking unmarried sons and daughters with them, leaving the main house for the successor's elementary family. In time those sons and daughters who moved their residence with their parents leave again from this *inkyo* house, but one of them takes over the house built for *inkyo*. The old couple may remain with the son (or daughter) who remains in this house after his or her marriage; or the old couple may again change their residence back to their successor's house (the main house from which they came) as dependants, leaving the *inkyo* house to be taken over by their younger son. The important point is that this system entails succession to the *inkyo* house by a younger son (or son-in-law), and such a household will become independent from the main house. In this case the land allotted to the *inkyo* may never be pooled together with that of the main house. Structurally *inkyo-bunke* entails fission of a household,[1] while the other *inkyo* system implies only a residential arrangement within one household. The practice of *inkyo-bunke* results in an increase of the number of households in a village, and is possible only when one household has enough land for the establishment of another household. Hence limits to the availability of land restrict its practice.

The *inkyo* system, including *inkyo-bunke*, is the custom distinguished by the residential arrangement in which old parents leave the main house at their retirement, transmitting the rights to the successor. The distribution of the *inkyo* system as shown by the ethnographic information obtained, tends to local concentrations, and because of this, it has been usually explained as a local custom, a culture item attached to a particular locality. However, its incidence suggests to me that in large part it has been determined by economic factors of a more general kind. First, actual ethnographic data on the villages with the *inkyo* system reveal economic situations very similar to those described above. Secondly, on the whole the distribution of the *inkyo* system reveals a situation where productive activity in farming is manageable by the labour of an elementary family, and a woman's economic contribution is significant for the household economy.

---

[1] *Bunke* means a 'branch household', which will be discussed in detail in Chapter 3.

Thirdly, the *inkyo* system is not restricted to such villages as those described above, but may be practised by some relatively well-to-do households in villages where it is not generally common. This custom is also known widely all over Japan, though not generally practised. Even in a locality where the *inkyo* system is rarely found, people often remark: 'We cannot practise an *inkyo* system because of the lack of house-site land', or 'Though we do not practise it generally, some well-to-do households do make an *inkyo* house', etc. Among households on a larger scale an *inkyo* arrangement tends to be more delayed than among households on a smaller scale. For example, among big landowners whose farming establishment is more complicated and larger in scale, the head normally tends to keep his office until a considerable age, since the leadership does not require physical labour from him. This delays the time of *inkyo*, since it would be certainly a disadvantage to have separate residences and form separate economic units while the head is still fit to conduct affairs.

So far I have presented the interpretation and generalizations from the available ethnographic data of the *inkyo* system,[1] with particular reference to the household succession rule. The issues which I have not taken up in this discussion, such as whether the *inkyo* system once prevailed all over Japan, or whether it originated in a particular stratum or locality, need further ethnographic and historical investigation.

FATHER AND MOTHER IN THE HOUSEHOLD STRUCTURE

The succession rule which entails a sharp distinction between brothers as successor and non-successor amalgamates the statuses of father and (successor) son into one continuum. The headship of the household in fact is often taken by the father and the son jointly. At a certain stage of the domestic cycle of the household, when the successor is already married and has a child, the father and the successor normally hold *de facto* headship jointly: the son manages the farming, while the father represents the household externally. The latter's activity is replaceable at convenience by the former's. As the father gets older all the activities of the head

---

[1] The major works concerning the *inkyo* system are included in Bibliography II for Chapter 1.

gradually shift to the son, and thus the father becomes *inkyo* (retired), and a dependant of his son like other members.

The time of the father's retirement in terms of handing over the property (including the right of handling income and expenditure of the household) varies widely according to the locality as well as according to individual households. Among the farmers it is normally around the age of sixty. This comparatively early retirement from the headship is closely related to the structure of the farmer's household, for its economy greatly depends on actual physical labour. If the head does not hand over the headship in spite of his old age, there often exist antagonisms between him and his successor son (who may be over forty), and other villagers also disapprove of it. Among households of the upper strata of the society, whose economy does not depend on physical labour of the household members, the transmission of the headship tends to be delayed much later than among the farmers. In such cases, naturally, the father tends to have greater authority than in the ordinary household.

The final shift of the headship (handing over the rights in the household property and the full responsibility for household management) from the father to the son has a great significance for the external relations of the household as well as for interpersonal relations among the household members. As already mentioned, the property attaches to the household, not to an individual.[1] The head of the household is a kind of a caretaker of the property, responsible for it only during the period he occupies the headship: he acts as the head by virtue of holding the office of headship. It is expected that he will not dispose of the property, since the property is meant to be transferred to his successor. If he should happen to lose the property by his mismanagement, he would say, 'I don't know what excuse to make to our ancestors (predecessors)'. This embodies the basic traditional Japanese concept of household property. The head exercises his authority in correlation with his responsibility, not through any right of possession.

In most cases, the office of headship is occupied by the father

---

[1] The absolute right of the head, as an individual, over the household property and the household members was introduced by the old Civil Code under the term *koshu-ken*. This modern law contradicted the traditional ideology of the Japanese *ie* institution. In spite of this law, the traditional concept of household property continued, though there were some who abused this legal right.

of the family residing in the household. However it should be noted that his authority over the household members is validated by his *office* as the head of the household, not by his being the *father*: the authority of the head resides primarily in the office rather than the person. For example, on his retirement the father loses all his authority over the household members, and his position becomes one of a dependant of his son who succeeds to the headship. Also, the household is represented externally by the name of the current head, although his predecessor, his father, is still alive. The father will not sit any more in the seat of the head (*yokoza*, which will be explained later in the text). Because the all-important decisions will now be made by the new head (son), family members begin to think of the son as the most important figure, and begin to disregard the retired father.

In this feature, a Japanese father's legitimate authority differs greatly from that of a Chinese father, who normally keeps the headship till his death. Even if he were to hand over household management to his son during his own lifetime, the Chinese father remains the legitimate and spiritual authority who leads family members and continues to receive utmost respect from them. The father's opinion still has great importance in the management and he is always consulted. Also, the household continues to be recognized externally under the name of the father so long as he is alive. His handing over the management does not terminate his authority as the head of the family. It is with him till his death. However, the *de facto* leadership of the father as the head of the family does not sharply exclude the rights of sons, as it does among the Japanese. In the Chinese family system, the rights in the family property are considered to be held by the father and sons or brothers (grown-up patrilineal members) who form the unit of the family, though the father is the legal owner of the family property. For example, a disposal of the family property is normally made only by the consent of these members, and transfer documents are signed by the sons together with their father. (It should be noted too that in China all sons of a family have equal rights, which again differs from the Japanese case.) Among the Chinese, the central core of the family is father and sons (or brothers), while among the Japanese, it is the head (father) and his successor (the particular son).

The Japanese father occupying the office of the headship may exercise relatively greater power than the Chinese father, since in Japan the rights and authority of the man in the office of head-ship have marked differences from those of the other members of the household. This privileged position of the father as the head of the household is seen in various aspects of household life.

For example, there is the fixed seat of the head, called *yokoza* in peasant households, at the centre of the dining room; no other person is allowed to occupy it even when the head is absent. (Villagers say 'Anyone who sits on the *yokoza* is either a foolish priest or a cat'.) He may also gain extra privileges through out-standing economic achievement. This, for example, is demon-strated in a custom which prevailed in many villages in Kyushū, though no longer practised today: a head who contributed a great deal to building up the household's property used to have especially good meals which were not shared by other members of the household. It was the custom in most Japanese households until the last war, that the head was not only served first at meals, but also was given the best part of the meal. The order of taking the evening hot bath also gave first place to the head: all other members had to wait, even till very late at night, if the head had not come back home.

The father, as head of the household, was often regarded as a figure to be much feared by other members of the household. As the proverb has it: 'The things that one has most to fear are *jishin, kaminari, kaji, oyaji* (earthquake, thunder, fire and father).' The household with a firmly authoritarian father was highly regarded, and treated as an ideal model for the majority, and indeed this was enforced and influenced by the legal (and ethical) pattern established by the old Civil Code (under the term *koshu-ken* as already mentioned), which reflected the feudal ideology of the preceding period. In these households, every activity of the individual member was regulated under the leadership of the father. The father was the sole figure to make final decisions, and he often made them unilaterally. He could even decide upon his successor: in an extreme case, he could appoint as his suc-cessor an adopted son-in-law, superseding his real son. The tradi-tional Japanese conception, which regards the household rather than the family as the most important sociological unit, modifies the structure of the family itself.

Through these aspects it is clear that the authority of the

Japanese father derives from his being head of the *household* (the residential and economic group), rather than from his being the *father*, the head of the *family* (kin group).

The degree to which the Japanese father exercises his authority as head of the household is therefore conditioned by the economy of the household: a functional degree conditioned by productivity of the property and his own capability as economic contributor. In households which have no significant property or which do not form distinctive productive units, the father's (head's) authority tends to be decreased. This kind of household is found in rural areas where agriculture is not the only means of livelihood; and also among the poor sectors of the society living in a 'hand-to-mouth' economy. Another example of such a household is that of the modern white-collar worker, who lives on a salary without depending on his father's household property. In such a situation, a household is simply a house occupied by a family. It is natural in such a household for the father's authority as head to be minimized, and there is hardly any discrimination among brothers, or between brothers and sisters: without household property, succession does not have any economic and social significance, so the relationship between the father and the (successor) son becomes less institutionalized. The degree of the father's authority as the head of the household is paralleled by the degree of discrimination among the brothers.

However, among traditional Japanese, the ideal image of the father as the head of the household reflected a man of distinguished authority as exemplified in heads of well-established households holding considerable property. This ideal pattern, supported legally by the old Civil Code and ethically by the feudal ideology, greatly influenced the pattern of the majority of Japanese households, even those not having significant property. This can be seen in the rapid decline of the middle-class father's authority, effected by the legal and ideological changes after the war. The present weakness of the father's authority, reduced to a degree which the Japanese could never have imagined before the war, substantiates the thesis that the authority commonly believed to be vested in the father as a person was instead derived from his office and the household economic structure.

Even before the war, the nature of Japanese piety toward the father was quite different from that of the Chinese, though the moral precept of piety toward fathers took its forms of expression from the Chinese, imported from China during the feudal era. The piety and loyalty shown by Japanese dependants towards the father was in the nature of that shown to the leader of a kind of economic corporate group, but combined with family sentiment. The Japanese ideology which regards economic and residential factors as being no less significant than the descent factor is also expressed by a common Japanese proverb, 'More important than real parents are one's foster-parents'. According to native Japanese thinking, one should be filial towards one's parents because of their fostering care, not just because they are one's parents. This is indeed unlike the Chinese, among whom piety was owed primarily to one's real parents, under any circumstances. Even in pre-war times the behaviour of Japanese children toward their parents often surprised Chinese who visited Japan, because of the lack of respect toward parents as measured by Chinese standards of conduct. The son's attitude towards the retired aged parent was particularly out of keeping with that of the Chinese.

Throughout historical periods, and in various strata of society, the Japanese father's authority never completely rested in his person; it depended on his performing the actual role of the head in household management. This is very different from the father's status in a society where the descent factor plays an important role.

The lesser importance attached to criteria of descent, which restrained the father from completing his authority as a person, determines the crucial weakness in the position of the Japanese mother. The father, occupying the headship, has an important position in the household structure, but the mother is the least important figure in the household. She could be replaced at any moment without leading to any confusion or to the dissolution of the household structure.

Before the old Civil Code came into force, the *de jure* status of the children of the household was not necessarily established by being born from the womb of the mistress of the household, the wife of the head: any child could be a *de jure* child of the household, if the correct relationship of the child to the head (father) was established. Whether born to a concubine or to any other woman, a child suffered no social or legal discrimination compared with a child born to the wife of the head, provided that the head recognized him as his son or daughter. This seems one reason why wives and concubines were legally equated.[1] Children were considered as members of the household, rather than as the off-spring of a particular married couple. The sociological importance of the mother was thus minimized. The mother who left the household on divorce had no legal right to take her children with her—this was also the law till the new Civil Code was established after the war. 'The womb is a thing to be borrowed' has been a proverbial saying among the Japanese since the feudal age. It has been thought this expression is based on the feudal ideology which despised women by placing them in a lower status. However, in my view, this is not simply based on, or created by, the feudal morality itself; rather the feudal concept developed on the basis of native kinship ideology.

Japanese ideas concerning the mother's status might give the impression of a case of extreme patrilineality, to the extent that 'the mother has no kinship ties with her husband's children but is bound only to their father as an affine', as in the case of the Lakher presented in the recent discussion by E. R. Leach (1961b, p. 14). But there is *not* the same logical structure involved: one should remember here that the Japanese system differs from a patrilineal system.[2] In a strict sense, it is not *fathership* (kinship) which gives the sociological status to the child, but *headship* (legitimate co-resident membership). The crucial point involved in Japanese kinship structure is that kinship tie with the mother—or even with the father—is not essential for the sociological recognition of the child.

However, the father certainly has an advantage over the mother as a result of the structure of the household, being placed as the head, or the potential head, who cannot be easily replaced. This fact appears clearly in divorce: divorce was only possible from the husband's side (the exception being the case of a husband who

---

[1] Concubines had the same legal rights as wives as recently as 1889 (the Meiji period dates from 1868).

[2] Further, there is even an ideology extremely opposed to that of the patrilineal system. According to data found in ancient literature (such as *Kojiki*) composed in A.D. 712, the son and daughter of one woman by two different fathers are regarded as committing incest if they have sex relations with one another, while offspring of one man by two different mothers are not. This is indeed in contrast to that of the Lakher patrilineal system described by Leach (1961b, pp. 14–16).

was an adopted son-in-law married to a daughter of the household). Divorce in practice probably occurred more often in the earlier stages of marriage—before the wife established her firm position as the mistress of the household. The wife as daughter-in-law with her middle-aged mother-in-law in the same household, was in a situation that often led to divorce. The favourite reason for divorce, besides incapacity for child-bearing, was that the wife did not fit into the traditional 'ways' of the husband's household.[1] However, this expression was used to justify the mother-in-law's advantage in the conflict with the daughter-in-law.

The conflict between the mother-in-law and daughter-in-law arises from the interpersonal relations derived from the household structure. In comparison with the co-operative friendly relationship between the head and his successor (whether the latter is the former's real son or son-in-law), the relationship between the mistress and her successor often involves hostility. The son, being the successor of the father in this type of residence, will occupy the role of the father as the head of the household, so that the mother looks to him as a surrogate for her husband, on whom she can depend entirely. But the son's role as husband to his wife is often overlooked by the mother. In fact the son placed in such a position has to face the conflict of his roles as son and as husband. The most difficult situation arises when he has a weak personality and is therefore torn between mother and wife. This situation places these two affinal women in jealous competition centred on the man, in which the mother usually dominates the newly arrived young wife. Traditionally, the only solution was the expected obedience of the daughter-in-law to the mother-in-law. In this context, the well-known conflict between the Japanese mother-in-law and the daughter-in-law (particularly the wife of the successor, who resides in the same house with the mother-in-law) can be understood. For this system involves more structural elements for conflict between mother-in-law and daughter-in-law than those normally found in other societies. Indeed the conflict would become much less if there was transmission of the mistress's office to the daughter-in-law from the mother-in-law. The *inkyo* system discussed in the foregoing

---

[1] Every household is so distinctive a social unit that each develops its own 'ways', which naturally present difficulties to the newly married wife.

section offers the best solution for such a conflict. Normally the transmission of the office of mistress is parallel to the transmission of the headship, though it does not necessarily take place at the same time—it may be delayed.[1]

In the case of an uxorilocal marriage (with adopted son-in-law) in which the successor of the mistress is her own daughter, the relationship is a very friendly one. There is a special term for a woman in this position: *ietsuki-musume* (the daughter attached to the household). Her advantageous position often develops in her a quite different personality from that of a virilocally married woman, so much so that *ietsuki-musume* are thought to be easily identifiable on casual acquaintance. Further, the woman who has married a non-successor is also at an advantage since she becomes the mistress of a household from the beginning of her matrimonial life. (Hence in fact such a marriage is preferred by a woman as well as by her parents and is much more easily arranged than the marriage of the successor residing with his mother.)

In order to get a secure position in the household, a woman *must* become the *mistress* of the household. A wife as the mistress of the household can have a chance to rule the household operationally as a non-competing figure. She can not only control the domestic affairs of the household, but also can in a sense share the power of the headship held by her husband or by her son. In a Japanese family, there are no rules which define the wife's role and responsibility exclusively as distinct from that of the husband. Hence the power and influence of the mistress depend on the relative strengths of personality of herself and her husband. In some cases the husband's voice dominates in the family, and in other cases the wife's does, though she often does not show such power externally. In the absence of the head, his wife certainly would assume the headship of the household. A widow whose son is still minor in age acts as the *de facto* head of the household, without depending on her kin. (She hardly needs to look for protection to her brother: her role as the head of the household

---

[1] The symbolic custom of the transmission of the office of the mistress found in some localities is called *hera-watashi* (see Sasaki, 1926): the mother-in-law hands over to her daughter-in-law the spatula (*hera* or *shamoji* in standard Japanese), a kind of spoon made of wood by which cooked rice is distributed into each member's cup by the hand of the mistress at meal times. Even today a *shamoji* is used as a symbol of the mistress (in a very large size for a placard), held up in demonstrations by the National Association of Wives.

makes her quite independent.) A woman enjoys her position as *the mistress*, rather than as wife, mother or sister. Her status thus acquired through household structure also seems to be related significantly to the fact that she makes great contributions to her household's economy by working in the fields as her husband does.

The structure of the household produces a sociological weakness in the wife's initial position. But when she succeeds to a secure position as the mistress of the household she usually has the chance to overcome her handicap as a wife, and thus are the power and influence of women discreetly maintained in Japanese society. Further, as in the case of the father, actual economic contribution also gives an advantageous position to the wife: her labour can be important in the household economy, or she may have brought substantial property at her marriage.

It is extremely difficult to describe *the* status (in the sense of power and prestige) of Japanese woman in the household. It can be very low, or very high—it all depends on the situation in which she is involved. The following factors have to be taken into account: her status in the household (whether she is the mistress or not); the degree of her economic contribution to the household economy; the degree to which status differentiations in the household are institutionalized; the economic situation of the household she has entered, as well as that from which she came; competing personal relationships among the household members; her character, personality and ability; local customs; the ideology prevailing at a given time. The complex of all these factors determines her actual power and prestige in the household. Above all the most significant element is whether or not she holds the position of mistress. The status of wife or mother gives her little authority unless she is the mistress of the household, just as a father has little unless he is the head. While the absence of the descent principle gives her a very weak position as a mother or wife, at the same time it gives her unlimited possibilities of exercising power as the mistress.

This analysis reveals a very different picture from the stereotype of the traditional patriarchical family system of Japan, which produced a widespread belief that the status of Japanese women was a lowly one, the wife and daughters being placed at the bottom of the hierarchy. This was indeed the ideal pattern propagated among the mass of the population by the old Civil Code. This stereotype, which is normally looked on as the traditional Japanese pattern, should not be considered as the basic feature of the traditional family in Japan, but one developed under specific conditions and for specific historical causes on the basis of the native household structure. Furthermore, such a stereotype of a Japanese woman's position has been exemplified mostly by women of the middle class in urban areas, where women did not engage in productive work, but remained at home and carried out domestic duties. In contrast, the mistresses of peasant households whose contribution to the household economy was especially great had considerable power and influence, though they did not show them overtly.

The household structure discussed above represents the principle of Japanese social structure in its concise form. It is the economic and residential factors that play the important decisive role in shaping the organization. Indeed these are the crucial elements in the complex picture of any form of social organization in Japan. Further, this discussion reveals that the Japanese kinship system, normally designated as 'patrilineal', differs greatly from a patrilineal system as ordinarily defined, though it has something of a patrilineal *look*. The non-patrilineal elements in its function will be seen to be more pronounced in the following discussion.

ANALYSIS OF THE CONCEPT OF SHINRUI

I have emphasized the strong sociological solidarity of the household against the weak relations of collateral kin. The weakness of kinship ties, however, is a relative matter. For example, among the members of the same household the immediate family members are usually and clearly distinguishable from the other members by their rights and obligations. This is also the case in the local community. A set of households whose members are related through kinship, are operationally distinguishable in a given local community, and this distinction is recognized in the term *shinrui*.[1] A *shinrui* includes a certain number of households

---

[1] The term *shinrui* (or *shinseki*), which is now standard Japanese and has been used widely all over Japan, was originally derived from Chinese. Indigenous terms for *shinrui* are *itoko* (cousin) or *oyako* (parent-child), which are still used in

whose family members are related to ego through the bilateral extension of kinship. Though it is not a constant group of kin, yet it has important functions: it is the *shinrui* which assemble, and are indispensable, for weddings and funerals. (The implications of the function of *shinrui*, which have great influence on the social organization, will be discussed in Chapter 4.)

The range of a *shinrui* normally includes bilateral first cousins. The category of *shinrui* is somewhat analogous to that of *kindred*. However, if kindred is defined 'to refer only to cognates and never extended to embrace affines' as suggested by Freeman in his recent work (Freeman, 1961, p. 202), a *shinrui* is not a kindred

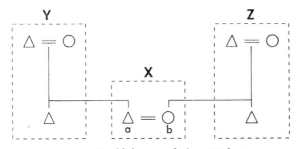

FIGURE 2. Establishment of *Shinrui* Relations

because it embraces affines as well, though it is based on the kindred category. In fact *shinrui* involves marriage relationships no less importantly than cognatic relationships.

For the understanding of this Japanese concept of *shinrui*, the unit of a household is of prime importance. Though a *shinrui* is recognized in terms of kinship relations and with reference to a single person, the function of *shinrui* is carried out on the basis of household units. A *shinrui* is recognized as a set of households, not simply as an aggregate of kin. A kinsman who is a member of ego's own household is not called *shinrui*. A *shinrui* arises

many parts of Japan (Yanagita, 1943, pp. 71–83). In a locality where *itoko* is used for *shinrui*, *oyako* is used only for the actual parents and children relation; likewise where *oyako* is used, *itoko* is used only for real cousins (Ariga, 1947, pp. 52–70).

Further, in some localities the term *shinrui* (or *shinseki*) is applied in a slightly different context from the one defined here, as will be shown later. A set of households related through closer kinship is distinguishable from any other category of group or relationship. In this discussion I use the term *shinrui* for this set: in practice *shinrui* and *shinseki* are the terms applied to this set by the majority of Japanese.

through the marriage of a member (kin) of ego's household.[1] In Figure 2, the household X, formed by the marriage of *a* and *b*, establishes a *shinrui* relationship between Y and Z households, and X also becomes *shinrui* for both Y and Z. In fact in many localities, the wedding ceremony is termed '*oyako-nari*' ('to establish a *shinrui* relationship').

The kin who are normally included in the range of *shinrui* are shown in Figure 3. The affines in Figure 3 are no less important than the cognates. This concept is better understood when Figure 3 is compared with Figure 4, where the same set of kin are shown as the members of households linked by the marriages of those who are or were members of ego's household. Differentiation by cognates and affines is overshadowed by the concept of household—in fact for the Japanese it is never recognized as

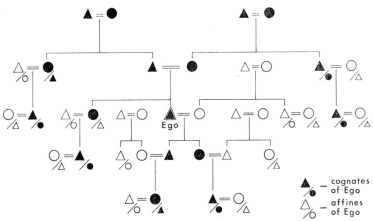

FIGURE 3. Category of Kin Normally Included in *Shinrui*

prominently as is the difference by household. It is the household, rather than descent links, that gives the frame of organization in which individuals are classified. In Figure 2, once the household X is established, *a* and *b* are primarily regarded as members of X, rather than of their respective families.

In this connection, one should note the significance of marriage as implying the shift of sociological group membership of either a woman or a man. Since marriages in Japan are predominantly

---

[1] The local term *enka* used for *shinrui* in Kumamoto prefecture manifests the Japanese conception of *shinrui*: the literal meaning of *enka* is 'affinal household'.

virilocal, the shift of membership is usually on the part of the bride, and it is symbolized in dramatic acts by the bride at the marriage ceremony. When she leaves her parental house, she is dressed up in a *white* ceremonial *kimono*, the same colour as the shroud in which corpses are dressed. The meaning of this is that she will not return to her parental household alive: by her marriage she changes her membership forever from the household of her father to that of her husband. In fact she will be buried in the grave of her husband's family, never in that of her parents, unless she is divorced without remarriage. In some localities, the bride also steps over burnt straw at the departure from her parental house, which symbolizes that she will not be able to return, just as burnt ashes can never become straw again. The essence of such customs, I think, lies in the symbolic change of household membership, but does not necessarily mean the cessation of the actual relationship between her and her parental family. In fact (to take the case shown in Figure 2), by her marriage her parental household Z begins to have significant relations with Y as well as with her new household X, as I presently describe. Actually she maintains a close relationship with members of Z; there would be frequent visits between them and occasional exchanges of gifts. (In many localities, a woman's parental household provides more gifts than the husband's.)

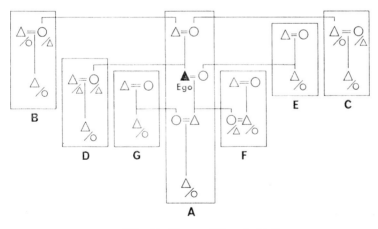

FIGURE 4. *Shinrui* in Terms of Household Category

Now to come back to the main issue, the important point here is that the husband and wife belong always to the same household, whether the marriage is virilocal or uxorilocal, whether X (independent house for a couple) was established by the economic help of Y or Z, and whether they take the surname of Y or Z.[1] This household membership criterion, with its great degree of sociological independence from descent criteria, entails an identical degree of social distance between consanguines and affines. The distance between *a* and the members of Z has to be considered operationally the same as that between *a* and the members of Y; and this is exactly the same in the case of *b*. Thus ego's affines are equated with ego's cognates, though there is the slightest cognatic bias. For example, at the death of a member of Z household *a* takes exactly the same role as in the case of the death of a member of Y household. The same principle also appears in kinship terminology: the parents and siblings of ego's spouse are addressed in exactly the same terms as his own parents and siblings (see p. 33 and Figure 5). Because of the strong concept of household, Japanese tend to ignore the sociological distinction between cognates and affines. Though certainly they are aware of the difference, it is minimized in actual functional contexts.[2]

This kinship structure, in which affines and cognates are of almost equal consequence, cannot be regarded as showing an important structural relationship of the affinal group *vis-à-vis* the cognatic group, as appears in South Indian kinship (Dumont, 1957) in which affines stand as a constant group to supply spouses to ego's cognatic group. Japanese kinship structure is the antithesis of South Indian kinship structure, in which the affines are clearly

[1] This is reflected in the surname system by which the husband and wife never remain legally with different surnames: when a wife does not change her surname by marriage (normally in uxorilocal marriage as in the case of an adopted son-in-law), it is the husband who changes his surname to that of his wife. The Japanese system differs from the Chinese system, in which the wife continues to use her father's surname after her marriage in addition to her husband's, and also from the English system in which normally only the wife changes her surname, to that of her husband.

[2] The distinction between cognates and affines is seen in legal regulations and official tabulations in various periods of history, but clearly derives from the influence of Chinese and western usages. For example a new legal term, *inseki* (Chinese derivation) was made for affines when the old Civil Code was compiled at the time of the modernization. There have been considerable discrepancies between these regulations and actual practice of the people, particularly in the rural population, who have largely maintained their local usage.

recognized, and sharply differentiated from the cognates, and both groups bind each other structurally, regardless of the replacement of individuals. In the Japanese system, the *de facto* and *de jure* relationship with a household of affines usually rapidly decreases after the death of the individual member through whom the affinal relation is established. Close relationship with households of affines is kept through individuals, not through a kinship network as a whole. With cognates too, kinship relations are maintained through the individuals of the household, rather than through the descent network.

The functions of *shinrui* are carried out on the basis of a household. The *shinrui* of the members of a household tends to be framed along the lines of the *shinrui* of the household head, rather than of each individual member. The recognition of kinship itself with reference to each individual does not always establish *shinrui* relationship, unless it is supported by some activity. It is the kin of the household, not of the individual, that are most significant socially. Therefore, the range and the gradation of the *shinrui* for an individual gradually change according to the life cycle of that individual, in which alterations in his status in the household are involved. For example, a man, as a head of the household, sees the changing composition of his *shinrui* symbolically appearing in two major events: one is his father's funeral and the other his son's marriage. Some *shinrui* members appear for the former but disappear for the latter, and in place of them, new *shinrui* members appear. For the former were those *shinrui* recognized with reference to his father, and in the latter, with reference to his son. The funeral of his parent would be the last occasion on which his distant *shinrui* through his parents (such as cousins of his parents) come to his household. His son's wedding marks the beginning of the association with *shinrui* new to him (such as his son's wife's *shinrui*). In the case of a woman, before her marriage, her *shinrui* is recognized as that of her father; then, if she marries virilocally into another village, the *shinrui* of her husband stands closer to her, while her previous *shinrui* tends to fade; finally, after the retirement of her husband from the headship, or by the death of her husband, her *shinrui* is gradually framed on that of her son, while her husband's distant *shinrui* will be fading. Contact with these distant *shinrui* is normally ended on the death of cousins, nephews and nieces.

In theory the number of *shinrui* would constantly increase by the marriage of members of the households involved in the *shinrui* relationship, and at the same time, the death of individuals would decrease their number. Hence the range of a *shinrui* is kept fairly constant with reference to a household, though its composition gradually changes. It therefore seems clear, by this process, that a *shinrui* is not a group but a category.

The *shinrui* relationship will not extend along the simple lines of 'relatedness' through cognatic and affinal relationships. The recognition of a *shinrui*, the outer limit of the category, is precisely governed by the economic and moral rights and obligations of the members to each other, in which the varying degree of gradation has significance according to the closeness of the relationship among the members of *shinrui*. Normally, *de jure* *shinrui* are recognized as those households of relatives which exchange the mortuary offerings (*kōden*), presented by each household of a *shinrui* to the household where the funeral is performed. The degree of gradation among the households of a *shinrui* is clearly seen in the different amounts of mortuary offerings.[1] One of the best examples is drawn from Koh village, where the mortuary offerings are still measured by the traditionally fixed quantity of rice, as follows:

At the death of ego's (and spouse's)

parent	1 *to* (10 *shō*)[2] of rice;
sibling	7 *shō*;
uncle and aunt	3 *shō*;
cousin	1 *shō*;

(In the case of members of the *shinrui* other than the above-stated persons, the amount of their offerings of rice is decided by a meeting of the *shinrui*, and is in accordance with the above standard.)

In Koh village marriages are traditionally arranged mostly between members of the village, so that the majority of the villagers are related in one way or another. But they make a sharp distinction between recognized *shinrui* among whom the mortuary offerings are exchanged, and simply related people. The cousin is the last person to present a mortuary offering.

This example demonstrates the accepted standard range and

[1] Today the mortuary offering consists of money, but in traditional form consisted of rice. Normally the expense of the funeral is met by the total mortuary offerings received.   [2] 1 *shō* equals 3·18 pints.

grading of categories of a *shinrui* in terms of kinship distance in Japan. According to my study of the 'lists of mortuary offerings' (*kōden-chō*)[1] of several households in different villages, the gradation in the amounts of the mortuary offerings in the pre-war period reveals a pattern strikingly similar to that in Koh village.[2]

It is important to note here that according to this gradation, cognates and affines are placed in the same grade. In fact, the household from which the spouse came stands as one of the most important *shinrui* to ego's own household, no less important than the household of his own sibling. When this affinal household is to be found in the same village, it would be the first to help in an emergency. Thus the affines in this category are regarded as among the closest *shinrui* to ego's household.

In the grading there is also no discrimination between the paternal and the maternal sides, or between the sexes. This bilateral extension of the cousin range seems the basic pattern in Japan. I even observed the same pattern in the lists of mortuary offerings of a village community where a strong patrinominal tendency is found in the formation of the local corporate group, *dōzoku* (see Chapter 3).

These characteristics in the composition of *shinrui* can be summed up, in kinship terms, as follows (see Figure 5): (1) Bilaterality: both paternal and maternal sides are symmetrically referred to and addressed by the same terms. (2) Range up to cousins: the range of kin referred to by kinship terms ends with cousins, grandparents and grandchildren. (3) Equation of kin and affines: the same range and terms apply to the kin and affines of ego's spouse. (Hence another set of kin—of spouse—should be added to the kin universe of ego in Figure 5.)

[1] It is the traditional custom throughout Japan for every household to keep lists of the offerings at funerals performed for the members of the household. This list records how each household of *shinrui* performed its duty at the funeral of a member of ego's household, so that a similar return can be made when a death occurs in any of these households.

[2] Today the degree of closeness of *shinrui* does not always accord with the different amounts of mortuary offerings, since the members of *shinrui* do not always engage in homogeneous economic activity even in villages. After the war, particularly, economic success or failure has modified the standard of mortuary offerings. However, the custom still prevails throughout Japan. Mortuary offerings are presented not only to *shinrui* members, but also to neighbours, friends and colleagues. The relative amounts of mortuary offerings of these people are measured also according to the closeness of personal relation and social status.

These three elements form the core of *shinrui*, on the basis of which an individual *shinrui* takes its actual shape according to circumstance. The bilateral character does not necessarily extend beyond the cousin range, and cousins stand at the furthermost point within the actual *shinrui*. In some cases a cousin would be equated in importance with a sibling, when there are no or few siblings. On the other hand, when there are many siblings, a cousin might have less importance as a *shinrui*. Remarks such as 'The relationship between cousins (*itoko*) would be as easily cut off as a thread (*ito*)', or 'One can carry on without cousins' are often heard in villages. In fact, beyond the range of cousins, a *shinrui* would be found in any shape according to the various circumstances of the household. The demarcation of the *shinrui* beyond or around cousins is indeed based on various economic and local situations, and not merely on a descent principle such as bilaterality.

As stated above, every household of Koh village has a fairly

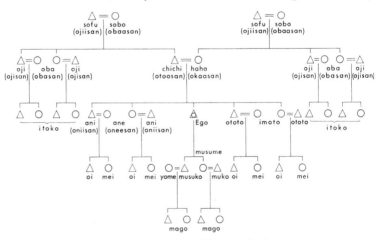

FIGURE 5. Japanese Kinship Terminology

(   ) = Term of address: those shown without such a term are addressed by personal name.

The only difference occasioned by the sex of ego is in the term of reference for ego's spouse: *tsuma* (wife) and *otto* (husband).

Affines who are called by the same term as that for consanguines—spouses of siblings and of uncles and aunts—can be differentiated by adding an adjective 'giri-no' (-in-law): such as *giri-no-ane* (elder sister-in-law). This applies only in reference, not address.

uniform range of *shinrui*, and this seems to derive from the fact that in this village the economic standing of every household is more or less equal, and the tendency towards village endogamy is great. But normally the range of *shinrui* would differ with the individual household. Whether *shinrui* is found in the same village or in another distant village has an important effect on its recognition. For example, in Koshiozu village, households up to second cousins in the village are recognized as *shinrui*, whereas households up to first cousins only are recognized as *shinrui* when they are in other villages. First cousins whose households are in a distant city tend to be excluded in the course of time. The local familiarity coming with similar socio-economic life, which makes it possible to maintain constant intercommunication, seems an important factor for recognition of the *shinrui* relation. The

Notes to Figure 5

1. Each individual term varies according to local usage and dialect, as well as with the different strata of society, but throughout Japan the general pattern is uniform. Figure 5 shows the terms in contemporary standard Japanese.

2. The basic pattern of Japanese kinship terminology is similar to that of English terminology, and the range and categories of kin referred to by kinship terms also correspond to English usage. One of the differences, however, is that there is no native term for *brother* and *sister* as one category. Siblings are differentiated respectively by their order of birth. *Kyodai* (brothers; and also used for siblings of both sexes) and *shimai* (sisters), used very commonly among Japanese, are derived from Chinese terms.

3. A parent is referred to as *oya*, a child is *ko*, as already mentioned elsewhere. Parents are also referred to as *ryōshin* (Chinese derivation).

4. Likewise *sofu* (grandfather) and *sobo* (grandmother) are derived from Chinese terms. Native terms which linguistically correspond to *chichi* (father), *haha* (mother) and others are *jii* and *baa* (or *jiji* and *baba*). *Sofu* and *sobo* are more generally used.

5. Terms of address are only used for senior members, and not for cousins. They are honorific forms of reference terms adding the suffix *san* (sometimes also prefix *o*). These terms of address may also be used for reference.

6. A common tendency in referring to kin is to make a distinction by residential (household) criterion rather than by kinship category. For instance, kin are referred to according to their residence: the uncle of one's house, and the uncle who resides elsewhere, such as *uchi-no-ojisan* (the uncle of my house), *tokyo-no-ojisan* (the uncle in Tokyo), etc.

7. Address terms such as *oniisan*, *oneesan*, *ojisan*, *obasan*, *ojiisan* and *obaasan* are also used widely in addressing non-kin (strangers as well as familiar acquaintances) according to their relative age.

RJ D

range of *shinrui* also differs according to social strata: a wealthy household tends to have a broader range of *shinrui*, while the poorer sector of the community tends to have a narrower range. When members of a *shinrui* reside far apart, they easily cease to interact, yet a wealthy household will maintain contact with quite distant *shinrui*. The maintenance of the *shinrui* relationship thus tends to depend largely upon the location of a household and its economic standing.

Shinrui is determined not only by the recognition of kinship distance, but also by the performance of duties and obligations between the households. Failure of the latter often leads to termination of the relationship, whatever be the actual kinship recognized. The maintenance of *shinrui* entails considerable expense, not only when it is necessary to make the occasional presentation of mortuary offerings and wedding gifts to *shinrui*, but particularly when a funeral or wedding is performed in one's own household. One should then give a big feast inviting all *shinrui*, according to the standing of each *shinrui* aggregate. In terms of intercommunication between *shinrui*, there is also an important custom among the rural population. Once a year on the occasion of a local festival (though the reason for and name of the festival may differ according to the locality) a household must distribute presents (home-made rice cakes, the kind of which varies according to the locality) to all its *shinrui* households, from whom the household receives similar gifts. It takes one or two days for the mistress of the household to prepare the cakes; her son or daughter-in-law will then visit every *shinrui* household to distribute a box of the cakes, and they enjoy meeting their *shinrui* and eating the cakes and other food offered. In the same way, members of various *shinrui* households come to visit ego's own household with a similar presentation. (Whether the exchange is done on the same day or on a different day depends on local custom.) While distributing and receiving cakes to and from various *shinrui* households, the people also enjoy criticizing the taste of the cake—the sweeter the better (hence more sugar is used to achieve greater appreciation). Such duties and obligations of *shinrui* also occur on other occasions.

Because of these economic obligations among *shinrui*, the economic standing of a household tends to determine the range of *shinrui*. A further point is that in order to carry out these functions, a *shinrui* household should be of equal standing with ego's household, since reciprocal gift exchange is involved. If one household of *shinrui* becomes very much less prosperous, it is difficult to maintain the *shinrui* relation. It is for this reason also that the Japanese consider marriages should take place between households of equal economic and social standing, as in fact normally occurs. (I shall discuss this point fully in Chapter 4.)

The limit or boundary of *shinrui*, which lies around the core of the cousin range, is largely determined by the local and economic situation of each household. Whether the recognized range is narrower or broader, according to the individual household, replacement of the members of *shinrui* occurs so that each household keeps its range of *shinrui* fairly constant, as already stated. But in some localities there is a custom of maintaining *shinrui* relationship with a particular household despite the distance of the kinship connection.

Such a household is called, for example, *ie-ni-tsuita-enka* (the household of a *shinrui* attached to one's household) in Kumamoto prefecture; or *ichino-shinrui* (the first *shinrui*) in Miyagi prefecture. A particular *shinrui* of this sort is the household which contributed to the establishment of one's own household. For instance, if ego's household was established by ego's great-grandfather the household where ego's great-grandfather was born is likely to be the first *shinrui*. In terms of kinship, the present head of this household may be a third cousin to ego, and is normally excluded from the range of *shinrui*, but one regards this particular household as one of the most important *shinrui*. Again if one's great-grandfather came to settle in the village from very far away, and had no relative near by, one's first *shinrui* could be that household in the village which gave help in the establishment of one's ancestral household. Thus in the absence of kinship, such a substitute relationship could be formed. In some cases two households regard each other as first *shinrui* because in the first generation their founders were siblings. Since every household recognizes as its first *shinrui* a household older than its own, or at least one equally old, a comparatively old household in a locality may have many *shinrui* households which regard it as the first *shinrui*.

It can therefore be seen that the term *shinrui*, which primarily expresses kinship and affinal relations, may be used for a particular relationship between households. In practice a particular local relation between households often overlaps with the *shinrui* relation, and the former plays an important role comparable to that of *shinrui*. Hence in some localities the term *shinrui* is also used for a household with which ego's household has a particularly close relation, as in the above instances.

However, as an analytical concept *shinrui* should be differentiated from local relations. From the theoretical angle, and in contrast to *shinrui*, the concept of *local corporate group* as another important element in the analysis of rural community, is introduced here.

Empirically, a local corporate group may or may not include a household of *shinrui*. It is essentially formed on the criterion of neighbourhood; a household of *shinrui* would be included if it happened to be a neighbour. It is very rare for a set of *shinrui* alone to form a local corporate group. Theoretically this is impossible unless all households of *shinrui* are clustered in a particular residential area in a village, and marriages occur only within the group. There are some ethnographic reports stating that *shinrui* form an endogamous group, and operate as a local corporate group. But I suspect that such a local corporate group would be formed mostly rather than exclusively of *shinrui*.

Not only in theory, but also in fact, the concept of *shinrui* is clearly differentiated from that of the local corporate group (though a local term happens to be used indiscriminately). The *shinrui* is a category of kin, the boundary of which continually alters by the change of generations and by marriages of the members of the households involved. Its duties are rigorous, but the group is too unstable to serve as the basis of the whole social organization. The importance of the local corporate group, with its constant composition in terms of households, enters here. It is on a basis of local corporate groups that the village community is organized. The next chapter gives a detailed picture of village organization, and Chapter 3 describes the actual operations of local corporate groups.

NOTE

Shinzoku

Along with the category of *shinrui*, there is another category for a set of kin termed *shinzoku*, which is conceptualized in terms of *Goshintō* (Five Categories of Relatives graded according to their closeness to ego). The basic scheme of the *Goshintō* is shown in Figure 6. This scheme had its legal importance in terms of indicating a distance between relatives, rather than of delineating a set of relatives as a group. The frame of *Goshintō*, the pattern of the traditional legal usage in Japan, was effectively employed by the old Civil Code. The *Goshintō* was originally produced in the seventh century when the first firm state government was established in Japan. As a model, the mourning grades of the Chinese royal family of the Tang dynasty were followed, with some modification.

In comparison with the scheme of *shinrui* (as presented in

FIGURE 6. Major Scheme of *Five Categories of Shinzoku* established in 1917
Shading indicates membership of *Shinrui*.
(Other *shinrui* members are excluded from the *shinzoku*.)

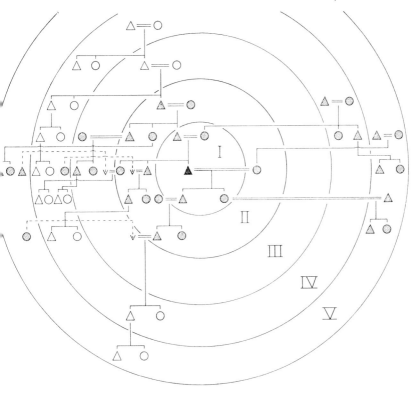

Figures 3 and 4), that of *shinzoku* (as shown in Figure 6) has a strong patrilineal influence, though it includes more affines than the Chinese patrilineal scheme above mentioned. It is interesting to note that some of the most important *shinrui*, for example, wife's parents and sister's husband, are placed in the fifth category of the *shinzoku*, the furthest distance among the *de jure* relatives in terms of *shinzoku*. Together with the patrilineal tendency, the important difference of *shinzoku* from *shinrui* is in its composition, which is based on the individual and disregards the household criterion that is so significant for *shinrui*. Later, the range of the *shinzoku* was extended by adding a sixth category: this reflects the difficulty of including all kin actually recognized by the native custom (in terms of *shinrui*) in the category of *shinzoku*.

The *shinzoku* took effect in the old Civil Code, particularly in the provision of the criminal law. But in the people's actual life it had hardly any effect; although they had been aware of the terms *shinzoku* and *Goshintō*, the majority of the rural population had no very clear recognition of relatives in terms of the Five Categories. The term *shinzoku* itself has been often used as a synonym of *shinrui*, without referring to the legal Five Categories. Because of such usage, the term *shinzoku* is often used in sociological literature in place of *shinrui*, without making any distinction in the concept. A further complication arises because Japanese scholars have been accustomed to refer to kinship relations in terms of the Five Categories. I suggest here, as T. Nakano did (Nakano, 1958), that the term *shinzoku* should be used only to refer to the legal frame of *Goshintō*, differentiated from *shinrui*: and *Goshintō* should be discussed only in terms of the legal frame, not in terms of the sociological frame.

2

Basic Village Organization in Historical Perspective

In studying Japanese kinship and local economic organization, whose basic features appear in the household structure, as described in Chapter 1, it is important to understand the historical background. In particular, the overall political organization of the Tokugawa period is significant, because it was at this time that the structure of rural Japan, as we now understand it, was taking shape.

The most important point is that the Tokugawa system established the *village* as the basic social and economic unit in rural Japan; and the *household* as a production unit responsible for revenue. An individual must be placed in the authorized unit of a household, and the household must be a member of a village, which represented the basic social and political unit of the peasant community. The resultant rights and ownership can be ascribed to a village at one level, and to a household at another, not to an individual. The structure and function of the *ie* (household), described in the previous chapter, certainly involve this historical factor.

From Tokugawa times a village (*mura*) formed a distinctive residential area, surrounded by fields, the cultivation of which was carried out by the villagers. The picture of a normal peasant household was as follows: each household possessed house-site land called *yashiki*—ideally of square shape—marked off from that of neighbouring households. Within this site, the dwelling house was built facing towards the south, and around it there were a storehouse and a cattle-shed where cows and other livestock were kept. In front of the dwelling house, adjoining the front yard, vegetable gardens were set out. Such a house was normally occupied by the elementary family with or without

41

parents and unmarried siblings of the husband or of the wife (cf. the composition of a household as discussed on pp. 1–7). Ideally the land in which such a household possessed the rights of ownership or of cultivation was estimated at about 1 *chō* (2·45 acres), which produced a yield of around 10 *koku* rice.[1] But the actual size of the holding and the rights varied according to an individual household or at a given time.

According to the records prepared by the Tokugawa Bakufu for the purpose of the revenue collection in 1734, the model village consisted of:

Total arable land	200 *koku* (50% wet field and 50% dry field);
Total population	120 (men and women 60 each);
Total number of households	24;
Total number of horses	6.

These figures give the following average for each household: arable land—8·3 *tan* (about two acres); the number of household members—five; and one horse to every four households. Further, the data reveal that twelve persons (2–3 households), 10 per cent of the village population, were craftsmen and merchants.[2]

The actual size of a village seems to vary considerably according to locality and time. The distribution of villages, varying in size from half a dozen to 200 households, reveals that size is in fair accord with the ecological and economic environment: the availability of arable lands, particularly of wet rice fields, seems to determine the number of the households in a village. Since the peasant does not go very far from his village for cultivation, and as he normally works in a field fed by water controlled by his

---

[1] 1 *chō* = 10 *tan*. 1 *tan* = 0·245 acre = 0·992 hectare. 1 *koku* = 4·9629 bushels.

The standard yield of 1 *tan* is estimated at 1 *koku*, the standard amount of one year's supply for one man.

The standard holding today also is estimated at 1 *chō*. However, the yield has more than doubled that of the Tokugawa period through technical improvements and the application of scientific methods.

[2] The detailed study of the records is presented in Oishi, 1962, pp. 187–96.

According to Oishi, there is another record, called *Suijin-roku* written by Katsu Kaishū, which contains data of arable land and population of the entire territory of Tokugawa Japan. The national survey of the population in 1804, recorded n the *Suijin-roku*, shows that the average of arable land held by a village is 408·57 *koku*, and that of the population is 404·94 persons. These figures reveal roughly one *koku* for one person, which is a little less in *koku* per person in comparison with that of the above data; and the size of a village is larger than the latter.

village, this arrangement has not altered much even today. Naturally in hilly areas the size of the village tends to be smaller, whereas in fertile delta valleys it tends to be larger. Quite large villages, some with more than 200 households, seem to have developed mainly during the last hundred years through technical developments in farming, and through the expansion of industrial enterprise into rural areas. It can be assumed that the number of larger villages in the Tokugawa period must have been much less than today, but that the number of villages in Japan has increased little since the later Tokugawa period.

During the Tokugawa period the village provided the basic rural organization by regulating peasant farming activities and by administering the civil affairs of the community; it was the most important unit of the administrative system of the feudal estates within the state organization. However, the term *mura* (village) is rather confusing, because of changes in the administrative system after the Tokugawa period. One of these important administrative reorganizations in Japan was that of Meiji 22 (1889), by which several *mura* of the Tokugawa were amalgamated into single units, and the term *mura* was also applied to this wider unit. Another change occurred after the war, by which the unit of *mura* became larger still so as to include many more villages than formerly. The unit of the *mura* in the Tokugawa period was known as *buraku* in general, and *ōaza* or *ku* as an administrative unit; it formed the nucleus of a larger local unit, *mura* or *chō*. After the war, in some cases, villages formed part of a *shi*,[1] together with its urban centre.

In spite of such changes in administrative schemes, in most cases the unit of the Tokugawa *mura* has persisted as the basic social and economic unit by which village life is largely determined. Since the economic life of the village depends on irrigation, the function of the *mura* has great significance both as the residential and also in many cases as the water-controlling unit. Hence in this book I employ the term *village* to refer to this important social and economic unit, mostly corresponding to the Tokugawa *mura*, and not strictly to the administrative units of following periods.

Within the scheme of the Tokugawa state administration,

[1] Administrative units in terms of *chō* (town) and *shi* (city) formerly applied only to urban areas.

villages were under their respective feudal lords (*Daimyō*), and all the territories of Japan were divided into roughly three hundred fiefs (estates of *Daimyō*) varying in size.[1] Each fief formed an autonomous political and economic unit, but externally accountable to the supreme authority of the Tokugawa Bakufu (the central government) at the highest level of the political system.[2] The Tokugawa political system was thus a centralized feudal system.

The internal organization of the *Daimyō*'s estate under the Tokugawa policy had great importance from the point of view of the social and economic history of Japan. One of the distinguishing characteristics was the clear-cut division between the urban and rural populations. The headquarters of the estate, where the *Daimyo*'s castle was situated, had developed, in the course of time, into a town or city. This residential area of the *Daimyō* and his retainers (*Bushi*) attracted merchants and craftsmen, while the rural areas were occupied only by peasants.

Before the Tokugawa period most peasants were serfs attached to the land owned by powerful local landlords, who were also the military men (*Bushi*). In an emergency these peasants were mobilized as their soldiers.[3] The Tokugawa feudal system reorganized these local semi-independent military officers, and incorporated them into the retinues of the *Daimyō*. Some of them remained in the rural areas and became peasants. Many of these rural *Bushi* were recruited into the administrative system of the

---

[1] There were some changes in the numbers of *Daimyō* during the period: there were 187 *Daimyō* in 1602; 233 in 1703; and 266 in 1866. The size of the *Daimyō* estates was expressed in terms of the authorized amounts of the rice revenue measured by *koku*. The following figures may give a rough idea of the size and distribution of the estates in 1703.

			Daimyō of more than 1,000,000 *koku*	1
,,	,,	,,	500,000 ,,	6
,,	,,	,,	200,000 ,,	15
,,	,,	,,	100,000 ,,	28
,,	,,	,,	50,000 ,,	51
,,	,,	,,	20,000 ,,	74
,,	less than		20,000 ,,	58
			Total	233

[2] Tokugawa itself had its own estates, the total of which amounted to 7,000,000 *koku*, geographically distributed in various areas. In this sense, the Tokugawa Shogun was also one of the *Daimyō*, though he held overall authority over the other *Daimyō*.

[3] There were also serfs of absentee aristocrats, and of temples and shrines.

feudal state: they were appointed as village officers to control the peasants, and were known as *Gōshi*. Some of the *Gōshi* continued the medieval practice of retaining serfs under their direct control, but the majority of the peasants became independent of their masters by conducting their own farm management. On the whole, the Tokugawa policy successfully kept the peasants under the direct control of the *Daimyō*: according to their holdings the peasants of a village were registered in a household with a duty to pay tax to the feudal lord.

Thus a clear geographical and occupational differentiation existed between the military men (administrative officers) and peasants, which was also expressed in terms of two distinct status occupations, namely, military service (*Bushi*) and cultivation of soil (*Nōmin*), which formed the basis of the national organization. The Tokugawa period is termed 'feudal', but it is not a feudal system in the sense of a pyramidal political structure in which retainers are granted rights in land from their master in return for service and tribute: instead it was more a bureaucratic system. The *Daimyō* held their estates under the Bakufu in return for service, without tribute. The nature of their service resembled that of governors appointed by the central government: they were responsible, under the strict control of the Bakufu, for the complete administration of the population of their estates. Further, the retainers of *Daimyō* received their salaries in *koku* of rice for their official services, and not in the form of land.

The bureaucratic nature of the administrative system, by which the income of the *Daimyō* and the salaries of his retinue were registered by *koku* of rice, might give an impression that a monetary economy was less developed in this period. But this was not so because of the widespread activities of the merchants. The rice received by *Daimyō* had to be exchanged for money for consumption purposes. Because of this the merchants played an important role and a monetary economy expanded rapidly all over Japan, centred mainly on Edo (modern Tokyo) and Osaka. Merchants in Japan had developed their activities to conform to, and within the scale of, this political system, attaching themselves to the ruling class, and not acting independently. It is here that a great difference between the premodern picture of Japan and that of Europe can be seen. In Japan the greatest merchants of this time were found among those under government patronage with special advantages, and were wholesale dealers who dealt mostly in rice and timber. They also contributed much to the development of city life by their wealth.

However, merchants were placed at the bottom of the national occupational ranking, morally despised because they were not engaged directly in production, and were not born into the honourable *Bushi*. Craftsmen, though they were a small percentage of the total population, were placed above merchants. Hence, in effect, there were four distinct status classes: at the top of this hierarchy was the *Bushi*, which formed the distinguished, intellectual élite of administrative officers, military men and scholars. Next were the peasants, who were most important in the structure of the national economy, on which the whole political system was built up. Then came the third rank, the craftsmen; and at the bottom, the merchants. According to the census at the end of the Tokugawa period, the percentage of each of the major occupational groups was as follows: the *Bushi* was 6 per cent, the townsmen (mostly merchants, but including craftsmen and others) 10 per cent, and peasants 80 per cent. The rest were various minor groups including priests, royal families and aristocrats (mainly families from which the officials of the Imperial Court came), etc.

Under this system peasants, as members of their respective villages, enjoyed village autonomy and great security. Each village was an autonomous administrative and economic unit, represented by its headman, and managed by a village council. The internal economy of the village was practically self-supporting. Thus a village represented a fairly closed political, economic and social unit. The peasant was supposed to devote himself to rice production, on which the nation's economy and political system depended, and was not allowed to engage in any occupation other than agriculture,[1] or even to produce crops other than rice beyond the authorized limit. Further, he was bound by other rules, such as a prohibition on the sale of land beyond the authorized amounts; and a limit on residential movement: particularly, a move to another estate was strictly prohibited.

Under the Tokugawa policy, which encouraged agriculture,

---

[1] It seems that a village included a few houses which engaged in blacksmithing and general dealing, but they were a very small percentage (see p. 42), and represented occupations ancillary to and usually necessary to agriculture.

the feudal lords also tried their best to increase production in order that their estates would prosper and their revenues increase. The construction of new irrigation ditches and improvements to farming techniques resulted in much more land being brought into cultivation, as well as in the yield of crops (mostly rice) being increased from the same plots of land. The arable lands of old villages had been greatly extended, and many new villages had been established during this period. As a result the landscape of rural Japan had greatly changed: in the medieval age, villages were normally clustered on the slopes of a hill under the fortress of a powerful local family, and only those areas irrigated directly from a river or a tank were cultivated. Now, the majority of villages were concentrated in the flat areas (large valley and delta plains), situated at the most convenient place for cultivation. The flow of the rivers was skilfully controlled and water was drawn further than ten miles from a river in order to irrigate more distant areas.

Furthermore, the political and economic changes brought about by the Tokugawa policy involved a genuine revision of the internal social and economic organization of the peasant community. The majority of peasants were no longer serfs or slaves; they cultivated their land under their own management. Every household became a separate productive unit, and in theory there was no social differentiation among the households of a village community. A village became a local autonomous unit well organized by its members, who were no longer merely culti-vators directly subject to, and managed by, the local master. Con-fidence was engendered in the peasants by their being made responsible for farm management under the new administrative system, and as a result state agriculture as well as peasant life greatly improved.

The successful Tokugawa system, which brought with it a long period of nation-wide peace, naturally resulted in a tremen-dous economic growth in both agriculture and commerce, accompanied by a swift increase of the population. This increase of population together with the expansion of the commercial economy resulted in a gradual shortage of land, despite the in-creased yield from crops and despite continuing land reclamation.[1]

[1] According to the survey carried out during the Kyōho (1716–34), the total of arable land had increased by 81 per cent from that of the beginning of the

Since Kyōho (1716–34) the fragmentation of land among households had gradually increased the number of households owning
less than the ideal holding. Anticipating this tendency, the Bakufu
issued a law in 1673 which prohibited the subdivision of holdings
of less than 10 *koku*, which was soon followed by similar regulations from local feudal lords. S. Oishi, economic historian,
measures the climax of the economic development and prosperity
of the peasants as occurring about 1670 (Oishi, 1956). At about
this time, it seems that all available land for cultivation had been
exploited, reaching a maximum production under the Tokugawa
farming techniques; and after that the increase of population was
beyond the land's resources. Thus, the latter part of the seventeenth century was the turning point in the economic history of
the Tokugawa period. By the eighteenth century the maintenance
of the integration of the community had come to pose a very
serious problem, and economic competition among households

Tokugawa period (the early seventeenth century); but that of 1884 (Meiji 7)
shows only 86 per cent increase from that same period. (See Oishi, 1956, pp.
83–84.) The national survey of arable land started in the later part of the sixteenth
century, before the Tokugawa period, but the national census of the population
was developed much later.

The embryonic forms of the census were introduced in the early Tokugawa
period by the Bakufu, and were called *Ninbetsu-aratame* (first taken in 1644) and
Shūmon-aratame (first taken in 1670). The *Ninbetsu-aratame* was taken by officials
who visited every village. In each village the record book, *Ninbetsu-chō*, was tabulated, in which was listed the name of the head of each household with his co-
residents (with indication of sex and age). This census followed the pattern of
tabulation established by the Bakufu, and aimed to further the control of the
agricultural population by the local lord for administrative and taxation purposes.

The second form of census, the *Shūmon-aratame*, was for the purpose of prohi-
biting and suppressing Christianity. This record book, also recorded village by
village, was called *Shūmon-aratame-chō*. It contained the names of the head of
each household and his co-residents, with sex, age, relation to the head and, the
most important item among them, the indication of temple affiliation of the
household. Both censuses included at the end the total population of each village
by household and sex, and the total number of cattle in the village. (It is important to note here too that the household and village were dealt with as the
most important basic units.)

Though these censuses were made for different purposes, in the course of time
they came to substitute for each other, and in many cases became one combined
record known as *Shūmon-ninbetsu-aratame-chō*, and played an important role as
a census register.

The first nation-wide census based on these records was taken in 1721, and was
repeated every six years. (Cf. Europe, where the first formal census was that
taken in 1754 in Sweden, followed by those of 1801 in England and France.)
During the Tokugawa period, the national census was taken 22 times (the 22nd
was in 1846). Some deficiencies of these censuses are found to be that first, most

of a village community was severe, to the disadvantage of sons of small owner-cultivators. The social consequences of such a trend were serious. About this time a differentiation in peasant statuses became common in most villages, resulting in titled farmers (owner) and dependants (tenants), as will be described in detail later.

Furthermore, this internal situation in the village was coupled with the development of commercial activities. The gradual advance of merchant capital and a commercial economy into rural areas, which exploited the interests of both agricultural production and agricultural life, eventually brought about a concentration of land ownership: the declining feudal law had little effect in checking this tendency. At the same time, merchants began to develop commercial enterprises in rural areas, as well as industries in the towns. By taking advantage of the expansion of a commercial economy and the development of commercial agriculture, wealthy landed farmers now tended to act as merchants and usurers. Some of them established rural industries. This tendency accelerated the expropriation of land from the poor, and wealthy landowners became a new economic class between peasant and feudal lord. Some of the big landowners owned land containing several villages, and they now developed a new

of them excluded children under fifteen (although some of them registered children from one year old, others from two, five, eight or eleven, etc.). Second, *Bushi* (including aristocrats) and their retinues and servants, and outcast lower population were excluded: the population of these special groups was entered in separate record books respectively under a different system. This excluded population was estimated to be some 1,900,000 of the total population of the later Tokugawa period, which is estimated to have been 34,800,000. The study of the population of the Tokugawa period is best presented by works of N. Sekiyama (1958 and 1959).

The manner of tabulation of these censuses shows that there were local differences in the details of information taken, though all contained the basic items above mentioned. Additional details sometimes included were: occupation, status, land owned (by *koku*), size and ownership of the house, number of cattle, names of father and of village from which wife and servant came, the length of employment of domestic and farm servants. Every year such incidents as the retirement of the head of a household, succession and inheritance, birth and death, marriage, change of permanent address, immigrants and emigrants of the village, were added by the local official. These provide indeed a wealth of information through which socio-economic study at the village level can be made. In some villages, such records have been well preserved, and detailed studies of them have been begun recently by economic historians. (Some of them will be discussed in the next section.) If social anthropologists can co-operate in this task, the results will be the greater.

method of increasing their income by letting the whole of their land out to be farmed by tenants. However, these were rather exceptional cases, and most landowners of this period were still farming landowners who cultivated their land themselves with the help of tenants or farm servants.

Coupled with this series of economic changes, an increasing demand for revenue further exploited the peasants. This revenue, which was 40 per cent of the yield in the earlier period of the Tokugawa, had been raised to 50 per cent, and even in some cases to 60 per cent,[1] since the middle of the period, in order to cover the financial difficulties of the feudal lords and the Tokugawa Bakufu. The development of a commercial economy and long-lasting peace had allowed the leisured class, the bureaucrats, to increase their expenditure, for they now tended to seek a luxurious city life. Furthermore, financial difficulties arose for the Bakufu, as well as for the *Daimyō*, on account of an increase in the number of new administrative posts. Expansion or reorganization of the administrative system, which helped to supply jobs for the growing numbers of the Bushi class, was responsible for this increase. As for local feudal lords, under the policy of the Bakufu they had been forced to make repeated large expenditures in order that wealth and power should not be allowed to accumulate in their hands.[2] Hence their financial difficulties too had increased towards the later period. As a *Daimyō* suffered, his retinue did likewise, particularly in the lower sector of the *Bushi* class; and as this loss could not all be covered by the raising of extra revenue, it finally brought about the decline of the whole Tokugawa régime.

Under these social and economic conditions of the later Tokugawa period, many poor peasants were finally forced to sell their land. Since the sale of land was prohibited by law beyond

[1] These figures on the revenue percentage were those laid down by the ruler as a goal for revenue collectors. They were not necessarily met by the actual percentage paid in by the peasants. Further, actual revenues differed from estate to estate. Some economic historians are of the opinion that 60 per cent was never realized: it was almost impossible in view of the peasants' situation in those days, and of the inefficiency of the declining administrative system.

[2] One such example was the system called *sankin-kōtai*, in which the wife and children of a *Daimyō* resided at Edo, the headquarters of the Bakufu, and the *Daimyō* changed his residence every other year between his estate and Edo. The trip was very costly for the *Daimyō*, as it had to be performed in a grand manner as befitted his rank.

the authorized amounts, most sales were done through a form of mortgage. Many landless peasants became the servants or tenants of wealthier ones, or labourers for growing manufacturers, servants of wealthy city dwellers (*Bushi* and merchants), or they became minor merchants and craftsmen. Among this section of the village population many families were broken up. At the worst, some of them sold their daughters. Much of the moving population went to Edo and Osaka, and other cities. However, since feudal law prevented residential movement and changes of occupation, those who went to urban areas were not a large percentage of the total. The majority were forced to solve their problems within their own community. The most serious situation here was the well-known tragic custom called *mabiki* (infanticide of new-born babies, or procured abortion), which was found in various parts of Japan. The rural situation was made even worse by the occasional famines of the latter part of the period, the historically well-known being those of 1732, 1782, 1786–7, and 1833–6. This series of events, which brought about the impoverishment of the peasants, eventually resulted in the nation-wide disturbances known as *hyakushō-ikki* (peasant revolts). Many *hyakushō-ikki* took the form of bringing complaints or petitions to the Bakufu or the *Daimyō*, thus bypassing the normal procedure of doing this through the village or local officials and district officers, in whose misconduct the peasants saw the cause of their intolerable existence; others took the form of escaping to other feudal estates and deserting their own villages. Most of these revolts met a tragic end, and sentences were indiscriminate and heavy: the leaders were mostly killed or exiled.

The Tokugawa era, which ended in nation-wide disturbances and in the grimmest conditions for the peasants, was succeeded by the modern Meiji period with its promise of great progress. However, the modern changes in the nation's political and economic system had little effect on the rural structure in which the life of the peasants was anchored. In spite of rapid industrialization at a national level, the traditional pattern of rural life had not changed. In other words, effective industrialization was carried out without affecting the basic social and economic composition of the village community: Japan's industrial revolution started without an agricultural revolution.

The backwardness of Japan's rural society—constantly discussed by economists and sociologists in terms of surviving feudal dues (pp. 178–9)—seems to be closely associated with unique features of Japan's industrialization, as a leading agricultural economist, T. Ouchi, has explained (Ouchi, 1951). Since industrialization in Japan was carried out on the initiative of the government, and much later than in Western countries, it therefore took a shorter time to reach its peak. Thus, the overall scale was quite small, and highly efficient techniques of production were adopted from the beginning, which resulted in the absorption of a relatively small proportion of the labour force. That is to say, the transformation of the nation to an industrial economy was carried out without reshaping the then existing rural economic and social structure. Factories which were established during this rapid period of industrialization could not recruit all the existing surplus population, in particular from the rural areas. At the onset of the industrial revolution Japanese peasants were thus less fortunate than their English counterparts, who could come to the cities to employment in factories.

The outstanding features of agrarian society in modern Japan can be seen in two aspects. First, the agrarian population and the average size of land-holding by households have remained fairly stable. The population engaged in agriculture has been maintained at 14 million from the Meiji period to 1955[1]; the number of rural households has been around 5·5 million and its total population around 30 million, with a small increase every year as follows:

TABLE I. Increase and Decrease of Agricultural Population

1920–5	Natural increase	2,650,000
	Social decrease	1,938,000
1925–30	Natural increase	3,045,000
	Social decrease	1,811,000
1930–5	Natural increase	3,030,000
	Social decrease	2,039,000

(Based on the census figures)

[1] The modern national census is available in Japan from the year 1920. If we trust the data of the national survey taken in 1872 (the early Meiji period), the agrarian population was then also 14 million (Namiki, 1960). This figure corresponds to 38·5 per cent of the total working population engaged in various occupations in 1955. However, recently it has decreased rapidly: 30·7 per cent in 1960, and 28·1 per cent in 1963. (Cf. 27·0 per cent in Italy in 1963; 20·7 per cent in France in 1962; 8·2 per cent in U.S. in 1962; and 4·0 per cent in U.K. in 1962, according to the figures of O.E.C.D.)

The arable land too, though increased to some extent, has been kept fairly stable: the total arable land, which was 5,384 million *chō* in 1905, is recorded as only 5,183 million *chō* in 1955.[1] Therefore, the average land-holding by one household has been around 1 *chō* throughout the last hundred years.[2] Though the rice production increased by an average of 4 per cent every year,[3] there does not seem to be enough space to allow for an increase in the rural population. It should be noted, however, that higher production involves further investment (an increase in the application of chemical fertilizers and the use of more developed agricultural tools); and the advent of an industrial economy has also necessitated an increase of income by reason of the probable higher cost of living. This means that agricultural villages in Japan have continued to present a fairly stable picture, without much increase or decrease in population or in the average size of holdings by household. This picture assumes that a substantial proportion of the population has left the villages for urban areas: this is estimated at around 400,000 every year.[4] Furthermore, those who left the villages were mostly second or third sons, who could not become successors to the household of their fathers or fathers-in-law. This kind of population flow from village to urban area has been an outstanding feature in Japan: it has been very rare for full household members to leave a village, except in the very poor sectors (see Nojiri, 1942). This pattern is understandable in terms of the household structure discussed in the previous chapter.

Secondly, the agrarian society did not change its structural composition: the industrialization of Japan did not entail any significant socio-economic differentiation in terms of large landlords and numerous landless. Instead, on the whole, it has been directed towards producing a large number of smallholders with five *tan* to one *chō*, who represent the middle strata of the agrarian society. The analysis and explanation of such a trend are an im-

---

[1] The total arable land of 1905 showed an increase of 0·85 per cent over 1789, but since 1905 there has not been any great change.

[2] Two-thirds of the total agricultural households belong to those holding under 1 *chō*.

[3] The increase of rice production, which was only 40–50 per cent during the 300 years of the Tokugawa period, showed almost a 40 per cent increase during the next 30 years (1883–1912); and by around 1940 it reached twice that of 1883.

[4] On the mobility of the agricultural population, see Namiki, 1959, and 1960.

portant subject with which a number of Japanese agricultural economists have been concerned. On the basis of these studies I present here a brief sketch of the land-holding situation over the last ninety years.

The new land system was established by the introduction of the modern national taxation system in 1872. The major changes involved in the system were: (1) the revenue of the Tokugawa system, assessed according to the yield of the year, the rate of which varied from estate to estate, was changed into the modern uniform land tax, i.e. three-hundredths of the land value (which was decided by the government, plot by plot); (2) the revenue which had been paid in kind was now to be paid in money; (3) the revenue from tenants, the payment system of which had varied according to local custom, was also brought under the unified new system whereby the landowner paid the government: a tenant paid tenant rent in kind to the landowner, and the landowner paid in money to the government; (4) those who were liable for direct taxation were given legal landownership: these were mostly titled farmers in the Tokugawa period. Hence, in spite of the changes brought about by the new system, the distribution of land holdings of the previous period was largely maintained.

The percentage of rented land to total arable land was said to be 29 per cent in 1872. However, this gradually increased to 36–37 per cent in 1883–4; 39·3 per cent in 1887; 40 per cent in 1892; and 46 per cent in 1930. Particularly during the eighties there was a rapid increase in smallholders who lost their land, thus becoming themselves the tenants of others. On the other hand, there had been a gradual increase in larger holders with more than one *chō* and five *tan*. Among the most noticeable trends was the rise of large landlords with more than fifty *chō*, many of whom were merchants and usurers, or wealthy farmers dealing in the same business, who collected forfeited lands in pawn. These large landowners eventually became non-cultivating landlords rather than modern large-scale farmers, letting the whole of their land to tenants on a farm management basis. The type of farm management remained unchanged, the cultivators being mostly small tenant-farmers, rather than agricultural labourers. From 1894–1905—which corresponds to the whole period of nineteenth-century industrialization in England— agrarian society produced a picture in which wealthy non-cultivating landlords were found in opposition to impoverished tenants. One of the major reasons for this has been said to be the fall in the rice market resulting from the government deflationary practices which had began in 1881.

The ratio of tenant-rent under the new system was 50–68 per cent, which was rather more than in the previous period. On the other hand, the profits of landlords were increased on the average from 28 per cent at the end of the Tokugawa period to 46 per cent in 1890, though these again decreased to 37 per cent in 1915, as is seen from the following table.

TABLE 2. Rate of Distribution of the Yield from Tenant Wet Rice Land

Year	Total yield	Received by landowner			Expenses of cultivator★	Tenant's share (living expenses)
		Land tax to Govt.	Owner's share	Total		
c.1860†	100	37	28	65	15	20
1873	100	35	34	68	15	17
1885	100	17	41	58	25	17
1890	100	12	46	58	24	17
1899	100	12	45	57	25	18
1912	100	11	44	55	22	23
1915	100	13	37	50	29	21

★ excluding family labour   † the end of the Tokugawa period
(Taken from Yamazaki, 1956, p. 72)

The interests of non-cultivating landlords were directed to the industrial field: accordingly, landlords' agricultural profits were mostly invested in industries such as silk-reeling, cotton-spinning, transportation, banking and stocks, etc., and not in the development of farming. Little of the immediate benefit of agricultural income had gone to the small tenant-farmers. Moreover, the flow of industrial commodities made their life more difficult. Since their living was kept constantly at a minimum level, they suffered greatly from occasional lean harvests and illness. Also, many poor peasants had heavily mortgaged their property, which was difficult to retrieve in one generation. The poverty of this lower sector of the peasants, which yet formed a considerable percentage of the agricultural population, had increased during this period and remained until the land reform after the war.

It was a very common story heard in many rural areas before the war, that the majority of villagers could not afford to eat their own rice, but sold it to meet minimum household expenses. In the ordinary way they used to eat barley and sweet potatoes, leaving a small amount of white rice for their festivals. Certainly meat and fish (except in fishing villages) and even sugar, were out of the reach of poor peasants. This was one of the reasons why the introduction of machines was delayed so long in Japanese agriculture, in spite of the rapid development of industry. The peasants had no money to invest in machines, nor space to use them in a land of small holdings. Agricultural improvements were introduced only to obtain rising yields: the production of better quality crops on the same land by hard work and by the application of chemical fertilizers made in factories, and not by the use of machinery.

The growth of large tenancies did not result in the growth of agricultural capitalists or in the extinction of many small ones, as happened in the seventeenth to nineteenth centuries in England. The smallholders still formed the majority of the agricultural population. Moreover, the concentration of lands, which was carried out rapidly during the eighties, reached its climax in 1919, and there then began a decline in the number of landlords: in 1936 landlords with more than fifty *chō* had decreased to 65 per cent of the 1919 figure. (These figures exclude data from Hokkaido and Okinawa.) The major reasons were the sudden fall of the rice market in 1920, and Government control of the rice price in 1921. The situation also became unfavourable to landlords because tenants' associations, which gradually became active after about 1921, began to combine against them.

However, whatever rise and fall there may have been in the number of landlords with more than fifty *chō*, it never exceeded 0·1 per cent of the total holders throughout these years. During the period 1919–36, nearly 50 per cent of landowners were minor holders with less than five *tan*. If those holders with five to ten *tan* are added, this becomes 75 per cent of the total. There therefore appears to have been no basic structural change in land holdings since the beginning of the twentieth century (Ouchi, 1960, p. 204), for this percentage also roughly corresponds to that of 1947, 1950, 1955 and 1957, though the percentage of tenants' land shows a radical decrease since the land reform.[1] One

[1] The percentage of tenant land is as follows: 46·7 per cent (1930), 45·5 per cent (1940), 46·4 per cent (1944), 9·4 per cent (1950) and 9·0 per cent (1955) according to the data quoted by Ouchi, 1960.

of the noticeable tendencies in relation to minor holding is the fairly high percentage of 'owner-tenants' (who cultivate rented lands in addition to their own land) as compared with owners and tenants, as shown below.

TABLE 3. The Number of Agricultural Households by Tenure

Year	Owner cultivation	Owner-tenant cultivation	Tenant cultivation	Total
1883–4	37·3%	41·8%	20·9%	100%
1888	33·4	46·0	20·6	100
1908	32·9	39·9	27·2	100 (5,261)
1920	30·4	41·8	27·8	100 (5,298)
1937	30·1	42·0	26·7	100 (5,575)
1947	36·5	36·9	26·6	100 (5,908)
1950	62·5	32·5	5·0	100 (6,136)
1955	69·6	26·4	4·0	100 (6,031)

( ) = Total number of households (thousands).
(Based on the census data quoted by Ouchi, 1960: excluding that of Hokkaido and Okinawa.)

On the whole the majority of the agricultural population, including a large percentage of tenants and owner-tenants, are *subsistence farmers* cultivating around five *tan* but less than one *chō*. In this respect, the agricultural community has remained basically the same since the Tokugawa period, despite industrialization at the end of the nineteenth century. Small-scale undertakings, characterized by family farmers, employing only a few or no hired workers, have been the general pattern of Japanese agriculture during the last three hundred years.[1]

[1] The greatest change in rural Japan since the Tokugawa era is that being experienced today. It is during the last few years that Japan's industrialization has been undergoing a great structural change, which really affects the rural structure. This is associated with the expansion of industry into rural areas, which has made possible the recruitment of a considerable labour force from the villages. At the same time post-war land reform has greatly affected the internal economic organization of the village. Indeed, the present changes in the rural areas are comparable in scale and depth, though not in the concentration of land ownership, with those experienced at the onset of industrialization of England. Today in rural Japan various problems are cropping up which have not been experienced before. For example, an acute shortage of agricultural labour is becoming a serious problem, yet there is little scope for development into large-scale farming, which could be efficiently carried out by the use of modern machinery in place of human labour, since all the present farmers are small cultivators who possess little capital. Despite the fall in the agricultural population, the number of households in rural areas, and the area of land holding by a household, seem to have remained stable. The present picture is that the majority of the younger genera-

Against this economic and historical background, I deal with rural Japan from the middle of the Tokugawa period to around 1950 in one structural sequence. To sum up, the Japanese agricultural community presents the following characteristics. A majority of the population has engaged in small-scale farming. Whether he is owner or tenant, the farmer is entirely responsible for management and cultivation; though there have been small minorities of non-cultivating, large landowners, and of farm servants. The total picture of the agricultural community in Japan has been fairly homogeneous without differentiation into distinct strata, such as gentry and landless peasants, as in the case of many other societies. I believe this overall composition of the agricultural community has much significance for the development of social organization in rural communities. For this reason this section will serve as a frame for the following discussion.

INTERNAL STRUCTURE OF THE VILLAGE

In this section I discuss certain important aspects of internal village organization which developed during the Tokugawa period, and which became characteristic of the village in the following periods.

(A) *Household composition in relation to farm management*

In the previous section I explained that the household was the most important unit in village organization. Here I present the detailed household composition of the Tokugawa peasant. On this subject, the study by K. Takao, an economic historian specializing in Tokugawa peasantry, gives a fairly detailed picture of a village near Osaka called Wakae (Takao, 1958, pp. 20–38).

Wakae village is found in the fertile valley of Kawachi district, and is one of the old villages situated at the political centre of the area, where a medieval castle belonging to one of the famous local families existed during the fifteenth to sixteenth century. Owing to the advantageous geographic and economic location,

tion are drawn to the factories, while their parents remain in the village engaged in farming. Alternatively, there are many households where the husband, sons and daughters are employed in factories or offices, while the wife cultivates their land, thus obtaining cash income, and supplementing low wages.

In this book I intentionally leave out the new features arising from present changes, not because they are irrelevant but because they are beyond the scope of this study. Methodologically, these new problems should be analysed on the same basis though not in the same context.

the village was already well developed at the beginning of the Tokugawa period. It then became one of those villages under the direct control of the Bakufu (the Tokugawa central government). According to the census of this village in 1644, obtained by K. Takao, the village consisted of 230 households with a population of 1,301—probably one of the biggest villages of that period.

Takao shows three types of household distinguishable in the village, each represented by an actual household found in the census.

1. Yamasaburō's household: this household was ranked as the ninth by its holding among the 230 households of the village, and possessed rice fields of 44·571 *koku*, which corresponds to three *chō* and four *tan*. The members of the household were in all nine persons:

> Yamasaburō himself (24 years old)
> his wife (22)
> his daughter (5)
> his two male servants (27) and (10)
> his four female servants (27), (24), (20), and (14).
> (The kinship relations among the servants are unknown.)

The household possessed one cow used for cultivating. The available labour force of the household was six persons: Yamasaburō and his wife, one male servant and three female servants. Normally one man can cultivate three *tan*, so that by these six persons one *chō* and eight *tan* could be cultivated: it was impossible for them to cultivate by themselves the total holding of three *chō* and four *tan* registered under Yamasaburō's name. It seems that the remaining one *chō* and six *tan* was cultivated by his tenants. Thus it can be assumed that Yamasaburō's household was of the owner-cultivator type with tenants, and was one of the well-off households by village standards.

2. Niuemon's household: this household had no land at all, and his house was rented from Yamasaburō. Niuemon had no cow. His household members were:

> Niuemon himself (53)
> his wife (47)
> his sons (27) and (15)

(K. Takao assumes that Niuemon might have other sons and

daughters as well as the above-mentioned two sons, who might have become the servants of other households. It must have been very difficult for him to feed all his children without having his own arable land. The poverty of this household can also be guessed from the fact that his son, who was 27 years old, still had no wife, while 24-year-old Yamasaburō, above-mentioned, already had a wife and daughter: poverty tended to delay the taking of a wife.)

The land which this family could cultivate seems to have been about one *chō*. Niuemon had to pay a share of the revenue to the lord as well as to his landowner. If they cultivated one *chō*, it would produce just enough to support their minimum needs. This household was one of poor tenants, dependent for labour entirely on family members.

However, the composition of this kind of household was also found among many owner-cultivators with small holdings of about one *chō*, which was more or less the standard holding of the period.

3. Chōzaemon's household: Chōzaemon was the head of the village, and possessed about eleven *chō* and six *tan* (150·78 *koku*). His household was the biggest in the village: the total number of members amounts to twenty-one:

Chōzaemon himself (37)
his wife (30)
his sons (13) and (5)
his male servants (56), (41), (29), (16) and (15)
his female servants (26), (25), (24), (18), (15), (14), (13) and (25)
sons of male servants (9), (8), (5) and (2)
(The kinship relations of these servants are unknown, but K. Takao assumes that this household consisted of the head's family and the families of his servants.)

The labourers available for cultivation were altogether thirteen persons, who could cultivate four *chō*. The rest of Chōzaemon's land seems to have been cultivated by his tenants. The revenue from the tenants would represent a large part of his income. This household can be said to be one of the large landowners by Tokugawa standards.

These three examples probably represent the three kinds of Tokugawa household farm systems found in many villages.

According to K. Takao the whole picture of this village in regard to land allocation and farming management can be summarized as follows. Out of the total arable land of the village, 58 per cent was held by households without servants, and with a composition similar to that of Niuemon's household. There seem to have been many smallholders whose land was cultivated by the owner-family members alone. It is generally agreed among economic historians and economists in Japan that the 'typical' peasant household of the Tokugawa period, and of the following periods, was of this type. Furthermore, out of the total arable land of Wakae village, 55 per cent was cultivated by the owners themselves, and the rest, 45 per cent, by tenants: the number of tenants' households was eighty-five, i.e. 37 per cent of the total. While in principle the peasant households of the village stood equal to one another, the actual size of the holdings varied considerably. Already there existed renting of land among the households in the village, though non-cultivating landowners were scarcely to be found.

(b) Different statuses among the households in the village

Detailed and tabulated data on the status of households in a Tokugawa village are available in the works of economic historians. One of the best accounts is to be found in the series of works by S. Oishi on Gorohei-shinden village in Nagano prefecture. The following discussion, mainly concerned with Gorohei-shinden, is based on his published works (Oishi, 1955, 1956) and on unpublished data which he kindly allowed me to use; also, I did field work in this village with him in the summer of 1961.

Gorohei-shinden village is situated in a fertile valley plain in Nagano prefecture, the economy of which mainly depends on irrigated rice fields. The village was established in 1630, at the beginning of the Tokugawa period, by the construction of a new irrigation ditch.[1] This village can be cited as one of the typical villages developed during the Tokugawa period: it contains major characteristic features of the Japanese village.

[1] The term 'shinden' literally means 'new field'. Gorohei was the name of the founder of the village. Most of these villages founded during the Tokugawa period bear the term *shinden*. A detailed account of the process of founding this village was given by Oishi (1952). The village was under the direct control of the Bakufu.

Gorohei-shinden village was a community of 133 households in 1713. The land allocation, according to the households in the village, shows considerable variation, ranging between forty *koku* and nil: out of a total of 133 households, seventeen did not own any land. As regards social differentiation, there were two distinct statuses: *honbyakushō* (titled farmers), and *kakaebyakushō* (non-titled farmers). The former were full members of the village, the officially registered members who were responsible for revenue payment and had a voice in the important details of village management; they were also candidates and voters for the positions of village officials. The latter lacked these rights and were in a dependent position. For the peasants it had great significance whether one was a *honbyakushō* or *kakaebyakushō*, since decisions concerning the share of the revenue for each household,[1] and the control of the irrigation water, both of which were of vital importance in peasant economic life, were in the hands of the *honbyakushō*.

The number of *honbyakushō* in 1713 in this village was only fifty out of a total of 133, and the rest, eighty-three households, were of *kakaebyakushō*. These *honbyakushō* were usually landowners (owner-cultivators). But it does not mean that they always had more land than the *kakaebyakushō*, as is shown in the following table (reproduced from Oishi, 1956, p. 99):

TABLE 4. Distribution of Lands by Households of *Honbyakushō* and *Kakaebyakushō* in Gorohei in 1713

land ('*koku*')	'*honbyakushō*' with tenants	'*honbyakushō*' without tenants	'*kakaebyakushō*'	total number of households
0	0	2	15	17
– 1	3	5	28	36
1– 5	15	4	30	49
5–10	5	5	8	18
10–20	9	0	1	10
20–30	0	0	0	0
30–40	2	0	0	2
?	0	0	1	1
Total	34	16	83	133

[1] The authorized amount of revenue from the village, and its quota from each assessable household, were registered in the village record, named *Nayosechō*. The revenue to the lord was assessed jointly by the village, and the village officers allocated a share to each household according to the actual yield of the household in every year, at a meeting of all household heads of the village.

Some of the *kakaebyakushō* possessed more land than some of the *honbyakushō*, though in general, *honbyakushō* owned more land than *kakaebyakushō*. For the understanding of this kind of land allocation, it is necessary to explain the working of title transmission in relation to land ownership at this period. The status differentiation between the *honbyakushō* and the *kakaebyakushō* was the result of the political and economic situation of the time. By the beginning of the eighteenth century, the number of the *honbyakushō* in a village came to be fixed. Hence in the course of time, owing to an increase in the village population, which resulted in the fissioning off of households, *kakaebyakushō* came to be created and their number increased. In this village in the earlier period, all households had been a kind of *honbyakushō*, but by 1713 it had produced eighty-three households of *kakaebyakushō*, increasing this number to 125 in 1745, 134 in 1758, and to 144 in 1866, while that of the *honbyakushō* had remained around forty-five throughout these years. This phenomenon in which the number of households with 'full membership' was expressed in terms of *honbyakushō*, was to be seen in most villages during the Tokugawa period. It seems to have been an expression of the internal economic structure of the village community, based on a balance between the number of households and the available rights and limited resources. Furthermore, the working of the transmission of 'full membership' is manifested in Japanese kinship ideology as influenced by household structure.

The title to rights (*kabu*) of the *honbyakushō* was attached to the household, not to the individual, and was held in the name of the household head. Hence a new household, fissioned off from a household of the *honbyakushō*, could not hold the title, even if the new head was a son of the *honbyakushō*. The *kabu* of the *honbyakushō* was inherited only by the son who succeeded in the household, never by other sons who left the parental household. Those sons who did not succeed to the father's household, and who set up new independent households at their marriage, had to become *kakaebyakushō*. As I have already explained, the working of the household constantly demands the fission of the collateral members other than the successor. There would always be the possibility of creating a *kakaebyakushō*, if a *honbyakushō* had more than one son who was not the successor in his household or in another household by adoption. An increase of *kakaebyakushō*, moreover, came not only from these extra members of *honbyakushō* households, but also from similar members of *kakaebyakushō*.

Such a status differentiation among sons, however, does not necessarily accord with economic differentiation, since the customary rule of inheritance normally practised at this time was that of equal division of lands. Thereby a *kakaebyakushō* might have considerable land inherited from a rich father, whereas there might be a poor *honbyakushō*. Furthermore, a *kakaebyakushō* might acquire lands by its own effort, while a *honbyakushō* might lose its land. Thus status did not always coincide with wealth. However, it was important that the title should not be based strictly on hereditary right only: it could be acquired by economic achievement. It was therefore possible for a *kakaebyakushō* to become a *honbyakushō* by purchasing the rights (*kabu*) of a *honbyakushō*, provided the villagers agreed. As a result, by and large, the *honbyakushō* were normally found more among the landed farmers. Nevertheless, at this stage, economic differentiation was not as significant as status differentiation. In fact, the former was not so great, because the feudal system as a rule did not allow for a landowner system,[1] though it slowly began to appear from this period onward as the state political organization began decline. The range to between landed and landless was small, as we see in the table. Further, there were no technical differences in farming management between these two categories: both were cultivators; and the profit was relatively small even though part of the land was leased to tenants.

In the course of time, however, economic differentiation gradually began to influence the overall village organization. This was stimulated by status differentiation which began to shape the rigid internal political organization of the village in the face of the growing shortage of net resources for an increasing population. The status differentiation tended to produce an unequal division of land, and to give a larger share to the successor than to other sons. Coupled with such internal developments of the peasant community, there were important external

---

[1] Big landowners who appeared in Wakae village, as previously discussed, were rather exceptional owing to the general conditions of the Tokugawa village in its earlier period. The land allocation seen in Gorohei village seems a more representative case at this time.

factors which enhanced such tendencies. Besides the limitation in the number of the *honbyakushō* in the village by the villagers themselves, there came the feudal law, as already stated, that a farmer holding less than ten *koku* should not be allowed to subdivide his land. Such a law was issued to prevent a decrease in the feudal lord's revenue income, since the Bakufu, as well as local feudal lords, now began to realize that minor holdings from which the revenue was expected to be small were increasing owing to the subdivision of the land among the peasants. The effects of this law in the actual village require further investigation.

S. Oishi assumes that subdivision of the land was actually still going on in spite of the above law. It seems possible for a peasant household, normally occupied by an elementary family, to have carried on their agricultural production if they owned five *koku* of land. The actual cessation of the establishment of new households in a village came much later than the time the above law was issued: it came when the villagers themselves realized that there was a limit to the number of households which village resources could carry, and that the majority of the households had reached the minimum holding for one elementary family. In fact, there was a reduction in the number of new households in a village towards the end of the Tokugawa period. The net available resources were limited by the then Tokugawa farming technique. Even if waste lands were available which might be turned into arable lands, the water supply for each village was restricted, and so cultivation would not expand beyond a certain limit. There are numerous data which reveal that the village itself checked the increasing number of households. I think this had more effect than the law of the feudal lord. It is surprising indeed how a village could keep the optimum number of households without overstepping the limit, and this can be considered as a further step in communal economic control by villagers themselves, particularly by the *honbyakushō*.

Whatever the checking force to an increase in the number of households in the village, or to further subdivision of the land, the question remained how to accommodate extra members born in the various households. As I explained in Chapter 1, the household structure required fissioning off if it contained more than two married brothers. The residential separation of such brothers involved subdivision of the household land. Without some such economic arrangement, a non-successor could hardly establish an independent household and the household would have to include a large number of family members. But actual data reveal that a household occupied by more than two married brothers (or married uncles and nephews) was very rare. As regards this issue, T. Furushima gives data on the development of larger households owing to the limitation of the number of households in a village (Furushima, 1947, pp. 116–18). In Hachite mura of Nagano prefecture in 1682, there were large households consisting of twenty, thirteen and twelve family members respectively, each of which included collateral kin with their elementary families. However, these households separated into smaller households seven years later: for example, the household of twenty members appears as four separate households in the registration taken after seven years. T. Furushima assumes that the change during this seven-year period from one household to four was due to the revision of the rules which allowed the number of households in the village to increase. As for the changes in the total situation of this village during the same seven years, the total number of the households increased from thirty-six to forty-six; the average number of household members changed from 6·6 persons to 5·5; and the number of large households of more than ten members decreased from three to one.

However, I think that if the number of households in a village had not been allowed to increase, it would have been impossible to continue to accommodate the increasing numbers (particularly married siblings of the head), considering the actual household in terms of its structure as well as of the capacity of the building. Furushima states, in relation to the above data, that large households tended to be found among the households of village officials: the upper strata of the village population. This fact, I think, involves the more spacious accommodation of the dwelling house and the desire of the descendants to be attached to the high status of their parental household. It would be difficult to accommodate more than one set of married collateral relatives in an ordinary peasant dwelling house. The household must divide sooner or later. Indeed the residential separation of grown-up sons and daughters, other than the successor, constantly appears throughout the period, in spite of various attempts to avoid the separation of a household with its consequent sub-division of the property.

Then how were these extra members accommodated? The best solution was for them to be adopted as successors to house-holds without sons. Even today there are quite a number of households whose heads are adopted sons—I have come across villages in which nearly one-third of the household heads were adopted sons or adopted sons-in-law. Certainly the death rate then was much higher than it is today, so that there would be more opportunity for extra members to be adopted. Those less fortunate members who could not find proper accommodation as an adopted son often had to remain unmarried, and worked as labourers for the natal household. Among the poor, many became servants of a wealthy household. In the very poorest families, children were killed as soon as they were born (*mabiki*), as mentioned in the previous section.

In this manner, a long-established and well organized village was maintained at the expense of the lower sector of the popula-tion; and in the course of time, the households were organized more rigidly into groups consisting of each *honbyakushō* and its dependent *kakaebyakushō*. A *kakaebyakushō*, whether he was a tenant or an owner of land, had to depend on the *honbyakushō*, through whom he could have access to the common rights of a member of the village. *Kakaebyakushō* were politically subject to particular *honbyakushō* within the village organization. In fact, their names were registered under the name of the *honbyakushō* to whom they were attached. Thus they formed a sub-stratum in the village composition. The manner of the allocation of *kakaebyakushō* varied according to the economic and political power of the *honbyakushō*. For example, the distribution of *kakaebyakushō* (134) in relation to each *honbyakushō* (the total number was 43) in Gorohei in 1758, was as shown in Table 5.

The relationship of *kakaebyakushō* to their respective *honbya-kushō* did not necessarily involve kinship, though kinship was likely to be found. It certainly involved economic relations, since a wealthier *honbyakushō* had a larger number of *kakaebyakushō*. Throughout the data it is rather difficult to find definite proof of the kinship relation between *kakaebyakushō* and their respective *honbyakushō*. However, the data do give the temple affiliation of each household, from which Oishi assumes that a *kakaebyakushō*

TABLE 5

The number of 'kakaebyakushō' grouped under one 'honbyakushō'	The number of 'honbyakushō'
11	1
10	1
9	1
8	1
7	2
6	2
5	3
4	5
3	4
2	7
1	9
0	7
Total 134	43

(Reproduced and rearranged from data by Oishi, 1956, pp. 106–15)

with the same temple affiliation as that of the *honbyakushō* to whom it belonged, could be considered as fissioned off from that *honbyakushō*. This assumption would not always be entirely accurate, yet the same temple affiliation certainly implies some form of social connection, which certainly involves the kinship factor since a newly created household always follows the temple affiliation of its original household. It would be safer to assume that a *kakaebyakushō* with a different temple affiliation from that of its *honbyakushō* is not a household fissioned from the latter. An example of temple affiliations of *kakaebyakushō* is shown in Table 6.

As this table shows, the relationship between the *honbyakushō* and its *kakaebyakushō* does not seem to be necessarily established on a kinship basis, but implies more a relationship of patron and client in terms of rights as a member of the village, rather than in terms of land ownership. Kinship criteria never seem to be the prime factor in the formation of a local group or village. This can also be seen in the composition of Gorohei village in the earlier period of its history, for example, in 1667, as shown in Table 7. This was the time when the villagers had ample opportunities of expanding their cultivation by reclaiming waste land, and the village welcomed more farmers coming to settle there.

TABLE 6. Distribution of *Kakaebyakushō* Grouped by *Honbyakushō* with an Indication of Temple Affiliation, in Gorohei in 1758

Each italic figure represents the name of a *honbyakushō* household.
The number of *kakaebyakushō* which have the same temple affiliation as the *honbyakushō* to which they are attached are indicated in the brackets. Those whose temple affiliations are not known are indicated by ?.

'Honbyakushō'	1	2	3	4	5	6	7	8	9	10
Number of 'kakaebyakushō'	(1)6	1	6	0	0	(2)	3	0	(6)1	(1)

11	12	13	14	15	16	17	18	19	20	21
(1)1	(5)	(5)	(3)1	1	2	0	(2)1	(2)	(4)	(7)3

22	23	24	25	26	27	28	29	30	31	32	33
(8)1	(4)	(3)1	(2)	(3)	(4)2	(1)	1	0	(4)	(2)	(5)

34	35	36	37	38	39	40	41	42	43	Total	43
0	(1)	(1)	0	1	(6)5	1	8?	2?	3		134

(Reproduced and rearranged from data in Oishi, 1956, pp. 106–15)

There was certainly no status differentiation among the households such as *honbyakushō* and *kakaebyakushō*. It is not known how a local group was interconnected, but a set of households can be grouped by some particular relation, as can be seen from Table 7.

Out of a total of thirty households, six households (8, 11, 27, 28, 29 and 30) were independent, having no particular relation to any other household. Among the rest, a linkage between households is found in various ways: kinship, fictive kinship, close acquaintance, etc. In Japan a high degree of independence of households, and an absence of an exclusive kin group (and of any type of kinship principle) seem to have been the distinctive features of the local group and village composition throughout different periods and varying economic conditions.[1]

[1] There were also important local groups known as *Goningumi* (The Five Men's Association) in the Tokugawa period. This group form was created by feudal policy as the sub-organization of the village within the administrative network maintained by the feudal lord. It was based on the *honbyakushō*, and feudal policy deliberately avoided including kinsmen or close friends in the same group, in order to subject each household directly to political control. The group contained several *honbyakushō*, not necessarily five in number, though five was a nominal standard. A head was appointed from among them, and the group was given joint responsibility in various activities of the peasants, particularly for collection of revenues. This system played an important role in the

[footnote continued on p. 71

TABLE 7. Composition of Gorohei Village in 1667
(Reproduced from Oishi, 1955, pp. 10–11)

Name of household head	Relation between household heads
1. Takeuemon	
2. Yozaemon	Brother of Takeuemon
3. Kiyozaemon	Takeuemon's sister's husband
4. Kuhyōe	
5. Hyōzaburō	His father and Kuhyōe's father were brothers
6. Yosozaemon	Kuhyōe's aunt's daughters' son
7. Gonuemon	Kuhyōe and Yosozaemon invited him to settle in this village
8. Sahyōe	
9. Monnojō	
10. Kuzaemon	Monnojō's mother's nephew
11. Shōhyōe	
12. Yogozaemon	
13. Shōzaemon	Brother of Yogozaemon
14. Jirohachi	Yogozaemon's father's adopted son
15. Riuemon	
16. Denshiro	Son of Riuemon
17. Tarozaemon	
18. Sauemon	Son of Tarozaemon
19. Magouemon	?
20. Hansaemon	Sauemon's brother (Kiuemon)'s wife's cousin
21. Jinuemon	
22. Hanshirō	Jinuemon's wife's son
23. Kakuuemon	
24. Saheiji	Ritual son of Kakuuemon
25. Yogouemon	
26. Mouemon	Adopted son of Yogouemon
27. Montarō	
28. Kouemon	
29. Kiuemon	
30. Hachiuemon	

This kind of social structure theoretically involves a high possibility of change in group composition in accordance with changes in economic circumstances. For example, as I have already described, the *kabu* of *honbyakushō* was not handed on strictly by inheritance but could also be purchased; and *honbyakushō* of a village did not together form a constant, exclusive status group. A poor *honbyakushō* at any time might reduce its status to that of a *kakaebyakushō*, while a rich *kakaebyakushō* might become a *honbyakushō*. It is important here to note that the patron and client relationship between the *honbyakushō* and the *kakaebyakushō* was theoretically adjustable in the face of changing economic situations.

In fact during the Tokugawa period, there had been considerable changes in the fortunes of households. The historical data in Table 8 give an example of such changes in a village during half a century, showing changes of land holdings of households in Saraike village near Osaka during the period between 1644 and 1702.

The above example shows not only the changes in holdings among the households, but also the general tendency for an increasing degree of economic differentiation among them, an increase in the percentage of landless households, and on the other hand, an increase of holdings by a few households of the upper strata. These phenomena were found in many villages during the course of the Tokugawa period, particularly towards the end of the period. In this connection the data from Shimodaiichi mura in Hyogo prefecture also provide a good example.

Economic ups and downs of a household have been fairly normal occurrences in a village community throughout various historical periods. Yet what is important to notice about these changes is the high degree of independence of the household. Even a household of one's close kin, or of a close neighbour, seldom offered one help to their own detriment, and envied the rise of another household, and vice versa. Yet though the individual household has a high degree of independence, it is

feudal administrative control over the peasants, particularly in terms of prohibition of Christianity, efficient collection of revenues, and maintenance of the public peace. Detailed studies on the *Goningumi* are found among works by economic historians (see Bibliography II, for Chapter 2, at the end of the text). However, the actual relationship between the *Goningumi* and locally developed corporate groups has not yet been thoroughly investigated.

TABLE 8. Changing Process of the Holdings by each Household in Saraike
(Reproduced from Takao, 1958, p. 64)

Dotted lines indicate the fissioning off of a household: for
example, household 26 fissioned off from household 1, and
were alloted 9 *koku* from the latter.

	1644	1665	1678	1690	1702
Number of households	11	?	22	27	28
Number of landholders	11	14	13	10	10
Number of landless	0	?	9	17	18

| Landless | 0 | ? | 9 | 17 | 18 |

bound to be organized within the frame of the village structure,
in which the rise and fall of each household economy, and status
ranking or differentiation are significant. Indeed, it is the village
frame, not kinship or any other principle, which sets a pattern
for the organization of the peasant community. The village was
certainly made a distinctive unit by the policy of the Tokugawa
administration.

TABLE 9. Distribution of Holders by *Koku* in Shimo-daiichi in the Period 1685–1871

(Reproduced from Takao, 1958, p. 193)

	1685	1762	1807	1851	1871
				1	1
80 *koku*					
70					
			1		
60					
50					
	1			2	1
40					
		5	1	1	2
30					
	4	2	6	2	2
20					
	19	9	6	8	7
10					
	10	14	9	4	5
5					
	1	17	20	24	17
0					
	?	?	2	?	6

(c) *System based on the water network*

The irrigation system in the Tokugawa period, which is largely followed even today, was as follows. The rice fields cultivated by the villagers, scattered around the village, were divided into a number of plots called *hitsu* for the actual cultivation. Each plot was carefully measured with regard to the fertility of the soil (normally divided into three types) by the potential yield of rice (in *koku*), and registered in the name of its owner and cultivator (in either case in the name of the household head). The normal size of a plot (one *hitsu*) in this village was 0·7–0·8 *maki*.[1] This plot, usually of square shape, represents the optimum

[1] It was the usual practice of this period that the size of a paddy field was registered or measured by its potential productivity, *koku*, rather than by the area measure (*tan*) of the land. There were also local differences in practice in the measurement of a plot. In this particular area, the productive quantity of each *hitsu* was expressed by *maki* (which literally means 'sowing'). 0·8 *maki* is a field where young plants grown from 8 *shō* (see p. 32, note 2) of paddy seeds can be transplanted. The conversion of *maki* to acreage is difficult, because the

size and shape of an operating unit of irrigated fields under the Tokugawa agricultural technique. It is a convenient size for cultivation by two or three persons, which is the normal labour force available in one household; and also it is the ideal size for spreading the water evenly, and for making a flat field on the mild slopes which are normally to be found in Japan. The milder the slope, the larger the size of plot tends to be. Each plot, having once been brought into irrigated rice cultivation, becomes an indivisible unit within the network of the water flow. (The layout must be revised if it is to be divided. Fragmentation by sub-division of the land among the farmers normally will not result in any actual division of a plot.)

All these plots are united by the water flow: the irrigation system was such that the same water flowed through every plot. The controlling rights in this water were held by the village.

Details of the network of the water in Gorohei-shinden village in 1771 were as follows. The water of this village was brought from the upper stream of the Kakuma river, eight km. away from the village, along the canal constructed by the villagers when the village was established. This water was divided into three streams at the entrance to the village in order to feed three separate sets of fields belonging to the village (owned by different households). The following data are concerned with the fields fed by the biggest of the three branch channels. This water feeds 105 plots altogether, the sizes of which range from 0·1 to 1·5. Each plot is numbered according to the flow of the water; and the water flows regularly from No. 1 to No. 105, and again back to No. 1 from No. 105 after a week's interval.

The details of the allocation of these 105 plots, according to ownership and tenantship, are as follows. These 105 plots were held by 41 households, and cultivated in the names of 82 house-hold heads: out of these, 27 were owner cultivators, and 55 were tenants. Table 10 shows the number of plots and of tenants.

Out of eighty-two cultivators, three held three plots each; seventeen held two plots each; and the rest held one plot each. (Some of the cultivators may cultivate other plots in the fields

quantity of paddy seeds did not always accord with the size of the field: a better field required less quantity of seeds than an inferior one. However, roughly speaking, the average size of one plot of this village in the Tokugawa period fairly corresponds to that of the present-day national average, for which statistics show about 0·34 acre.

1. Paddy fields after transplanting. The dark 'island' at the upper left is a village in Hiraizumi (Miyagi Prefecture).

2*a*. A main irrigation stream at Goroheishinden village (*see* pp. 74–9).

2*b*. Threshing paddy after harvest (Nagano Prefecture). This kind of machine is now common throughout Japan.

3*a*. A modern-style farmhouse at Haru Buraku (Oita Prefecture). On the right is a storehouse, and behind the glasshouse are the cowshed and granary.

3*b*. Couple at work in a modern greenhouse in Koshiozu (*see* pp. 122, 142).

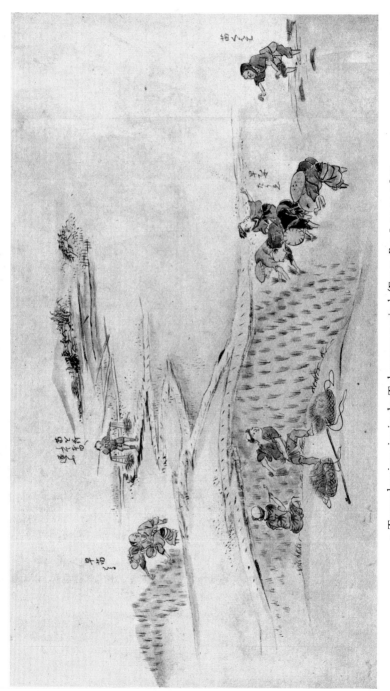

4. Transplanting rice in the Tokugawa period. (From *Ronō-yawa*, 1843, by courtesy of the Historiographical Institute, University of Tokyo.)

TABLE 10. Distribution of Plots by Owners, with the Number of Tenants,
in Gorohei in 1771

(Reproduced and rearranged from the data in Oishi, 1955, p. 8)

Number of plots belonging to one owner	Number of tenants belonging to one owner	Number of owners
13	10	1
7	5	1
6	4	2
6	3	1
5	5	1
5	4	1
4	4	1
4	3	2
3	3	2
3	2	1
3	1	1
2	2	1
2	1	3
2	0	2
1	1	5
1	0	16
Total 105	55	41

fed by another branch stream, so that the distribution of these
plots according to owners and cultivators does not accurately
represent the picture of the village as a whole.) The actual distribution of plots and cultivators according to the water flow is
shown in Table 11.

As this scheme shows, there is no great difference between a
larger landowner and a small one, or a tenant. Both owner and
tenant remain on the same level as cultivators, and aligned
according to the order of the water flow. Each is entirely responsible for the cultivation of the plot for which his name is registered as the cultivator. This system may be closely related to the
Tokugawa farming technique: the efficiency of the farming
depends greatly upon constant close attention to the field which
one cultivates; and it is difficult for one manager to supervise a
great number of plots by employing temporary replaceable
labourers. Further, the decisive factor in this system is the manner
in which water is allocated. Even though a cultivator may own
a large amount of land, the water, without which cultivation is
impossible, is out of his control. Therefore, as Oishi emphasizes,

TABLE 11. Distribution of Plots and Cultivators according to the
Water Flow in Gorohei in 1771

(Reproduced and rearranged from the data in Oishi, 1955, p. 8)

1	*2*	*3*	4	5	6	7	8	9	10	11	12	*13*	14	*15*	*16*	17
95	89						98	61				91		27	23	28
															24	

18	19	*20*	21	22	(23)	(24)	25	26	(27)	(28)	*29*	30	31
		73					57	54				104	
		83											

32	33	*34*	35	36	37	38	39	40	*41*	42	43	44	45	46	47
				55										52	

48	49	50	51	(52)	(53)	(54)	(55)	56	(57)	*58*	*59*	*60*
53												

(61)	62	63	*64*	65	66	67	68	(69)	70	(71)	72	(73)	74
				69	71								84
													94

75	*76*	77	78	79	80	*81*	82	(83)	(84)	(85)	86	*87*	88
							92						

(89)	*90*	(91)	(92)	93	(94)	(95)	96	97	(98)	99	100

101 102 103 (104) 105.

Note: Figures show the number of the plot according to the flow of the water. The italics indicate owner cultivation. Figures in brackets indicate a plot already shown with another figure, because it belongs to the same cultivator who cultivates the earlier number: for example, (23) and (24) are cultivated by X, who cultivates plot 16. Further, 16 and 23 belong to X; and he also cultivates plot no. 24, which is owned by another person. X is an owner as well as a tenant.

whether one is an owner-cultivator or tenant-cultivator, farming management is completely subject to the control of the water flow; that is, to village control.

Water allocation has great significance at a particular season: that is, at the time of transplantation in the spring, when abundant water is essential. This transplantation time is restricted to a very few days: it should be done under the best climatic conditions in the local agricultural calendar. It is said that the ideal period for this is a maximum of ten days, which often become about a week because of the weather conditions at the time. Hence all plots should be fed by water in or around this time, and the transplanting, which requires concentrated labour, should be done while abundant water is available in each field.

Because of this, as Oishi states, a cultivator tries not to have adjacent plots, as can be seen from the distribution of plots in this village. While plot 1 is fully fed by the water, plot 2 will be also fed by the water either gradually or simultaneously: when the transplantation of plot 1 is finished, plot 2 would be already losing the water at its best. Hence ideally, when more than two plots are cultivated by the same person, these should be situated with considerable distance between them in the water flow, so as to make the best use of water and labour in each field.[1] In the above-mentioned distribution scheme of 105 plots according to cultivator, I found only one case where the same person had to cultivate two adjacent plots: the case of 23 and 24. To my question concerning this, Oishi explained that although this is indeed an exception in the total scheme, the areas of 23 and 24 are 0.9 and 0.4 respectively, totalling 1.3. This is a manageable size for one cultivator: there are plots of even 1.5, so that the net labour needed for these two plots can be equated with another large plot.

The limited water flow through the fields cultivated by all the villagers makes it essential that it should be distributed equally to each field. Therefore the timing of the water supply to each plot is carefully calculated by the number of plots and according to the size of each plot. The interval of the water supply and the quantity of the water to each field varies according to the available quantity for that year, and the number of plots to be fed. But whatever the manner of distribution may be, the order of the water-flow among the plots is always adhered to. The village rule is very strict on this point. No one is allowed to have water as freely as he desires, unless abundant water is available. Everybody wants sufficient water because water virtually decides the annual yield. When there is not enough water, the order becomes more strict. There may be quarrels among the villagers attempting to get more water; and some of them might even

---

[1] This does not mean that a man works alone, but that he is the man responsible for the management of a particular plot. Actual transplantation is done in co-operation with other workers, in a team which is formed according to mutual convenience.

steal water for their fields. To understand this I now explain the way in which water is fed into each plot, as I observed it in Gorohei village: the same technique as was used during the Tokugawa period is still adopted today.

The plots are lined up along the contour, the level of the plots decreasing gradually from No. 1 to No. 105. In Figure 7, when plot 1 is fed by the water, the valves A and C are closed. Then at the turn of plot No. 2, valve A remains as it is (this will remain closed till No. 5 is fed), and C is removed, while D and F are closed, so that the water flows straight to No. 2 from the entrance E, and so on.

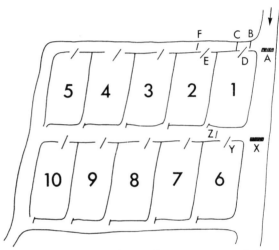

FIGURE 7. Basic Scheme of Irrigation in Gorohei

In theory the water is fed into each field in turn. But actually the degree of the opening and closing of valves depends on the available quantity of water. When the water supply is abundant, the valves are not completely closed, so that some of the water can flow to other plots simultaneously. For example, plots 1 to 5 would be fed almost simultaneously; or while plot 1 is fed plot 6 is also slowly fed by water through the interstices of A. The manner and frequency of valve changing depends on the amount of the water supply which varies by the year as well as by the season. In this village, traditionally, all the plots were fed in a week, with a major change of the valves three times in 24 hours: i.e., at early morning, noon, and just before going to bed. This means that roughly 15 plots out of the 105 are fed within 24 hours; and 5 plots at each major change of the valves. A villager thus says, 'My field has always been fed during the night since my grandfather's time.' The regulation of the order of the water in this village represents one of the well-arranged cases. Other villages do not necessarily have such regularity, but the basic pattern of controlling water is similar: the order of the plots to be fed by one flow of water is always maintained in the system of irrigation. The flow of the water is carefully arranged by the village council, and watched and supervised by two persons on duty under the responsibility of the irrigation official(s).

Water could be stolen by opening the closed valve to one's own field, or closing the valve to other fields, when nobody is around, particularly at night. This could easily be done since the valves are fixed only by stones and straw: the removal of even one small stone could eventually result in a considerable flow of water. But such malicious conduct can easily be detected: the person on duty often comes round to see that everything is in order, and also each person will carefully watch the flow of water to his own field, particularly when the water supply is scarce. It is said that the villagers can tell if someone is stealing water by the slightest change in the sound of the water flow.

The fields cultivated by the villagers are normally distributed around the village to which the right to the water belongs, though land ownership may be scattered beyond the village area. Some of the villagers may cultivate a field in a neighbouring village, but even today the majority of villagers cultivate fields around their own village. This system certainly makes a village one distinct social and economic unit; without being a member of the village it is difficult to carry on wet rice cultivation. The fact that individual farming is directly linked with village organization, as appears in the network of the water flow, and the way in which households are inevitably bound to each other by water, determine the form of the village organization: internally it involves severe economic and political competition among the households, and externally it presents the village as a tightly knit organization. This situation has been enhanced by the constant shortage of water as well as of fields, which has been a very common phenomenon in most villages in Japan since the middle of the Tokugawa period.

In such an economic situation, there is more competition among households over their rights than in the accumulation of wealth. Though outstanding economic achievement could attract rights, this would be difficult to accomplish in a short period. Rights are naturally held by older households; and a household with full rights acquired high prestige in the course of time, provided it had not fallen too low economically. That is why an older household in a village normally has higher prestige than a new one. At the same time, the limited availability of rights in the village produces an exclusive attitude by the villagers to a newly established household. If by any chance an outsider is allowed to become resident and establish his household, whether he be wealthy or not, he is not allowed any rights in the management of the village: he is placed at the lowest status in the ranking of the households in the village. This situation also applies to a household fissioned off from an existing household in the village. It is usually very difficult for such a household to acquire an economic and social status akin to that of the original household. S. Oishi explains that this kind of new household, whether a newcomer to the village or a new one created by fissioning off from an older household, inevitably means a lesser share to the existing households of the village. Even with an increase in production from the same fields, it means a decrease in the vested rights of the existing households (Oishi, 1956, pp. 18–19).

In a village where every household cannot enjoy full rights, certain households develop high prestige from the maintenance of their rights for a long time. This prestige has kept its importance within the village political organization, which is built upon a delicate ranking system among the households. Hence, even after the abolition of the title of *honbyakushō* of the Tokugawa, a very similar social and political situation has continued in many peasant communities.

The development of status differentiation, however, depends on the historical and economic situation of a given village community. As I emphasized elsewhere, every household, as an independent property-owning and farming unit, theoretically stands equal to any other as a member of a village. Superiority over others is made possible only by the social and economic advantage historically accumulated by the household, and can be maintained only by constant economic and social superiority over others. Thereby a village maintains continuous egalitarian competition among its households. Certainly this long-lasting economic and social superiority of one household over others might give the impression of a constant status differentiation in a village. But it is not impossible for a household to raise its status from lower to upper, though it may be very difficult and take many generations; and also superior status can be lost through economic decline. The relative ranking in household status in a village, which normally exists in the majority of villages in Japan, is theoretically changeable and is always relative within the framework of a village community. Therefore it should not be wondered at if, in a given village community, no status differentiation existed which formed hierarchical political relations among the households; or that status differentiation in a given village should disappear following a great change in the economic life of the village.

A village is always organized into sub-groups, despite the degree of status differentiation existing therein. These are local corporate groups consisting of a set of households, the formation of which largely depends on local inter-household relations rather than on the state administrative system. For a household, this group serves as a means of maximization of economic, political and social activities. At the village level it serves to support the ranking system and to stabilize political power relations within the village community; or it serves to maintain the balance of competitive power relations among the households and groups of households on which the village organization is built up.

The analysis of such local groups reveals important elements of social structure in a rural community. The next chapter is entirely devoted to this subject; I there use numerous data collected from field observations by Japanese scholars during the last fifty years, and by myself quite recently. It also deals with more detailed data of periods later than the Tokugawa dealt with in this chapter.

3

Analysis of Local Corporate Groups Within a Village

Within the frame of a village community, each household has several other households closely connected to it in daily life as well as through economic activities. A set of these households forms a fairly constant corporate group, and is a distinct functional sub-unit of village organization. The size of such a corporate group tends to suit its function. A group may change its composition: when the group becomes too large, it may split into smaller units. But normally it continues over generations, for so long as the economic and social relationships between the households remain fairly constant. The functional importance of such groups has become weaker as industrialization has expanded, but they played an exceedingly important role until recent years in shaping the structure of the village community. Analysis of them reveals significant elements in the kinship and economic organization of rural Japan.

The structure of the group itself exhibits several constituent elements. The most common is that of neighbourhood, somewhat akin to a ward. Coupled with this, a group may be linked either by kinship or through particular types of economic relations. In order to simplify the analysis, I now discuss three major principles which unite particular sets of households as a local corporate group: *dōzoku*, *oyako-kankei* and *kumi*. Each principle does not necessarily represent a type of actual local group, but rather serves as an analytical concept. In practice, two or three principles may be found to overlap; and the actual strength of each varies according to the local situation.

A. DOZOKU

Composition and structure of dōzoku

Dōzoku is a set of households, consisting of the main household

82

and branch household(s). As already stated in Chapter 1, among Japanese households it is the normal procedure for a son other than the successor to live separately from his parental household upon marriage. The establishment of such a household is often arranged by the parental household, whose head builds a house on part of his house-site land, and apportions cultivated land to the member who is about to become independent by marriage. The household thus newly created is called *bunke* (branch household) and the original one, *honke*, and the group of households in the relation of *honke* and *bunke* is called *dōzoku*.[1]

It is important to note here that genealogical relationship alone cannot form a *dōzoku*: it must be accompanied by an economic relationship. This economic relationship need not necessarily be in terms of ownership of land, but could be the allowance of tenant rights, or any other form of economic help from the original household which enables the branch household to carry on an independent household life. Furthermore, a branch household can be established not only by a son but also by a daughter whose husband has become an adopted son-in-law, and even by a servant who has worked for a considerable length of time in the household (he is equated somewhat to an adopted son). Hence, the genealogical relationship is not strictly recognized in terms of descent (based on individuals) but of *household*, and this genealogical relationship should accompany the economic involvement. For instance, if a new household is established by a son without any economic help from his parental household, this household will not form a *dōzoku* with its parental household, though the genealogical relation is clearly recognized in terms of father and son. Villagers distinguish between such a household and what is known as *bunke*: the former is called simply the household of a younger brother, or of a son; in some localities (Miyagi prefecture) it is called *dokuritsu* (independent), as against *bekke* (branch household). Hence, though a *dōzoku* normally appears in the form of a patrinominal group, a branch household usually having the same surname as the original one, theoretically it is not a patrilineal or patrinominal group. There are also instances where two households with different surnames form a *dōzoku*, whereas the fact that two households have the same

[1] *Dōzoku, honke* and *bunke* are standard sociological terms: different terms are used locally corresponding to each of these terms.

surname does not necessarily mean that they form a *dōzoku*.

The definition of the *dōzoku*, in spite of numerous researches on this subject, has never been clearly set forth in terms of current social anthropology: the structure of *dōzoku* has not been clearly analysed. This is the reason that the *dōzoku* is often referred to as a 'lineage' or 'patrinominal group'. One of the reasons that Japanese scholars termed the *dōzoku* a patrinominal group is that according to the old Civil Code the term *bunke* was applied, against traditional usage, to all households of sons or brothers regardless of the economic arrangement made by the parental household.[1] Because of this Civil Code usage, the expression *bunke* has sometimes been used socially, but there has been clear differentiation between households with and without economic arrangements at time of fission, particularly among the rural population. In practice in a village community, a set of patrinominal households without this economic relation differs greatly in its inter-household arrangement from one with it—the former involves almost no corporate elements. The patrinominal grouping itself, without other criteria, has no functional significance in social organization. Certainly a set of households with the same surname often recognize the genealogical links among them, but such a group does not always form a corporate group. The genealogy itself does not serve as the basis for the formation of a local group. Because of the fact that a set of households in a village frequently share the same surname and recognize a genealogical link with one another, and even more because of the influence of the legal usage mentioned above, many of those scholars concerned with the study of *dōzoku* have referred to it as a patrinominal group. Further, Japanese sociologists, being unfamiliar with the kinship analyses of social anthropology, carelessly equated *dōzoku* with a patrilineal lineage, though many of them were well aware that a *dōzoku* was a group of *households*, not of individuals who were classified by patrilineal descent. In English translations of the works of these scholars the *dōzoku* is usually presented as a patrilineal lineage. On the other hand, most western scholars who dealt with family and kinship and

---

[1] In Japan there have occasionally been such discrepancies between the regulations of the old Civil Code and actual practice based on traditional usage: some of them I have already mentioned: the concept of *shinzoku* and *shinrui* (pp. 39–40), and the headship of the household, *koshu-ken* (p. 17).

village community in Japan failed to see the structural significance of the *ie* institution as the basic element of the *dōzoku*, and simply applied the term 'family' to *ie* and 'lineage' to the *dōzoku* group.[1]

I do not object absolutely to the views of all those who substitute 'patrilineal lineage' for the *dōzoku*, since among them some are well aware that the actual composition of a *dōzoku* often includes fictive kin members.[2] However, if analysis of the *dōzoku* remains at this level—applying concepts of *descent* and *lineage* in such a loose way—the basic working of Japanese kinship and the nature of local groups in the village community will never be grasped. Furthermore, such rough treatment causes the researcher unnecessary difficulty; and he may miss the significant and basic points in comparative studies, particularly when comparing Japanese with Chinese or Hindu family and kinship systems. The *dōzoku* is *not* a patrilineal lineage. I have demonstrated this important point in earlier essays (Nakane, 1962 and 1964b): I have analysed how the *dōzoku* structure differs from a patrilineal lineage as commonly defined in social anthropology, and have analysed the structure and composition of the *dōzoku* by comparison with that of the patrilineal lineage, and pointed out significant differences between the *dōzoku* and Chinese and Hindu patrilineal lineage organizations. In the following dis-

---

[1] Examples of such interpretations are found in almost all works so far published; as recently as 1964, for example, Johnson states: 'The *dōzoku* is a large lineage consisting of patrilineally related *ie* with a main stem family and a number of clustered dependent stem families . . .' (Johnson, 1964, p. 840). Further I contend that neither is the *dōzoku* a survival of the lineage group. Careful examination of data found in various local documents in the Tokugawa period never reveals the existence of lineage groups (for example see pp. 67–71). Smith also fails to see this point: he assumes local groups in a village community of that period are simply lineage groups or survivals of the lineage group (for example see Smith, 1959, pp. 53, 54).

It is interesting to note that while those who have hitherto dealt with Japanese social organization have failed to see its essential structure, Freedman, a specialist in Chinese systems, clearly understands the nature of the *dōzoku* structure of Japan when viewed against the lineage system of China; he states: 'Japan, in contrast, presents an entirely different system. The *dōzoku* is not a lineage, in the sense of a group made up of all the unilineal descendants of a focal ancestor, but a line running throuth a succession of main families (*honke*) to which branch families are attached' (Freedman, 1963, p. 290).

[2] For example, the *dōzoku* 'is a hierarchically organized corporation of families patrilineally related (fictively or otherwise) in which the stem and its branches are mutually bound by complex relationships of reciprocal obligation' (Befu, 1963, p. 1331).

cussion, I want to demonstrate in more detail the structure of *dōzoku*, and to make clear my theoretical point on the issue.

To begin with, it is important to examine the formation of the *dōzoku*. A *bunke* can be established when a household is able to provide economic help for the establishment of a new household for one of its members. If economic circumstances allow, either *honke* or *bunke* enjoys the possibility of establishing its *bunke*. In the course of time a *dōzoku* might grow to more than half-a-dozen households in all; and this set of households is distinguished as a group from other households in a village. Figure 8 is an example showing the composition of such *dōzoku* members in relation to kinship.

This diagram is not from any single set of data, but presents a combination of various factors actually found in many existing *dōzoku* for which records are available. This hypothetical *dōzoku* is formed by seven households (A–G). Households of x, y and z are excluded, though their parents and sibling(s) are members of the *dōzoku*, because they married out of the group and joined their spouses' households elsewhere, which may (or may not) have formed other *dōzoku*. Although there is a general tendency for virilocal residence on marriage, members who marry out are not always female. For example z is excluded, while e is included in the *dōzoku*, because z became the adopted son-in-law of another household elsewhere, whereas the husband of e became an adopted son-in-law of a^2 (he married into the household built by a^2 and was given a portion of his land). Beside e's case, c, the adopted son of a^1, continued his membership in this *dōzoku* group, bringing his wife in and being given a house and a portion of the land by a^1. Further, the *dōzoku* itself is neither an exogamous nor an endogamous unit: marriage between the same *dōzoku* members may or may not occur, an example of which is seen in the marriage of g and b^3's sister. Both cross-cousin and parallel-cousin marriages, as well as uncle-niece marriages, may take place. Above all, the arrangements involved in this *dōzoku* situation are the outcome of internal as well as external economic and political factors; it is not a particular descent principle which determines the composition of the *dōzoku*.

As can be clearly seen from this figure, the *dōzoku* is not a descent group like a lineage or ramage in Firth's sense (Firth

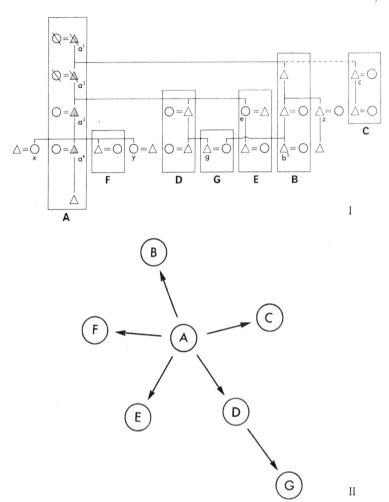

FIGURE 8. Relations of Households of a *Dōzoku*
Kinship Relations of the Individual
Members in the *Dōzoku* (I)
Relation of the Branch Households to the
Main Household (A) (II)

1957; 1959, pp. 213–14). The structure of the *dōzoku* is theoretically different from that of a descent group. Firstly, sons and
daughters who become members of households other than that

of the *dōzoku* of their parents by marriage or adoption are excluded, while spouses who marry members of the *dōzoku* are included. Secondly, the genealogical relation is traced through heads of households, not through individual members. Theoretically, an individual belongs to a *dōzoku* because his household forms part of the *dōzoku*, not because he, as an individual, is a member of the *dōzoku*. Hence all members of a household, whether related through kinship or not, are automatically included in the *dōzoku* group if their household forms a part of the *dōzoku*. Thus the *dōzoku* may include members who are not consanguineal kin, such as wives, husbands and servants, on the ground that they are members of a household which belongs to the *dōzoku*.

Thirdly, this genealogical relation between household heads has significance for forming a functional group only when both households have (or once had) an economic relation, and both are located in the same village. On the fissioning of a household, the newly established household is either given a portion of the land of the original one, or becomes a tenant of the original household, or makes an arrangement for constant economic help in exchange for labour. If there were no such economic relation between households so linked by kinship, as father and son or brothers, they probably would not form a functional group. On the other hand, if a semi-permanent economic relation were established between two households which were in no way related, they could form a *dōzoku* together with other households related by kinship and economic ties. (This does not necessarily mean that economic relations between two households always constitute a *dōzoku*. Whether an economic relationship creates a *dōzoku* or not depends on its particular nature. This will become clearer in the course of discussion.) Furthermore, a household of a son or brother in another village or distant urban area is not incorporated in the *dōzoku* (though they are *shinrui*): in this point the difference between *dōzoku* and *shinrui* can be seen clearly. The *dōzoku* is essentially a local group, the function of which is found within the scope of the village,[1] and in a normal situation

---

[1] A *dōzoku* of merchants, of business men, or of landords with large holdings, certainly will encompass the much wider geographical area that corresponds to their economic activities. The present discussion deals only with the ordinary agricultural population.

the set of households which forms a *dōzoku* is made up of neighbours living in a certain area within the village. Thus, the *dōzoku* draws essentially upon economic and residential factors. The kinship factor alone does not necessarily generate a *dōzoku*. Moreover, the *dōzoku* system is not a universal institution which covers an entire population like a lineage system. The absence or existence of *dōzoku* is closely related to the given economic conditions.

Dōzoku may sometimes seem to be no more than the members of a patrilineal lineage with their wives. For example, a man's real son is usually the foremost candidate for the establishment of a branch household, being born into the same household as the head. Hence, a *dōzoku* naturally tends to be formed by a set of households of father and sons, and/or brothers. But these are chance occurrences: theoretically *dōzoku* involves the possibility of stepping out of the domain of the descent group—it is not a closed descent group. The composition of the *dōzoku* is indeed sufficiently flexible to meet varied economic conditions.

Though a *dōzoku* is distinguishable as a group by the genealogical relations of its households, the degree of cohesion as a group varies greatly with the particular conditions of a particular period. The essence of the relation between households of a *dōzoku* is between *two* particular households, linked directly. For example in the *dōzoku* formed by five households A, B, C, D and E, whose genealogical relations are shown in Figure 9, the relations of A–B, A–C, A–D are not equal to those of B–C and C–D. B, C and D are the members of the *dōzoku* because of

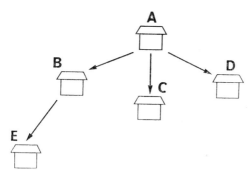

FIGURE 9. Basic Scheme of Relations between Households of the Dōzoku

their relations with A, not because the heads of these households are/were brothers or cousins. E is a member of the *dōzoku* through its relation to B: the relation A–E is much weaker than A–B or B–E. Normally, as the generation of the household head changes, the relations between households tend to become weaker. When B establishes E, the relation B–E becomes stronger than that of B–A. The important genealogical relation is the one established between the two households directly linked to each other, and the frame of the full genealogy which links all households of the *dōzoku* is not so important.

Within a *dōzoku* group there is a high degree of independence between households, which, I think, constantly tends to weaken group cohesion. The first generation of a branch household normally maintains close contact with its parental household by whose help it was established, but as generations change in both households this becomes more a matter of genealogical memory without much feeling of economic obligation, and after several generations have passed even the genealogical memory may become uncertain. For a branch household the most important ancestor is the first person who occupied the headship of the branch household where they actually live, not the ancestor of the main household. The cohesion of a *dōzoku* group as a whole is not easily maintained by genealogical recognition alone. In other words the composition of a *dōzoku* in itself has no structural force in maintaining the group as a functional unit. Many examples might be cited, such as the set of households distinguished from others as a group by genealogical and economic relations at their establishment, which once formed a *dōzoku*, but which now lack any corporate function. In some cases such a group cannot trace clearly (for nobody can remember) its genealogical relations: i.e. the history of the fissioning of these households has been forgotten. A set of these households may or may not form a single local group (*kumi*: which will be discussed in detail in section C). If they do form a local group, it is because they are located in the same area (not because they belong to the same *dōzoku*); and in such a case the local group most often will also include households which were not a part of the original *dōzoku*.

The *dōzoku*, according to my definition, is a set of households which recognize their relationship in terms of *honke* and *bunke*, and which, on the basis of this relation, have developed a corporate function as a group. In the course of time, a set of households which once formed a *dōzoku* might gradually drift apart, as just mentioned; or a *dōzoku* might come to interact closely, and acquire cohesion as a distinctive local group: this could be called an 'effective *dōzoku*'. Between these extremes there is of course considerable variety in the degree of function of individual *dōzoku*.

In the case of an effective *dōzoku*, the organization is always based upon the status differentiation as well as the economic differentiation between the main household and the branch households. If the *dōzoku* in Figure 8 is effectively organized, then the six households B–G, being the branch households (*bunke*), stand as subordinates to the leader A, the main or stem household (*honke*). Branch households are again classified into two categories, according to the relationship to A (the stem): those directly fissioned off from the main household by the immediate members, including adopted ones—B, C, D, E and F; and those indirectly related to the stem by the fissioning off from one of the branch households in the former category—G. Thus a clear hierarchical order is established among the households.

Classification based on the genealogical relations of branch households to the main household becomes a significant factor when and if a *dōzoku* is effectively organized as a whole. The *dōzoku*, in the absence of any structural cohesion as a definite group, such as through lineage, can only be organized as a functional corporate group by the economic and political power of the main household, utilizing status differentiation according to the genealogical frame, with the main household at its apex. Status differentiation among the households is based on a recognition of the legitimate authority of the main household which has economic and political superiority as well as the highest social prestige assigned to it as the oldest house among the group.

Normally in an effective *dōzoku*, the main household keeps a major share of the land when a branch household is separated off from it by fission, so as to be able to act as the non-competing head of the group. In fact, the weakness of the economic basis of the branch household is the primary reason for its subjection to the main household. Thus the *dōzoku*, the main household of which alone has a superior economic basis, develops a hierarchical structure through the subordination of the branch households. It is on this basis that the cohesion and the function of a *dōzoku* can be maintained.

The prestige given to the head of the main household is based on the notion that he is the representative of the direct line: it does not matter whether he is the real son of the late head, or an adopted son, or a son-in-law. In the Japanese conception he is the direct descendant of the founder of the household because he holds the position of head of the main household—he is the legal successor in the office. The initial kinship relation is secondary. The head of the main household, though he may be brother or cousin to the heads of branch households, is not 'brother' or 'cousin' in the structural sense, but 'master'.

The degree of differentiation between main household and branch household is also manifested in the modification of kinship terminology. In an effective *dōzoku*, the head of the main household is addressed as 'father' (*dodo*), and his wife as 'mother' (*aba*), while the heads of branch households are addressed as 'uncle' (*onji*) and their wives as 'aunt' (*unba*). Among the children, regardless of their relative ages, sons of the main household are addressed as 'elder brother' (*ani*) by the children of branch households, and sons of a branch household are regarded as younger brother by the former, being called by their personal names without using a kinship term.[1] In general among those people who develop effective *dōzoku* there is a widespread usage of three particular classificatory kinship terms: *father*, *elder brother* and *uncle*. For all members the *father* is the man who occupies the post of head; the *elder brother* is his successor. The rest of the male members are all called *uncle* by everyone, including one another. *Uncle* signifies generally male kin who are not in the direct line, and not necessarily only the parents' brother.

The kin who fall into the categories of 'brothers' and 'cousins' are divided into two structural categories in terms of household ideology: one is that of 'father-eldest son' (the head and his successor), and the other is that of 'uncle-younger brother' (non-successor). In Japanese sociological usage, the former category is expressed by 'the main line' (or direct line) and the latter by

---

[1] There are many similar practices among *dōzoku* in Japan, but these particular data are drawn from Fukutake, 1949, pp. 72–74. He adds that these kinship terms cited are used among the upper strata of the village population; among the lower strata different terms are used, but in corresponding fashion.

'the branch lines' (or side lines). This classification appears as the decisive factor in determining the status of members of a household and of *dōzoku*. Structured vertically, and accompanied by economic differentiation, it produces a hierarchical organization.

A further degree of institutionalization with greater discrimination between main and branch households is found among the more highly developed *dōzoku* in which the superior activities of the main household have been carried on for a long time. For example, marriage between members of the main household and of a branch household should be avoided. This is related to a widely prevalent notion, held also by those who are not concerned with the *dōzoku* institution, that marriage should take place between households of reasonably similar status. Therefore if a marriage takes place between members of a main and a branch household, it implies the degradation of the status of the main household to that of the branch household. In fact among minor *dōzoku*, whose main households have not attained any markedly superior status within the households of the *dōzoku*, such marriages do occur. The avoidance of marriage between main and branch household members shows the degree of power and prestige of the main household, as well as of the *dōzoku* as a whole. Such a powerful main household tends to have marriage relations with an equally influential main household of another *dōzoku*.

Such tendencies also appear in ritual conduct. A powerful main household monopolizes the conduct of ceremonies: for example, only the head of the *dōzoku* is allowed to officiate at the ceremony of the *dōzoku* shrine; and wedding and funeral ceremonies of members of the *dōzoku* are carried out under the leadership of the head of the main household. In another sphere, all members of the *dōzoku* usually have the same design on their family insignia, since this will stress the notion of one household (*ie*). But a powerful main household may possess family insignia a little different in design from those of the branch households, in order to show the differentiation between them (Fukutake, 1949, p. 78). Again, the main household has a surname with different letters from, but the same pronunciation as, that of its branch households.[1]

When the main household thus gained economic and social

[1] This is the case in one of the biggest *dōzoku*, called Nakamura-Ittō in Koshiozu village in Aichi prefecture, as I myself discovered.

power over its branch households, the *dōzoku* was recognized as an exclusive local corporate group with strong economic and social functions, and with much political influence in the village. In an extreme case a *dōzoku* may include most of the population of a village; on the other hand, more than two effective *dōzoku* may be found in one village, and it is quite normal, in a village where a *dōzoku* exists, for there to be households which do not form a *dōzoku*. Further, the degree of effectiveness and of institutionalization of *dōzoku* shows a great range, and the history of individual *dōzoku* demonstrates considerable variation. This mostly depends on the character of the leadership and of the economic basis of the main household, but also upon the history and economic organization of a given village, which is discussed in the following sections.

Inclusion of households of non-kin in the dōzoku

One of the characteristics of the *dōzoku* organization is its inclusion of non-kin members. As I stated in the previous section, the structure of the *dōzoku*, which is free from the descent principle, provides for the inclusion of a household whose members have no kinship at all with the rest of the *dōzoku* members; such a household might be that of a servant who was furnished with an arrangement similar to that of an adopted son, or of a tenant who established a tenancy on land owned by a household of the *dōzoku*, and was then given a house on its house-site land. By such economic relations a genealogical relation may be established with one of the households of the *dōzoku*, and thus the household of a stranger merges into the *dōzoku* group.

Particularly before the Meiji period, outstandingly wealthy *dōzoku* tended to include these households of non-kin, most of them former domestic or farm servants of the main or branch households. Some of them had been raised to the status of an adopted son, but the majority were treated as secondary members of the household when compared with the immediate members. And these secondary members had been given an arrangement for the establishment of their households analogous to a branch household of an immediate family member. An outsider might become a branch household by the establishment of a tenant relation with one of the households of the *dōzoku*, but without having been a servant of the latter. Such members of a *dōzoku* normally cultivated the master's land as a tenant or as a labourer whenever required. The degree of independence of this kind of branch household was certainly less; and this helped to strengthen the internal organization of a *dōzoku*: the more economically dependent a branch household was upon the main household, the easier became the control of the main household over the branch household. A high degree of dependence among these branch households necessarily involved elements of the patron/client relationship between the main and branch households, akin to that found in a medieval rural community.

Consideration of data from *dōzoku* which included non-kin members has produced much argument as to whether the *dōzoku* should be regarded as a descent group or not. Many scholars have tended to divide *dōzoku* into two types: the descent group, and that which included non-kin. (Some of them restrict the use of the term *dōzoku* to the latter case only.) I do not see any point in such a typological classification, because there are no structural differences between the two 'types'. First of all a *dōzoku* which does not include the household of servants and tenants is not thereby a descent group, as has already been discussed in the previous section: the structure of the *dōzoku* itself involves the possibility of inclusion of non-kin, which is the result of economic and situational factors. As a justification, there were also very effective *dōzoku* with branch households of immediate family members, who acted as tenants of the main household, which is a position similar to that of branch households of servants and tenants. Thus to classify members of a *dōzoku* in terms of kin or non-kin has no structural significance. Discussion on *dōzoku* should be directed along the lines of economic and historical analysis, rather than those of kinship alone.

The inclusion of households of servants and tenants in the *dōzoku* organization was closely related to the employment and land-tenure systems. Domestic or farm servants of the pre-Meiji period used to live in the same household as their master, without regular payment, as if they were members of the master's family. When they became of marriageable age, they were given a spouse by the master's arrangement. When they became middle-aged, they were given an independent household and land (usually as a tenancy on a long-term lease, rent-free) as a reward for their service. The amount of the portion given to these servants was dependent on the years they had served, and on the economic condition of the master's household. Thus, after their residential separation from their master's household, they mostly became tenants of the master. Usually the land leased to them was not sufficient to provide for their household, so they continued to receive economic help from their master's household, and in return gave free labour on their master's farms.

The master and his family were also cultivators, so superficially the two categories (family members and the servants) were assimilated. This land tenure system, with no technological differentiation between landowners and tenants, coupled with an employment system whereby servants received no regular payment but a kind of pension in land, seem to be the major factors making for the inclusion of non-kin members in the *dōzoku*. For this purpose I want to give a detailed analysis of the data concerning one of the well-documented *dōzoku* which included many servants' and tenants' households. This is Saito *dōzoku* in Iwate prefecture, surveyed by K. Ariga.[1]

The main household of Saito *dōzoku* is called *Ooya*, literally meaning the main or major household. This household was first established by a man who was a *Bushi* (entitled to bear arms), who settled in this Ishigami *buraku* in the middle of the seventeenth century and became a farmer.[2] Originating from this

---

[1] Ariga has been working on this Saito *dōzoku* over the past thirty years, and his findings have been published in various essays and books. Here I refer particularly to those of 1938, 1939, 1943, 1958, 1959 and 1960. Among all the accounts of Saito *dōzoku*, the *Nihon Kazoku-seido to Kosaku-seido* published in 1943 is best known and now stands as the classic text of *dōzoku* studies. Those who have dealt with *dōzoku* (including western scholars) almost without exception refer to or quote from this book, and thus Saito *dōzoku* has become well known. The references found in English-language works, however, are not reliable: there are often misleading and partial translations. The reasons for these inaccuracies are first, that Ariga does not employ terms of current usage in social anthropology and second, the Japanese terms he uses are quite clear to Japanese readers but difficult to render into adequate and accurate counterparts in English. I myself have had to make a considerable effort to present his researches in terms of current social anthropology. In doing this I appreciate greatly Professor Ariga's most kind co-operation. To assist me in clarifying details he also gave me his unpublished data, which I found invaluable for the anthropological analysis. I hope that Ariga's work thus gathered and presented here may serve others who will deal with Japanese rural society, and not merely for my own present study.

[2] This man has been regarded as *the* ancestor of the Saito *dōzoku*, though they can trace back their genealogy beyond him. Although these distant ancestors prior to him figure in stories of family lore, he is in effect 'crowned' as head of the first generation to settle in their village.

main household, Ooya, forty branch households in all had been established from the time of its settlement up to 1935. In 1935 when Ariga made a survey there, the total number of households in Ishigami *buraku* was thirty-seven, of which thirty-four belonged to Saito *dōzoku*. (Saito *dōzoku* consisted of forty-one households together with the main household, but five of them were in Nakasai, a neighbouring *buraku* of Ishigami, and two were in other villages far from Ishigami.)

In 1935, Ooya possessed a wet rice field of one *chō* and two *tan*, a dry field of two *chō*, and also engaged in the manufacture of lacquer. The Ooya household consisted of twenty-one members altogether: the family of the head of Ooya, and two families of servants. (Figures in brackets show respective ages.)

Family members of Ooya:

Zensuke (the head) (49); his wife (45)
his sons (25), (13), (10), (9), (5)
his daughters (18), (6)
his eldest son's wife (21) and daughter (2)
his mother (72) and his sister (52)

Servants:

A man (54), his daughter (23) and his daughter's husband (28)
A man (26), his wife (24), their daughters (5), (1) and a son (1)
(Servants had married by arrangement of the master; each family was given a small room (*hiya*) in the house. Their economy was completely dependent upon Ooya, and they were the labour force in Ooya's enterprise.)

It was said that at the beginning of the Meiji period this household included four families of servants, and that the second and third sons of the head also shared the common residence after they had each acquired a wife and children. These kin members, like servants, were also engaged in the labour of the household until each in the course of time was established as a branch household. In basic operations, the immediate kin members and servants were in the same category. However, the differences between them appeared clearly in the arrangements made when the branch households were established, as I describe presently.

The households of Saito *dōzoku* in Ishigami *buraku* were classified as follows, according to their statuses:

Main household: Ooya

Branch households: (the genealogical relations are shown in
Figure 10)

   Category I (7 households altogether)
      Bekke (fissioned off from immediate members of Ooya):
         Sakaya; Nakayashiki; Tahyoe; Himashi; and Atarashie
      Mago-bekke (fissioned off from immediate members of
         Bekke): Keijirō and Kotarō

   Category II (26 households altogether): A–Z
      Bekkekaku-nago⎱ (fissioned off from servants of Ooya or
      Bunke-nago ⎰   Bekke)
      Yashiki-nago⎱ (tenants' households of Ooya or Bekke)
      Sakugo ⎰

Relations of the households of Category II with the households
of Category I and Ooya are as follows. (The letters show each
household corresponding to Ariga's data, and the year of establishment is given in brackets.)

   Households attached to Ooya:

      Bekkekaku-nago: A (1863); B (1912); C (1928)
      Bunke-nago: D (1926); E (1877); F (1840); G; H (1897);
         I (1905); J (1810); K; L (1921)
      Yashiki-nago: M (1912); N (1933); O (1843); P (1918)
      Sakugo: Q; R
   To Sakaya:
      Bunke-nago: S; T
      Yashiki-nago: U; V; W
   To Nakayashiki:
      Bunke-nago: Y
      Yashiki-nago: X
   To Tahyoe:
      Yashiki-nago: Z

Among the households of Category II (A–Z), kinship links
between households are found as follows:

A–B   F–D   C–K–Q–R   U–Y–O–Z   J–M
                          ╱＼╱   │
         P–E–G–L–S   H   W–V
                │
                N

Only three households (I, T, X) have no kinship link with other households in the *dōzoku*.

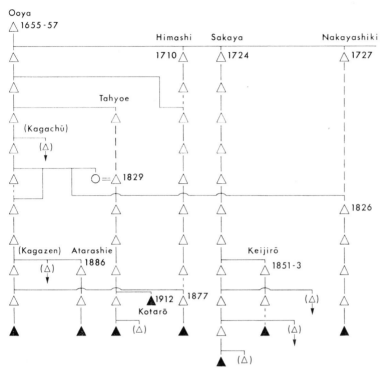

FIGURE 10. Genealogical Relations of Household Heads of Saito *Dōzoku*
(Reproduced from the data collected by K. Ariga in 1935)

The vertical line indicates the succession of each household.
The year indicates the establishment/re-establishment of the household.

▲ Present head of the households in Ishigami *buraku*.
(△) The first head of a branch household established in a neighbouring *buraku*.
↓ Line continued.
– – – – Adoption.
— — — Interval without a member of the house.

Kagachū established branch household. Hence the number of *dōzoku* households in this figure is fifteen in all.

The status differentiation among the households of Saito *dōzoku* is also clearly expressed in the arrangements at the graveyard as seen in Figure 11.

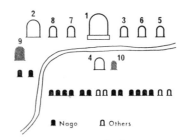

FIGURE II. Graveyard of Saito *Dōzoku*
(Reproduced from Ariga, 1939, p. 312)

1. Ooya   2. Sakaya   3. Nakayashiki   4. Tahyoe   5. Himashi
6. Atarashie 7. Kagachū   8. Kagazen   9. Keijirō 10. Kotarō

The internal classification of the various households of the
dōzoku not only indicates the status of a household, but also
differentiates between the amounts of land and property given
to households at the time of their fissioning off, and their duties
and obligations. It also indicates the degree of economic security
achieved after the separation.

According to Ariga's data, which mainly deal with the direct
relationship of Ooya to each branch household, at the establishment of Bekke considerable property was given from Ooya,
including a house with residential area, some moveable property,
some fields and a portion of forest, which made it possible for
them to have an economy independent of Ooya. They had no
obligation to give their services in agricultural labour to Ooya,
though they kept close social and ritual ties with this household.

The difference between Bekkekaku-nago and Bunke-nago lies
in the length of time they resided in Ooya household: the founder
of the former household was taken in when a baby, whereas the
latter became a servant at four or five years old. The arrangements made for them by Ooya when they became independent
were very similar but were more favourable to the former than
to the latter. Each was given a house, movable property and agricultural tools, and lent some portion of land free for cultivation.
They kept close economic and social contacts with Ooya (or
Bekke). Economically their life was not so independent as that
of Bekke, since the land they cultivated for themselves was not
sufficient for their families. In fact they received economic aid of
various kinds. For example, they were allowed to borrow money

from Ooya without interest and to borrow rice in the period of shortage (before harvest). They were helped with fertilizer and seeds; they were lent clothes, furniture and necessary materials on occasions such as birth, marriage or funeral. Their children were often fed (as servants of Ooya) and were later given economic help when they became independent, as in their father's case. For these various kinds of help received from Ooya, they had an obligation to provide seasonal labour (fifteen to sixteen days per year in 1936). Because their economic weakness was relieved by Ooya's help, their social life was closely controlled by Ooya. Their marriages were arranged by the head of Ooya.

Both Yashiki-nago and Sakugo were branch households, the members of which had not been residential members of Ooya or Bekke, but had established tenant relations with one of these. The difference between the two categories was that Yashiki-nago was a branch household whose house-site belonged to Ooya's residential area, while that of Sakugo was their own. The degree of obligation to Ooya (or Bekke) of Yashiki-nago was almost the same as that of Bunke-nago, but they did not get as much help as Bunke-nago from Ooya. Sakugo's obligation to Ooya in seasonal labour was half that of Yashiki-nago, and they received less help.

Thus, major distinctions were drawn: first, between branch households sprung from immediate members of the main household and those originating from non-kin of the main household; then, between those households whose heads were once residential members (servants) of the main household and those whose heads were non-residential members (tenants). The economic security of each category is graded accordingly. For instance, in a case of famine, the household first allowed to starve was Sakugo, then Yashiki-nago; Bunke-nago (including Bekke-kaku-nago) were most protected. However, the degree of independence was in the opposite direction, towards increasing autonomy from Bunke-nago to Yashiki-nago, and then to Sakugo, the last-named finally leaving the *dōzoku* and becoming independent farmers as their economy developed.

The difference between Bekke (including the Mago-Bekke) and the rest (Bekkekaku-nago, Bunke-nago, Yashiki-nago and Sakugo) was not only between kin and non-kin, the former being an immediate member of the household and the latter servants or tenants. There was also an economic difference—the former was an independent holder and the latter were tenants. The differentiation among those households having a basic economic status as tenants clearly corresponded to residential factors: household and residential site. From Ariga's description of the relationship of these households to Ooya or Bekke, the differentiation can be shown systematically as follows (see Figure 12). There were three major factors: (1) all these households cultivated Ooya (or Bekke) land; (2) there was a difference according to whether the head of the household had ever been a resident of Ooya (or Bekke) household or not; (3) there was a difference according to whether the household was within the residential site belonging to Ooya (or Bekke) or not. According to the situation in terms of factors (2) and (3), the arrangement of (1) differed in the terms of the lease in return for labour service; or payment of tax with reduced or no labour service.

According to the combination of these three factors, the relationship to Ooya (or Bekke) was determined. In Figure 12, A, B and C represent a typical arrangement of these three categories respectively. The households of A and B were established within the residential area of Ooya (normally the house was built by Ooya and belonged to Ooya); but the difference between the two was that the head of the household A was once a servant (and a residential member) of Ooya, while that of B was not. This was the difference between Bunke-nago (A) and Yashiki-nago (B). C was the third type, Sakugo; the household was situated out of the residential area of Ooya (normally the house was built without help from Ooya, and belonged to the head of C). The head of the household, like the head of B, had never been a residential member of Ooya household.

Naturally the children of these tenants' branch households would be also involved in the *dōzoku* organization unless they left the community or had an economic establishment independent of the *dōzoku*. In such arrangements we can see the theoretical extension of the basic procedures described above. There are four major arrangements possible, as shown in D, E, F, and G of Figure 12.

D. The head of household D was the son of the head of A, who followed exactly the same procedure as his father: he served in Ooya household, and later was given the same arrangement as his father.

Thus he became Bunke-nago. (Another son of *A* would occupy or succeed the household head of *A*. But household *A* was in the possession of Ooya, hence a son of *A* had no right to succeed to the household unless he had a similar relationship to Ooya as his father.) Thus actual kinship is modified by economic and residential factors.

E. *E* was derived also from *A*, but this son of *A*, without serving in Ooya household, was allowed to establish his household by Ooya within this residential site. Because he did not become a residential member of Ooya household, his household relationship to Ooya became similar to that of *B*, Yashiki-nago. What is important is not the kinship relation involved, but the actual economic and residential factors.

F. The father of the head of *F* was formerly of the category *A*, but later he purchased the residential site from Ooya. When his son married, he built a house for his son's family in his own residential area. However, he had no land to give or lease to his son, hence his son again became a tenant of his master, Ooya. Thereby his son's household also became a part of the *dōzoku* in terms similar to those by which Sakugo was related to Ooya.

G. The basic process was the same as with *F*, but the residential arrangement between father and son was different from that of *F*. The head of *G* was formerly of the category *A*, but he later purchased his residential site from Ooya, where he built another house. Instead of giving this new house to his newly married son, he himself moved to the new house with his wife and unmarried son, giving his older house (built by Ooya) to his married son. Thus, the father transmitted the headship, which automatically accompanied the right of household and tenantship, to his son. This residential arrangement is *inkyo*, already explained in detail in Chapter 1 (see pp. 11–16). The difference in this household from that of case *D* should be noted—in this case (*G*) the possession of the household with its site lay with the tenant, not with Ooya, so that the father could transmit his right to this son, who had never been the servant of Ooya. The father who had lost the legitimate relationship with Ooya by his transmission of the headship to his son, again became a tenant of Ooya. As a result, his relationship to Ooya became of category *C*, Sakugo, while his son maintained the older relationship to Ooya in place of his father.

The variations from *D* to *G* present alternative arrangements of the tenants' households for the next generation, according to the degree of independence of each household within the *dōzoku* network. The distinguishing feature is that in the network of the *dōzoku* organization, the relationship to Ooya is established in

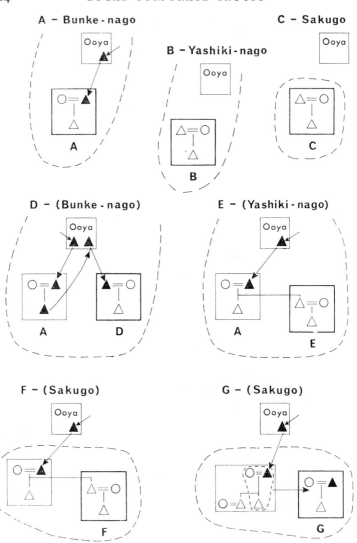

FIGURE 12. Variations of Household Relations in Saito *Dōzoku*
(Produced by the author according to Ariga's description)

terms of the household: individual relationship is subject to household relationship.

The distinguishing household criteria also appear in the following manner. When any such tenant's household becomes vacant, any individual (with his family members) who was allowed to occupy it was placed in the same relationship to Ooya as the original household, with corresponding economic qualifications and regardless of their descent. Thus, the relation of any household to the main household established through residential and economic criteria played a far more important sociological role than any actual kinship relations involved. This shows one of the important aspects of the principle of Japanese social organization: actual kinship becomes a negligible factor by comparison with the residential and economic factors.

However, tenancy did not always result in the formation of the *dōzoku* organization. Perhaps economic and residential factors are responsible for the formation of a social institution such as *dōzoku* only when these factors are expected to have considerable stability over a long period—i.e. for more than the lifetime of any single person—and when the master's household already forms part of a large functional *dōzoku*.

The constitution of the *dōzoku* was further cemented by the religious unity of its members. Most of the effective *dōzoku* used to have their own shrines. The existence of a *dōzoku* shrine was an indication of the effectiveness of the *dōzoku*; at least it showed that the *dōzoku* was once 'effective' as a local corporate group. This unity, ideologically perceived as one *ie*, was also expressed in the fact that those households of tenants who formed the *dōzoku* regarded the ancestor of the main households as their ancestor also, and participated in the ceremonies of the main household.[1] In Saito *dōzoku*, the most important ancestor is the founder of Ooya, who settled first in this Ishigami *buraku*. Indeed this ancestor of the main household is treated as the ancestor of the *dōzoku* as a whole.

However, each household which belonged to a *dōzoku*, and carried on the ancestor cult in terms of the *dōzoku*, normally had its own ancestor as well. Since each household is a distinct unit even in the framework of the *dōzoku*, and even though a branch household is directly linked to the main household through kinship, it regards its own founder as its own particular most im-

---

[1] However, they normally maintained their own temple affiliation. In the village there were always two kinds of religious institutions: shrine (Shintō) and temple (Buddhist). Every household had its separate affiliation with each of them. It was the shrine that had the more important relation to the organization of local groups and the village community.

portant ancestor. This is also the case with a tenant branch household.

This point touches the essentially functional aspect of the Japanese ancestor cult. The recognition of the ancestor in Japan usually refers to the actual founder of the household (*ie*) in which the present occupants live: this recognition does not go back to extremely remote ancestors, unless the *ie* is a household of distinguished aristocrats who can trace back a clear pedigree to an ancient period of Japanese history. Among commoners, ancestors are regarded more in terms of local and economic factors than in terms of genealogy. It is the founder of the *ie*, and those who died as the members of the household, who are celebrated as ancestors.[1] Because of this tradition, every household after the second generation has its own ancestor. Hence in the case of a branch household of an effective *dōzoku*, there may be a double ancestral ceremony—one relating to the main household from which it branched off or with which it has established a local genealogical relationship; and the other relating to its own household. Such double recognition of ancestors not infrequently exists among branch households. If a *dōzoku* is very effective, and the main household is economically and socially distinguished, the ancestor cult of the whole *dōzoku* plays a very important role as compared with that of each branch household. Ariga reports that even in 1935 the branch households of the Saito *dōzoku* used to gather at the main household for the seasonal festivals; they conducted very few ceremonial activities of their own (Ariga, 1959, p. 10).

Branch households regard the ancestor of the main household as their own ancestor because they form a corporate body for their major economic activities, not because they can trace back their actual descent to a common ancestor. This corporate body is formed by the concept of the extension of a household, which justifies their notion of the genealogy. This genealogy, which is differentiated from that of a descent group, has meaning in terms of the present economic corporate body. The ancestor is

[1] Some old influential households in a village possess a written genealogy which may go back to a distinguished Bushi in the medieval age. However, this early part of the genealogy is often added later in order to increase the prestige of the household: most of such genealogies are not factual. (Indeed there were instances in the later Tokugawa period where a landlord, having grown wealthy, bought a genealogy from a poor *Bushi*.)

the guardian and protector of the living members of the corporate body, of which its smallest unit is the household.

The ancestor is the justifying authority for the co-operation of the living members. How an individual is related to the ancestor in terms of descent is not primarily important. The term 'ancestor' which usually conveys the notion of descent, is subject to economic and local factors. The modification of a category originally connoting descent by economic and local factors seems a widespread native principle in Japan. This concept of ancestor and the function of ancestor worship among the Japanese are in decided contrast to those of the Chinese, among whom the patrilineal kinship principle strongly adheres, so that they do not allow inclusion of non-patrilineal members, and a set of ancestors of a localized lineage is recognized as one of the segments of a wider unit.

Further, it should be recalled that, as in the case of Saito *dōzoku*, the members of the *dōzoku*, including those who had no kinship relation, were buried in the same graveyard belonging to the main household (see p. 100). Though not always so well arranged as the graveyard of Saito *dōzoku*, the graves of a set of households which form a *dōzoku* are normally found in a distinctive cluster within the grave area of a village. (Indeed the arrangement of graveyards in the village reveals in a longer perspective the local groupings of the households in the village.) In this manner their group consciousness is also explicitly expressed.

Another manifestation of the strong consciousness of a local corporate group not necessarily based on the kinship relation is in its participation in the shrine, for such participation includes households which are not related through descent. Those households which form a distinctive corporate group other than in a *dōzoku*, as they may in some cases, also share the same shrine as that of the common ancestor of the group, on the grounds that he is a common guardian deity for the group (see Ariga, 1959, p. 14). This kind of shrine has the same basic function as that of the *dōzoku*. But in the latter case the group is more institutionalized, and the shrine has a further function—that of justification of its internal organization. Whether in *dōzoku* or non-*dōzoku* local corporate groups, shrines play an important role in group unity.

As demonstrated in the foregoing discussion, the inclusion of non-kin members in the *dōzoku* is also logical, in view of its religious foundation. I think this system, in not restricting membership to kin, is of great advantage to the economic management of the main household in a society where there is considerable mobility of population. Adequate replacement of labour is most efficiently achieved by this means. At the same time, for landless peasants it is a great advantage for there to be no sharp discrimination between kin and non-kin.

Some actual cases of how newcomers came into a *dōzoku* group will give a clearer picture of this process.

Acceptance of a non-kin member from outside the village (*buraku*), Ariga states, would seem to require someone to give a surety for that person. In spite of a detailed survey in Ishigami *buraku*, he failed to find any document involving such surety. In the later period of the Tokugawa it appears that it was necessary only to have an oral introduction from a man of high status. The examples from Ishigami seem to indicate that people came into Saito *dōzoku* through the verbal introduction of someone who, being of the same status as a member of Ooya, acted as surety for the newcomer (Ariga, 1943, p. 390).

Further, Ariga states that if a servant saw no possibility of being allowed by his master to form a branch household at the termination of his service, he would leave the house before it was too late to make a career elsewhere. But under the circumstances of the Tokugawa period it was almost impossible for a poor peasant to establish an independent household by himself. Hence, if a peasant left his master's household, he had to find another master who might in the end set him up in a branch household. The possibility of a servant establishing a branch household had its limits. If a household had no land to spare for a branch household, a servant would not stay long. There was thus a tendency for constant renewal of servants (Ariga, *ibid.*, p. 391). Within the society, those in possession of land and those not so were adjusted to one another by the residential mobility of the latter. For these operations the *dōzoku* played an important role in solving social and economic problems.

Those persons who were engaged temporarily, without expectation of a branch household from their master, were indeed in the category of 'servant'. But those who were treated as members of the household and were expected in due course to have branch households, stood equal to the immediate family members of the household in terms of economic organization. Both kinds of members were unpaid labourers (while they were in the master's household) with a kind of a pension (establishment of branch household with a portion of the master's land given or leased). Therefore, the general relations between family members and servants, including tenants, was closely related to the labour structure—there was no differentiation in farming technique between employer and employees; all were cultivators.

Normally the immediate members of the household had more advantageous arrangements than did the servants, but the principle was the same. The case of Saito *dōzoku* clearly shows the different treatment. At the establishment of a branch household those who were immediate family members were given sufficient land and property to be independent. Those in the category of servants were not given sufficient land for independence, their labour was expected from time to time, and they still had to depend on economic help from the main household (see pp. 100–2). So far as land allotment was concerned, the former was *subdivision* while the latter was *lease*.

However, in other cases in which the main household had not the land for the establishment of branch households that Saito *dōzoku* had, the arrangement made with the branch households was called *nago* (tenant), though they were the households of sons of the head of the main household. Such cases were found among *dōzoku* in comparatively poor areas where the penetration of the monetary economy had been delayed, forcing the branch households to depend on the main household economy (Ariga, *ibid.*, p. 277).[1] In general, too, regardless of the fertility of the land, similar cases were found among many poor *dōzoku*, whose main household resources were so limited that they could not easily afford to establish branch households. In such a situation, the brothers of the man who succeeded to the headship were considered simply as a labour force. Also the time of branching off tended to be delayed: brothers stayed at their natal house after

[1] In some cases a branch household of the immediate members entered the category of *nago* through the decline of its economy. Therefore the categories of tenant and independent farmer were not indications of non-kin and kin branch households: the most important factor was the economic one.

marriage and begetting children—they were often over forty years of age before they founded branch households. Though they might each get an independent residence and a small plot of land, these brothers could not carry on an independent economy under that arrangement. The land and other property given to these branch households by their established head was considered as payment for labour service during their stay at the main household. The brothers were told that if they worked well they would get a larger share when they had an independent residence. This conception was exactly the same as that in the case of servants.

The equation of immediate members and servants also can be seen in another context: for example, in the Nosa *dōzoku* surveyed by Ariga. This *dōzoku*, unlike the Saito *dōzoku*, was formed only by related members of the main family: servants were always taken from among the relatives of the household. These servants at their branching off benefited from the same arrangement as did the immediate family members, though the latter had a rather larger share than the former. The time of branching off was also the same for the two kinds of members. Both sons and servants were allowed to branch off at the statutory age of forty-one years; until then they worked for the main household. Ariga states that these servants, who came from households related through kinship to the main household, in fact fell into the category of adopted sons and daughters. Such was the actual status of what were called *hōkōnin* (servants) in this period (Ariga, *ibid.*, pp. 92–95).

Discrimination between immediate family members and servants was basically in a similar category. The high frequency of adoption cases was derived from the same notion. Before modern times it was rather difficult to draw the line between adopted members and servants, in default of a clear legal procedure. Among the members of a *dōzoku* (and household), if we place adopted sons between real sons and servants, we can see more clearly the link between the immediate family members and servants; they are in the same category from this point of view. The widespread practice of adoption and the employment of servants—particularly in the later Tokugawa period when the *dōzoku* was functioning strongly—added more strength to the labour force required by the household. The immediate members formed a significant labour force, but not always sufficient. Permanent land-working servants in this context should be differentiated from temporary domestic servants.

One point remains to be cleared up—that is, why servants were engaged only from among kin in the case of Nosa *dōzoku*, whereas in other cases, as in the Saito *dōzoku*, non-kin servants were employed. I think this is neither a structural nor a local difference, but one in which economic factors were involved. As Ariga describes it, the area of Nosa *dōzoku* was poor in resources; the climatic conditions were not fit for wet rice cultivation, and they had to depend on dry fields. Owing to low output, a larger area and more labour were needed for cultivation (Ariga, *ibid.*, pp. 93–94). Before the Meiji period, this *buraku* was occupied only by relatives of the Nosa family. Such economic conditions probably did not attract strangers, and at the same time kin were numerous enough to be employed by their more fortunate kinsmen. Perhaps, if there had been a shortage of kinsmen, strangers might have been taken. As it was, there may have been no space for their inclusion. There was a balance between the limited possibilities for the people born in this *buraku* and the resources and labour required.

In general, it seems that the inclusion of non-kin depended upon the economy of the main household, and on the availability of kin for its needs. A wealthier household, particularly in its period of economic expansion, had more need to employ non-kin. If Saito *dōzoku* had had more kin who sought employment, this might have decreased the branch households of non-kin. The availability of kin does not mean simply the number of kin in the community, but the number of poorer kin who could constitute a labour force. If kin were all equally well off, none would become tenants. The most important factor for the formation or increase of non-kin branch households was the amount of the labour force required at a given time.

The inclusion of households of non-kin members into a *dōzoku* also meets the economic situation of the village community where poor households exist which cannot provide for the establishment of branch households for the extra members. Sons of such a household seek a tenantship in other households which may lease land, and with which they may establish the *dōzoku* relationship. The result of establishing such a relationship is often that they become servants of the household. In a community where no alternative was open to the secondary sons other than engaging in cultivation, a most desirable solution was for them to become tenants as well as members of a *dōzoku*, unless they could become adopted sons or adopted sons-in-law of other households which would provide property for them as successor in the household or as the head of a new branch household. At worst, a secondary son might remain unmarried as a labourer in his natal household. In some cases, he did have an informal marital relationship, but his family of procreation would not be recognized by society. Normally if a great degree of economic differentiation existed in a community, an effective *dōzoku* would result. A successful wealthy man tended to attract his kin as well as non-kin, who would give him their labour in return for economic dependence upon him, and also would become political allies under him. The unfortunate had to depend on the more fortunate, either kin or non-kin, within the community. Hence, the *dōzoku* tended to be formed from the upper strata of the community. It was the general tendency for more prosperous *dōzoku* to include many households of kin and non-kin in their number, while minor ones might consist only of a small number of households of kin.

However, the inclusion of non-kin households in a *dōzoku* greatly decreased after modernization. Ariga states that since the Meiji period the change in farm management by large landowners (into a modern contract system of tenancy) and the availability of alternative economic means for small farmers and landless peasants, made it less necessary for them to depend on landowners and the *dōzoku* (Ariga, 1950, pp. 168–9). Thus, a change in the economic situation brought with it a significant change in *dōzoku* composition.

The economic and historical setting for the development and decline of dōzoku organization

The fact that branch households, whether of a real son, adopted son or servants, could scarcely carry on their economic life without depending upon the main household, provides the basis for the *dōzoku* hierarchical organization—the subjugation of branch households to the main, and the superior status of the main household—which made for tightly knit economic organization.

Accordingly, the *dōzoku* played an important functional role as a local corporate group, and maintained its cohesion.

In such a *dōzoku*, the main household usually possessed vast fields where its own family labour was not sufficient, and the cheapest labour supply came from these branch households. Thus the main household had the advantage of a permanent free labour force from the branch households. From the latter's point of view, they received economic help from the main household when they were in difficulty; in return, they had a duty to supply free labour to the main household. The following remarks well reflect such a relation.

'*Bekke* often visit *honke*, and are offered good meals there.'

'*Bekke* go to help *honke*'s work even without being asked.'

'When *bekke* have nothing to eat, they just go to *honke* and ask for rations.'

Thus their relation is a constant 'give and take' without close calculation—in the interests of both parties.

The actual working of a *dōzoku* was very complicated in comparison with a modern wage-payment system. All members of a *dōzoku* formed a constant labour pool under the leadership of the head of the main household, and formed the effective corporate body. Yet every household was a distinct property-holding unit. The cultivation of lands possessed or leased by each household was carried out by the joint labour force supplied by all members of the *dōzoku*, including those of the main household.[1] But on balance the branch households gave much more labour to the main household, than did the latter to the former. And, as already stated, this labour service was returned in economic help to the branch households from the main. In this way the economic interests of the main household were redistributed among the branch households. Moreover, the returns on capital and labour were low at this stage of farming technique.

Further, the creation of a branch household theoretically incurred loss of household property and land. The main household had no right to regain land apportioned to its branch households, without purchasing it. There was thus little opportunity for the

[1] In particularly busy seasons, i.e. transplantation in the spring, the main household might also engage wage labourers from, and exchange labour with, households other than its own *dōzoku*, besides employing the free labour of its branch households.

main household to accumulate elaborate economic interests, and even if its economic standing increased, it was always threatened by decline so long as its basic economy depended upon limited resources.

On the other hand, branch households might have an opportunity of raising their economic standing, though they were handicapped by their relatively small original share of the property as compared with the main household. In the earlier stages of the establishment of a branch household, it tended to depend upon the help of the main household since its economic basis was normally poor. However, this situation could be improved by good management and hard work and also by not having an obligation to help other households. A branch household could reach the point of independence after the accumulation of enough capital to buy from the main household or from others sufficient land for the family to live on; it would then usually operate an independent economy, though the social and ritual relationship might be maintained.

For example, in the Saitō *dōzoku*, household Y had already become semi-independent by the end of the Tokugawa period; it emerged from Sakugo (Bunke-nago) by purchasing the house-site land from Ooya. Hence the three branch households of Y did not form a part of Saito *dōzoku*, each of them acquiring land from Y without becoming tenants of the *dōzoku*. Likewise, after 1935 both S and T became independent farmers, and later W did too. There have been many such cases. In Koshiozu village, the economic history of households over the last hundred years shows that a new branch household often improved its economic standing over the original one within one or two generations. Unless the main household was extremely wealthy, such phenomena were quite common among *dōzoku*. The case of Saitō *dōzoku* where the main household had held its leading position for a long time is rather exceptional. Even in this Saitō *dōzoku*, *bekke* (branch households of immediate family members) maintained considerable independence from the beginning of their establishment, in comparison with those of servants and tenants. In fact the functional core of Saitō *dōzoku* was in each constituent group, consisting of tenant households directly attached to the main household.

Changes in the relative economic standing of the main and

branch households were one of the reasons why the *dōzoku* organization altered in the course of time. The main reason for the change or collapse of an effective *dōzoku* organization was not so much the prosperity of a branch household, as the economic decline of the main household. Since the pivot of the organization and its economic basis was the main household, its decline brought about the collapse of the whole organization. If the decline of the main household occurred when one of the branch households was rising, the latter would take the former's role. Thus a *dōzoku* might change its internal organization without the collapse of the whole unit. Since there was this possibility of an interchange of roles between the main and branch households, disputes sometimes arose among households of a *dōzoku* over which household should be the main household.

Other important factors caused considerable upheavals in the economic life of individual households in rural communities: principally, the series of great economic changes at state level after the middle of the Tokugawa period, and the expansion in merchants' capital which was accompanied by new developments in manufacture, and followed by industrialization. These factors certainly affected the economy of rural areas. In such a situation, a capable man could seize the opportunity of expanding his economy, while an unfortunate man could easily lose his wealth. The *dōzoku* organization should be understood in this context. One of the best examples is given in an historical sketch of the development and decline of several *dōzoku* in one village (Sawada *buraku*) in Okayama prefecture, recorded by Ariga (1943, pp. 33–41).

In 1935 Sawada *buraku* consisted of sixty households, of which three were vacant households. The majority of the households belonged to ten different *dōzoku*, as in the table on p. 116.

This Sawada *buraku* seems to be one of the very old villages of Japan, since Tokumori-jinja, the shrine of this village, is said to have been established in the fourth century. However, it is in the Tokugawa period that the composition of the village is made clear to us through historical documents, which are also relevant to the present situation.

During the Genroku (1688–1703), the main households of nos. 1–6 were already established; and among them, Ōtsuka, Sanga, Tabuchi, and Wajin were considered of equally high status;

Approximate order of settlement	Name of dōzoku and households	Number of households in each dōzoku
1	Ōtsuka	5
2	Sanga	4
3	Tabuchi	3
4	Yonesawa	4
5	Inoguchi	2
6	Wajin	11
7	Sugimoto	3 (1 vacant)
8	Ōbayashi	12 (1 vacant)
9	Uchida	2
10	Hatano	7
11	Hirose	1
12	Kosaka	1
13	Mokimoto	1
14	Kanajima	1 (vacant)
15	Kio	1
16	Takahashi	1
17	Atoyasu	1
	Total	60

Yonesawa and Inoguchi were placed lower than these. Soon after—almost at the same time as Wajin—Sugimoto, Ōbayashi, Uchida and Hatano came to this village from neighbouring villages. These four families brought with them considerable wealth, so that they were able to establish their households without help from previous settlers in the village.

The rest (11-17) came later than these wealthy family groups. They were rather poor and their settlement was effected through starting a relationship with one of the wealthy and powerful households in the village, who acted as a protecting sponsor. This kind of settlement was termed *nurewaraji* in olden days. The order of the settlement of these minor households is not clear. As Ariga traced it back it is as follows: Hirose came at the Tenpo famine (1832–6); Kio and Takahashi came during the Taishō (1912–26). The year of settlement of Kosaka, Makimoto and Kanajima is not known; they might have come earlier than Hirose. Atoyasu was a servant of the main household of Tabuchi, but on the decline of the Tabuchi household, he emerged and established his own household in 1933.

The distribution of the households shows a tendency for those now belonging to the same *dōzoku* to be clustered in the same residential area: this tendency is particularly noticeable among the *dōzoku* of Sanga, Wajin, Ōtsuka, Yonesawa and Ōbayashi. Each *dōzoku* has its own shrine, which is situated near the main house, or on the hill owned by the main household. From this early picture Ariga assumes that the village developed the establishment of effective *dōzoku* groups. These *dōzoku* had a fairly strong functional role as corporate groups through which the major village life was carried out. However, from the later period of the Tokugawa to 1935, considerable changes occurred in the internal organization of each *dōzoku* as well as in inter-*dōzoku* power relations. The rise and decline in prosperity of these *dōzoku* was as follows ('the present time' refers to 1935):

Ōtsuka: The main household had been prosperous until the end of the nineteenth century as a big landowner. (The members were also cultivators themselves.) They were also of high status as descendants of Samurai of the Middle Ages. However, by 1935, this *dōzoku* had lost its power, particularly the main household, which had declined and had become a tenant. Some of the branch households possess small plots of land, but all are tenant households.

Sanga: Like Ōtsuka, the main household had by 1935 much declined and became a tenant. The first and second branch households became powerful in the course of time, though recently the second branch household has begun to decline. Some branch households are smallholders, and others are tenants.

Tabuchi: This *dōzoku* had occupied the highest status in the village. The main household keeps the key of Tokumori shrine, and the well of this shrine is on the site of the main household. It is said that the members of this group once had higher status than the priest of the shrine, and also that the priest of the shrine came from among their members. During the Tokugawa period, the main household head once occupied the position of *shōya* (village headman). However this main household is now in decline, though it is still a landowner. The other two households of Tabuchi at present in the village are not direct branch households of the main household, but they are said to be descendants, together with the main household, of the common original household. They came from the neighbouring village, Kubota, after Genroku (1688–1703). One of these branch households is the biggest landowner in Sawada; and another engages in commerce, besides being a freeholder of land. In 1846 and 1850, according to the records, there were two direct branch households of the main household, but later they moved to Tsuyama city.

Yonesawa: It is said that the main household used to enjoy considerable wealth, but since it took a woman of another country[1] as wife, its status became lower and at the same time it lost its property. The households of this *dōzoku* are tenants at the present time.

Inoguchi: No particular information on this *dōzoku* is available; it seems that there has not been so much change here as in other *dōzoku*.

Wajin: Wajin *dōzoku* was once very powerful. In the latter part of the Tokugawa period, the main household and one of the branch households called Shinya occupied the *shōya* (headmanship) successively. The main household had been very wealthy and powerful till the end of the Meiji period (1912), but since then has been in decline. At present it is still a freeholder. On the other hand, the Shinya is a big landowner and is said to be the richest household in the village. Of the other branch households one half are freeholders and the other half are small landowners.

Sugimoto: This group, which settled in this *buraku* at almost the same time as Wajin, seems to have brought considerable property, and the *dōzoku* had been considered a very respectable one and also the richest in the village until the beginning of the Meiji period. However now all the households have completely declined.

Ōbayashi: This *dōzoku* had been very prosperous and large. It is rather difficult to know which was the real main household—either Nakaya (Ōbayashi) or Daihonke (Ōbayashi). Ariga thinks it was probably Nakaya because the Kabuuchi shrine (*dōzoku* shrine) is found within the Nakaya residential site, and Nakaya performs the ceremony. On the other hand, Daihonke had been very powerful till the end of the Meiji period. The saying is 'Wajin in upper Sawada, and Ōbayashi in the lower Sawada'. More recently Daihonke has declined. At present the powerful households are two branches of Daihonke, Kō and Otsu. Kō branch household is a big landowner (and a cultivator as well), and Otsu is also a big landowner (but a non-cultivator). One of the branch households at the next level is a land-owner, but three other branch households are freeholders, and a further three are tenants.

Uchida: No particular information.

Hatano: They were not prosperous throughout the period, and at present are mostly tenants or freeholders.

Thus, during the last two hundred years, considerable changes have occurred in each *dōzoku*. On the whole the function of the

---

[1] This means a woman of another feudal state. In the Tokugawa period each feudal state was an independent political and economic unit. Those who came from another state were considered foreigners and greatly handicapped. A marriage between different states hardly ever occurred.

dōzoku has been greatly decreased by the economic decline of the main household, and the internal organization has also changed with the economic change of each household. However, the majority of the households have remained in the same community, and some of the functions of local corporate groups are still maintained. Ariga states that at present there is no leader of each *dōzoku*, though some main households hold higher status. As a group they maintain a certain co-operation, and religious activities are centred on each *dōzoku* shrine. The main household takes the initiative in performing the ceremony and the feast is held usually at the main household, but the expense of feasts is met by the *dōzoku* households together, and not by the main household alone.

To sum up from the data on *dōzoku* collected by many scholars over the last fifty years, I draw the following conclusions in terms of their geographical and historical distribution. Geographically *dōzoku* show a fairly wide distribution covering various parts of Japan. However, the villages where the *dōzoku* existed seem to have had certain common economic and historical factors.

The data on effective *dōzoku* mostly come from villages where the major economy was directly dependent upon limited resources, and where the villagers had little opportunity of taking alternative economic action. Further, it was unlikely that *dōzoku* would be found among comparatively new villages developed after the Tokugawa period, or among very old villages already well organized before the Tokugawa period; *dōzoku* were found mostly among those villages where great expansion occurred during the Tokugawa period. Also, the formation of effective *dōzoku* was mostly concentrated in the period from the later Tokugawa to the Meiji. Concerning the function of an individual *dōzoku* itself, the span during which it played its effective role was normally around three generations: it was rare that its effective organization persisted over five or more generations.

These facts lead me to suggest that *dōzoku* must be closely related to a particular local economic situation in both the historical and political setting of the state. I conclude that the following two conditions are the most relevant prerequisites for the formation of *dōzoku*. First, *the community needs to provide substantial resources for the maintenance or the accumulation of wealth by one sector of the community. And it should be difficult for village members to obtain a living other than by dependence upon the limited resources within the community.* This situation in the village community involves differentiation of wealth. Indeed *dōzoku* tend to be found among those villages where considerable economic differentiation exists. Further, the greater the economic differentiation, the more possibility there is of forming an effective *dōzoku*. On the other hand, *dōzoku* are rarely found among poor hill villages or villages with minor fishing and gathering economies which are dependent on very limited communal resources. In such economic settings it is almost impossible for some of the members to accumulate substantial wealth, or at the same time for incomes to fall far below the village standard: there is thus little economic differentiation among the members of the community. Similar situations can also be found among very old villages where available resources had already been exploited before the Tokugawa period, and consequently where all households have fairly equal economies, sufficient to maintain themselves without surplus fields and house-site land. Again the *dōzoku* are not found, or have only a very weak function if they are found, among those villages near a commercial centre, nor in those villages where economic opportunities other than in agriculture have been easily available.

Second, *the existence of effective dōzoku seems to be largely determined by the earlier pattern of settlement of the village, and a high degree of stability in the economic organization of the village.* In order to create a *dōzoku* in the first place, a household must have an economic surplus of fields and of house-site land. The greater the economic reserve and the economic expansion of the household, the greater the possibility of the creation of *dōzoku*. The main household of an effective *dōzoku* is normally found among one of the oldest households in the village, which had already acquired considerable land and a large house-site in the earlier period of the village history (this mostly refers to the earlier Tokugawa period, the economic development of which indeed shaped the organization of the village community in the history of rural Japan). The study of Gorohei-shinden village reveals that households which form a *dōzoku* are the descendants of those who settled in this village at an earlier period of its history, and their predecessors had, or acquired in the course of time, large house-sites as well as fields, so that a set of households of the same *dōzoku* are found clustered around the main household. As this village was dependent mainly upon wet rice cultivation, land ownership and tenancy have been largely determined by the distribution of the earlier settlement. This stability seems to have produced a well-developed *dōzoku* organization among wealthier sectors of the village population.

On the other hand, an effective *dōzoku* has been less easily developed in a fishing or horticultural village, both closely connected with commerce and where the economy might be rather unstable. In such circumstances, the economic standing of an individual household tends to be changeable, so that it is difficult to create, or to maintain, the effective organization of a *dōzoku* over generations. An example of this kind of village is Koshiozu. Here the population and distribution of *dōzoku* are very similar to those of Gorohei-shinden village: in both villages about 50 per cent of the total number of households (150 approximately) form a half-dozen *dōzoku*. But in Koshiozu, *dōzoku* hardly functioned, as an exclusive effective group organizing all branch households under the leadership of the main household; and the economic standing of a branch household often became higher than that of the main household. There the really functional local corporate group has been formed in terms of neighbourhood, locally called *seko* (see pp. 142-43), though the majority of the households of one *dōzoku* belong to the same *seko*. In this village inter-household relationship in terms of *dōzoku* is recognized in practice as a relationship between two households, one of which was formed by fission from the other, rather than as a relationship linking several households together through a genealogy to an original household—although the group is recognized nominally in terms of *ittō* (*dōzoku*). The exclusive *dōzoku* group is far less developed here than in Gorohei-shinden village, where the *dōzoku* itself forms a local corporate group, termed *kuruwa*, and the main household maintains a significant ritual role in various activities, particularly those of funerals and marriages. In Gorohei-shinden the village organization was maintained largely by the balance of power of several competing influential *dōzoku* groups.[1]

---

[1] The local group of Gorohei-shinden village in the Tokugawa period, which was described in Chapter 2, consisted of a set of *kakaebyakushō* under each *honbya-*

These two villages, where I have carried out field work, reveal very interesting contrasts. Gorohei-shinden village, as already described in Chapter 2, is one of those typical wet-rice cultivation villages in Japan in which the basic economic organization has continued over the last three centuries. On the contrary, Koshiozu has undergone great economic change.[1] The fishing economy, which was largely responsible for the shaping of Koshiozu community, was rather unstable in comparison with wet-rice cultivation. Influential wealthy households called *amimoto* (capitalist, and the boss of a fishing team) had to risk their capital, which might be lost in the sea, and also had to feed in bad seasons a dozen smaller households who formed the fishing team. The ups and downs of these *amimoto* households are a well known story. In this kind of economy an effective *dōzoku* could hardly be maintained. Moreover, fishing requires that individuals have certain technical skills and this, I think, also contributed toward inhibiting a rigid hierarchical order among the households of rich and poor, or of main and branch. Indeed the personalities and interpersonal relations in these two villages are also very unlike: status-conscious and formal in Gorohei-shinden, and democratic and gay in Koshiozu.

Most households in rural Japan created a branch household as long as their economy allowed them to do so, though the group was not always effectively organized. Nowadays, a new branch household is rarely established in rural Japan, since most households have reached the stage where no surplus house site or fields

kushō. This group composition does not precisely coincide with a *dōzoku*: the *dōzoku* was gradually developed after the end of the Tokugawa era, in the re-organizing of old groups formed on the basis of rigid status differentiation within the Tokugawa framework.

[1] Koshiozu was originally dependent on potato and rice cultivation (fields there are not so favourable for wet-rice cultivation), and in the later Tokugawa period started *jibikiami* fishing, one of the best-known pre-modern fishing methods in Japan: a large net was spread along the coast by six boats, and the two ends of the net were drawn in by many people towards the beach, once enough fish were inside the net. This brought much greater profit than cultivation, and most of the villagers became fishermen during the following hundred years. However after the war, *jibikiami* fishing declined because it could not compete with modern highly mechanized fishing methods, which in addition exhausted the fishing grounds around the nearby coast. Then the villagers of Koshiozu found their living in a new application of horticulture: production of winter flowers, and of expensive fruits like melons, for which they had the advantage of a warm climate and easy communication with big cities. Now Koshiozu is one of the most promising modern farming villages.

are available; and also the chances of employment in industry draw off the surplus rural population.

However, the fact that no more branch households are created means not only that the economic limit of an individual household has been reached, but also that it is competing with other property-owning groups. The latter is the case with extremely wealthy landlords whose land covers several villages, and with Zaibatsu (a kind of *dōzoku* group which appeared with industrial enterprise in the earlier period of the industrialization of Japan). Among them, the establishment of a branch household used to be very rare, once a stable economic position had been attained.[1] In these households, non-successors become the adopted sons-in-law of other wealthy households; otherwise, they were just given the minimum provision necessary for their livelihood, and finally were dropped from the corporate group into which they were born. In an extreme case, some of these Zaibatsu secondary sons were not even allowed to take the father's surname. For these households, or corporate groups, the creation of a branch household was certainly disadvantageous, since it split the property by which they competed with others who were equally prosperous and powerful. Political allies were found among affinal relations of equally wealthy households, rather than by the creation of a branch household.

B. OYAKO-KANKEI

Another relationship between a set of households, closely related to the *dōzoku* conception, was *oyako-kankei* (patron and client relationship). *Oyako-kankei* is a relationship established in terms of master (*oyabun*) and client (*kobun*) through economic and political relationship between two households, regardless of kinship. However, it is very interesting that this type of association also takes the form of fictive 'father-son relationship': literally, *oya* signifies father (parent) and *ko* means son (child), *bun* signifies status and *kankei* means relation. This custom was widespread throughout Japan, though in differing degrees, and played an important role in village life, especially till the first quarter of the twentieth century.[2]

---

[1] See Oishi, 1956, for landlords; and Fukushima, 1962, for Zaibatsu.

[2] Today the basic concept of this custom is applied to interpersonal superior-subordinate relations in various modern organizations, and though the context

The relationship is normally established between a powerful and wealthy household and a poor one. In this aspect the relation is somewhat analogous to that between servants' and tenants' households which have been included in the master's *dōzoku*. But the *oyako-kankei* is not based on the ideology of fission of a household. Further it is normally expressed in terms of household, but is not necessarily binding upon the next generation. It is primarily established between man and man. However, the household structure being what it is, members of a household are automatically involved in the relationship established by their head. Thus the stability of the relationship often extends itself to the next generation. As T. Fukutake states in his data on Asao *buraku*, once the *oyabun-kobun* relationship was established it lasted a full lifetime, and the house of the *oyabun* is normally found to be the same house as that in which ego's father had been a *kobun* (Fukutake, 1954, p. 150). Further, he states that the relationship established between households normally continues from generation to generation. This is borne out in the following remark of villagers: 'The relationship of *oyabun-kobun* is established by households; thereby *oyabun* can be also a woman' (Fukutake, *ibid.*, pp. 153–4). Villagers often take for granted the stability of the relationship between two households and say, 'The *oyabun* of Household X is the Household A', and 'My father's *oyabun* was of that house, so I will ask that house to become my *oyabun*' (Furushima, 1953, p. 101). But this relationship will never be so strict as in the case of the *dōzoku*. It was considered reprehensible to change one's *oyabun* without good cause, but a change could be made, if really necessary, to a more convenient and influential *oyabun* from one which had declined in status and wealth. At the same time an *oyabun* who lost power could refuse to continue its commitment (Fukutake, *ibid.*, p. 154).

The *oyabun* are found mostly among influential households in the upper sector of the village community, and in general a *kobun* finds an *oyabun* among those households of higher rank than its own. However, as in the case of Ushio *buraku* in Shimane prefecture reported by S. Isoda (1954) those who seek their *oyabun* in the highest-ranked households are those of the middle ranks, who in turn play the role of *oyabun* to households whose

differs from that of the peasantry, the expressions *oyabun* and *kobun* are still used informally.

status and wealth are lower than their own. Normally *oyako-kankei* are so built that a man plays the role of an *oyabun* with one hand and with the other is a *kobun*. The organizing principle reveals a basic similarity to that of the *dōzoku*: the core of the organization is found in the direct linkage between the *two*, and multiplication of such linkages forms a group altogether.

Operationally *oyako-kankei* also bears a very similar function to that of the *dōzoku* in terms of (1) the actual relationship between the households of *oyabun* and *kobun*, and of (2) the formation of a local corporate group (centred on the *oyabun*'s household) within a village community.

An example of the actual operation of the relationship, described by T. Fukutake in his field survey in Yamanashi prefecture, is as follows. A *kobun* (client) used to discuss his affairs with his *oyabun* (patron), and seek intellectual assistance (such as help in reading and writing in the days before the modern educational system came into force) and economic patronage. In an emergency, *kobun* used to borrow from his *oyabun* ceremonial dresses, furniture, rice, etc., and also asked him to act as guarantor when borrowing money. Thus *oyabun* gave varied help and patronage to *kobun*, which was repaid by the latter's service to the former. *Kobun* should follow any order from his *oyabun* without question. On the death of the *oyabun*, the *kobun* took on a role similar to the *oyabun*'s real son (Fukutake, 1953, p. 150).

According to Furushima's report on Ainoshima *buraku* in Nagano prefecture, each *kobun* visits his *oyabun*'s house with an annual present at the end of the year, and in return *oyabun* invites *kobun* for a New Year's dinner and distributes gifts in celebration of the New Year. In the same way, during *Bon* (annual ancestor festival in summer) *kobun* visits *oyabun* with a present after visiting the graves of *oyabun*'s ancestors, and is offered dinner and gifts. It is said that 'the relationship between *oyabun* and *kobun* is closer than that between *shinrui*'. On the occasion of a funeral or wedding in *oyabun*'s house, *kobun* always goes to help in the preparation. On a like occasion in *kobun*'s household, *oyabun* conducts the ceremony. Any trouble in *kobun*'s household is carried to *oyabun* for counsel and solution (Furushima, 1953, pp. 102–3).

The relationship between the households rarely extends beyond the scope of the village community, and tends to be found among neighbours—clients' houses are likely to be found near the patron's house. The relationship was most commonly found between the households of landlord and tenant; and in such cases the landlord's household was always in the same community as that of the tenant. A tenant whose landlord resided in another village sought for his patron someone powerful in his own village, instead of his landlord. Hence the relationship could be established between tenants' households in a village where the population consists mostly of tenants whose landlords live elsewhere. Since the relationship does not originate in the apportionment or lease of land as is the case in the *dōzoku*, opportunities to establish it are more easily found.

Another common relationship is that formed between a newcomer and a powerful old household or *warajioya* in a village. This relationship is called *nurewaraji*, as mentioned elsewhere (p. 116). Such a relationship with one of the households of a village was essential in order for the newcomer to become a member of the village. There were two ways of achieving this relation: a man could establish his own household under the patronage of the *warajioya*, with which he established *oyako-kankei*; or a newcomer could marry a woman of the village, whose father then acted as a patron to him. According to K. Ariga, a newcomer in *nurewaraji* was usually lent a house with house-site land, agricultural tools and other equipment by the household which was his patron. At the village meeting, he was placed in the lowest seat. He had an obligation to help the patron's household in agricultural work and also in domestic tasks, including errands on such occasions as weddings and funerals in his patron's household. The first generation of the *nurewaraji* regarded such duties as especially important, but from the second generation onward concern for these obligations tended to decrease (Ariga, 1943, pp. 139, 396–7). If the patron's household formed part of a *dōzoku*, and leased its land to such a newcomer, the latter would probably be included in the patron's *dōzoku*, and the relationship would become more permanent. In this manner the *oyako-kankei* stands very close to the *dōzoku*, and the two could overlap.

Further, it is customary in a village where an effective *dōzoku* is found for the influential main household to play the role of *oyabun*. The main household may be regarded as *oyabun* of its branch households (which in turn are called *kobun*) and the weakened *dōzoku* organization then would be strengthened, as Furushima states (1952, p. 117; 1953, p. 99). Thus in some cases *dōzoku* and *oyako-kankei* coincide. Such an influential main household often includes *kobun* who do not belong in the *dōzoku*, thereby forming a larger and more powerful corporate group around the *dōzoku*.

There is also *oyako-kankei* which arises from a wedding: here the formal go-between at a wedding ceremony becomes *oyabun* of the newly married couple, as seen in Ainoshima *buraku* surveyed by Furushima (1953, pp. 100–2). In the selection of this *oyabun*, they look always for a household with higher status or more influence than those of the bride and bridegroom. At the wedding the *oyabun* in the role of go-between drinks the cup of *sake* by which the *oyako-kankei* is established ritually between the *oyabun* and the *kobun* (the couple). In Koshiozu *buraku* where I studied, such a go-between used to be the man who was already the *oya* of the young bridegroom, called specifically *yadooya*. It was their custom that young boys studied in the evening at a particular private house, the head of which was a man of high reputation as a learned and considerate person. This teacher was called *yadooya* and normally took reponsibility for his student's marriage, playing the role of go-between at the wedding ceremony.[1] Such an *oya*, normally about the same age as one's father, was considered more understanding than one's father, and boys used to take various personal problems to the *oya* for consultation.

Oyako-kankei is found not only between wealthy and poor or higher and lower status, but also between households of fairly equal economic and social status acting as friendly political allies. Because of its flexible and temporary nature, the *oyako-kankei* could be used in various political and economic relations between households, and was also very useful in meeting the changes in economic and political relations of households within a community. For example, this relationship helped an old established *dōzoku* organization to readjust to a new situation. Nagahama

---

[1] Besides these *oya* mentioned here, there are many other kinds of *oya* (the best collection of such customs is found in Yanagita 1943 and 1948). For example, a person who names a new born baby (god-parent) is called *nazuke-oya*. However, some of these *oyako-kankei* do not necessarily bind the parties by rigorous duty and obligations; they simply maintain a familiar, friendly relationship.

dōzoku of Mie *buraku* in Kyoto prefecture, described by Ariga, provides a good example here. This *dōzoku* once centred upon the main household, but later, following the decline of the main household, was reorganized around one of the branch households which took the role of *oyakata*. This *dōzoku* formerly consisted of six households in all, but when it was reorganized it included four new households other than *dōzoku* as *kobun*. Thus under the new *oyabun*, the former *dōzoku* group reorganized into *oyakata-kokata-kankei*, the status of the former main household declined to that of a *kobun* of its branch household (*oyakata*), and the group composition expanded beyond the scope of *dōzoku* (Ariga, 1943, p. 46). This illustrates another way in which *oyako-kankei* could overlap with *dōzoku*.

Further, it may be found in inter-*dōzoku* relations. For instance, a household which had its branch households as *kobun*, established the relation of *oyakatadori* (to establish a relation to an *oyakata*) with the more influential main household of another *dōzoku* in the village, as demonstrated by S. Kitano (Kitano, 1940, 1941). This case gives another example of how a household can play a dual role—as a dependant of a more powerful household and as a protector of humbler ones. Again a household of very high status, by a decline in its fortunes, might turn into a *kobun* of a wealthy household (whether or not the same *dōzoku*) of much lower status. In these ways the *oyako-kankei* serves a useful purpose in the reorganization and readjustment of household relations in the face of new economic situations. It has no charter such as has the *dōzoku*, and is therefore all the more adaptable to an infinite variety of circumstances.

The situation which makes for the development of the *oyako-kankei* is fundamentally similar to that of the *dōzoku*: i.e. where there is considerable economic differentiation among households in a community, and hence the degree of dependence of poorer households upon a wealthier and more powerful one is greater. The *oyako-kankei* involves the same structural principle as the *dōzoku*, but the degree of institutionalization is different: the latter has a genealogical background, while the *oyako-kankei* is established more freely and without prescribing any permanent relationship between the households. The *oyako-kankei* may or may not involve actual kinship, but kinship plays a far less significant role than in the case of the *dōzoku*. However, both institutions are products of local economic and political situations in which households are involved. Hence when such an institution loses its economic basis—i.e. when there is a change in economic power relations among the households of the group as well as of the community—it loses its function, and these households will be reorganized into another form of local group to suit the new economic and political situation. This explains why *dōzoku* and *oyako-kankei* have both declined owing to economic changes brought about by modernization.

In the course of time, as a local community has undergone various economic changes, household relationships within such a community have tended to adjust themselves to these changes. This has resulted in a multiplicity of terms for local groups in a village community. A new organization does not completely eclipse the former organization, since economic changes can never be wholly independent of the past; the change takes place gradually and not all at once. Some of the functions of the former local group might overlap with the functions of the new organization. The following is a good example of the multiplicity of group terms found in an actual local community, and of how these groups interact with one another, with particular reference to *dōzoku* and *oyako-kankei*. The data are taken from Asao *buraku* in Yamanashi prefecture, surveyed by Fukutake (Fukutake, *ibid.*, pp. 178–84).

Asao *buraku*, consisting of 139 households, presents five terms for household relationships within local groups: *koochi*, *kumi*, *maki*, *aiji* and *oyabun-kobun*. (See Table 12.)

koochi: A unit of the most functional local group (neighbourhood group) in the pre-war period. The Agriculture Association and Revenue Association were formed by this unit. It was also the basic unit for the election of members of the Village Council (formed by several *buraku*).

kumi: A neighbourhood group wider than the *koochi*: this *buraku* is divided into three *kumi*, and five *koochi*.

maki: A kind of *dōzoku* group: a set of households having the same surname.

aiji: A compound group—the term is applied only to the relationship between two households living on the same house-site land: such as a new branch household established within the house-site land of the original one, which forms *aiji* with the original household. Further, when one of the two households of *aiji* moved away, and a stranger occupied the vacant house, in this case also the two neighbouring households, who may or may not have a kinship relation, form *aiji*. Again, although the original household may have two branch households within its house-site land, these three together do not form *aiji*, since the term is only used for the relationship of two households. (The three households A, B and C are found on the same house-site land belonging to A; and B and C had branched off from A. In such a case, A and B, and A and C form the *aiji* respectively, but not any three together, or B and C.)

oyabun-kobun: patron and client relationship.

TABLE 12. Distribution of Households in terms of *Kumi*, *Koochi* and *Maki* in Asao *Buraku*

Kumi		Uenomura	Nakamura		Shimomura		
Koochi		Wade	Nakano-kubo	Nishi-mura	Honmura	Muko-mura	*Total*
Maki	Shinohara	2	15	12	7	1	37
	Irikono	30	1	1	—	1	33
	Shimizu	—	—	—	8	13	21
	Fukasawa	—	—	—	1	14	15
	Gomi	—	—	—	2	6	8
	Yomizu	—	—	—	5	—	5
	Sakurai	—	4	—	—	—	4
	(others)	8	1	2	—	5	16
Total		40	21	15	23	40	139

In this *buraku*, there had been traditionally seven *maki*, each of which largely corresponded to the present households of the same surname, though strictly the households bearing the same surname do not always form the same *maki* or *dōzoku* today. Once there were seven wealthy and powerful households, called 'the seven houses of Asao', each of which was the main household of a *maki* (*dōzoku*). However today, all except two out of the seven have declined or left the community. The function of the *maki* has accordingly weakened considerably since the beginning of the century, though households of the same surname show a fairly concentrated distribution by *kumi* as well as *koochi* even today. In place of *maki*, the most functional units as local corporate groups pre-war were *aiji* and *oyabun-kobun*.[1]

---

[1] The present situation is again different: the *aiji* and the *oyabun-kobun* relations are losing their functions.

I think *aiji* is the most clear-cut form of relationship found in *dōzoku*, the relationship of two households directly related through fission and/or sharing the same house-site land. The essence of the *dōzoku* relation is found between *two* households, the main and the branch households, and not directly between two branch households, or between all the households of a *dōzoku* together (see pp. 89–90). In this respect I see the structural link between the *aiji* and the *dōzoku*.

Further, the *dōzoku* organization was closely linked to *oyabun-kobun* in this *buraku*. The *oyako-kankei* seems to have developed as a substitute for the *dōzoku* organization in the face of the changing economic situations of households in the community. According to Fukutake, the loss of the function of the *maki* in the *buraku* was due to the economic decline of the main household, and to the inclusion of new households which did not belong to the *maki*. These new households, created either by marriage or immigration, always established a *oyabun-kobun* relationship with one of the powerful households in the village.

One of the *oyabun* in the *buraku*, who was the biggest landowner and possessed the largest number of *kobun* in pre-war times, was not one of the 'seven houses of Asao', but one of the branch households of one of the seven *maki*. Thus as the *dōzoku* organization declined, so a new economic power, the *oyabun*, appeared among the branch households, and became the centre of the new organization. Here we see the historic process of change in local corporate grouping from the *dōzoku* to the *oyabun-kobun* relationship, centred on a new rising household in place of the main household.

However, in some sectors of the *buraku*, the *dōzoku* organization could still persist if the main household maintained its wealth and power. But in the face of the new situation, this household also altered its role to become the *oyabun* instead of the main household of the *dōzoku*, and included also other households besides its branch households, in terms of *kobun* only. This main household, as the *oyabun*, had various kinds of *kobun*: there was a new household established by an immigrant, and another by an incoming bridegroom; there was a declined main household, one of the seven, who had once competed for power with this household; there were some of the branch households of such a declined *dōzoku*; there were even the main household's own

RJ K

branch households who wished to strengthen the weakened relationship of households within the *maki*.

Figure 13 shows one of the examples of distribution of the households involved in the *oyako-kankei* in this *buraku*. Eleven households of Nishimura *koochi* are the *kobun* of Shinohara *oyabun* (S) of the neighbouring *koochi*. Shinohara *oyabun* is at the same time the main household of Shinohara *maki*. Hence out of eleven *kobun* households, eight are of branch households of S: only one branch household of the Shinohara is not *kobun* of S. Thus old (*dōzoku*) and new (*oyabun-kobun*) units overlap. This diagram also shows one of the ways in which households are organized under the *oyabun*. Normally the *oyabun* and his *kobun* are found within the same *koochi*. But when there is no powerful household to be the *oyabun* in a *koochi*, the *koochi* boundary may be extended as in this case (but it rarely extends beyond the *buraku* range). In such a case the powerful *oyabun* who has *kobun* in more than two *koochi* appoints a small *oyabun* from among his *kobun* to be in charge of the *kobun* in the *koochi* other than his own, as Y in the diagram.

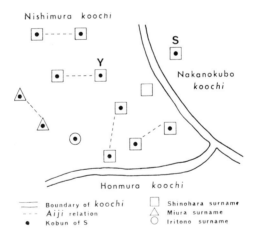

FIGURE 13. Household Relations in Nishimura *koochi* in Asao
(Reproduced from Fukutake, 1954, p. 196)

C. KUMI

Composition of kumi

In any village in Japan there have always been local corporate groups. It is essential for a household to have interaction with other households. The significance of this was greater in the days when the monetary economy had less importance, and the households in a village engaged in homogeneous economic activities. Regardless of the existence of *dōzoku* or *oyako-kankei*, neighbouring households tend to develop close relations which, in the course of time, take on a permanent character, forming a distinct local corporate group and a basic sub-unit of village organization. This kind of local group is generally termed *kumi*, though the name varies according to locality.

An effective *dōzoku* (including *oyako-kankei*) itself may form a *kumi*. However, a unit of *kumi* does not necessarily conform to the composition of a *dōzoku*. The basic necessity for the formation of *kumi* is neighbourhood: since the households of a *dōzoku* tend to be neighbours, the majority of these households are often found in a same *kumi* (as already described for Asao *buraku*, p. 130). Though a *dōzoku* could be effective enough to maintain a corporate function without *kumi*, when the effective power of a *dōzoku* declined, the households of the *dōzoku* normally reorganized into a *kumi*, which might or might not have included households other than those of the *dōzoku*. Hence a *kumi* may consist of one, two, or more *dōzoku*, together with non-*dōzoku* households. Further, there may be a *kumi* with no connection with a *dōzoku* (or *oyako-kankei*). For those households who do not form a *dōzoku* group (or *oyako-kankei*), a *kumi* becomes the most important corporate unit.[1]

Unless a *kumi* consists of households of an effective *dōzoku*, the internal organization of a *kumi* is democratic, contrasting with the hierarchical organization of an effective *dōzoku*. The internal organization of a declined or non-effective *dōzoku* is very similar to that of the *kumi*, even if it is formed exclusively of the *dōzoku*

[1] It was interesting to find during my field work that the members of households forming part of a distinctive *dōzoku* in a village said that the most important unit in this village was the *dōzoku*, not *kumi*, whereas in the same village other households who did not form a *dōzoku* said that it was *kumi*, not *dōzoku*. Thus the degree of importance of a particular local corporate group will vary for different individual households.

members, and it will operate in the same kind of way. Within a *kumi* each household is equal, and duties and obligations are essentially reciprocal. In this system also a household is the basic unit. For example, whether a household consists of two or five persons, each household should provide the same number of persons for the corporate activities of a *kumi*.

The size and function of a *kumi* differ with individual groups, and from village to village; they are closely related to the historical and economic situation of the household and village. The number of *kumi* in a village also differs: in a small village where the total number of the households is less than a dozen, the entire village is likely to form one *kumi*. The size of a *kumi* seems to be determined by its function. One of the most distinctive and commonly found functions of a *kumi* throughout rural Japan is mutual help in the performance of funerals. In fact, *kumi* is often expressed in terms of *soshiki-gumi* or *shini-gumi* (funeral association).

Indeed funerals of villagers especially need the help of neighbours, particularly when a professional undertaker—found only in towns—is not easily obtainable. In most villages in Japan the funeral is performed by the members of the *soshiki-gumi*. From the moment of death, the households of the *kumi* take over the entire responsibility in a corporate form. The major items to be carried out by the members of the *kumi* are as follows: report to the temple; notification to every household in the village and *shinrui* outside the village; the purchase of articles necessary for the funeral; the arrangement of the altar; making the coffin; digging the grave; hair-cutting and shaving of the people who attend the funeral; preparation of funeral meals for the people calling to condole; entertainment and accommodation for the relatives who come from outside the village; keeping an account of the expenditure, mortuary offerings, etc.

This requires the help of at least several households, with possibly two helpers from each. From my own observation, together with data collected by others, a *kumi* is normally formed of any number of households up to twenty-five. When a *kumi* is formed in a larger number of households, this may be divided internally into two or three groups, and at a funeral each has differentiated roles and degrees of help: for example, the group to which the household of the dead belongs takes the heavier responsibility, each providing a man and a woman for arranging the ceremony in the house and cooking the meals; and two other groups provide one person from each household for digging the grave and preparation of equipment for the funeral, etc. In this manner, within the households of a *kumi*, a particular set of households may stand closer to ego's household. A subdivision of *kumi* was also seen in Asao *buraku*, where *koochi*, the sub-unit of a *kumi*, is the most functional unit (pp. 129–30).

Very close households may be grouped as *tonari* (literally meaning direct neighbours) in many villages. These small sets of households may have clearly demarcated boundaries between each other, so as to divide a *kumi* into sub-groups. But there is also a system of forming a *tonari* centring on each household, so that groups overlap and are only recognizable with reference to a single household. Whatever the manner of grouping of *tonari* may be, the relationship of households of *tonari* is considered very close and important, comparable to that of close *shinrui*.[1] For example, it is usual to invite to a wedding feast only members of *shinrui* but the members of *tonari* are also often invited, or if not, are presented with wedding gifts. In a way, the *tonari* are more important functionally than the *shinrui*: first, because they are always available in emergencies, and since they share daily life, they know more about one another's circumstances than do *shinrui* (unless a household of *shinrui* is a member of *tonari*); secondly, the relation of *tonari* is permanent, forming a distinct durable group of households; the households of *shinrui* may change from time to time, but those of *tonari* remain the same in spite of generational changes in each household. There are many expressions which reflect the significance of neighbours as against *shinrui*:

'More important' are the neighbours than the *shinrui*';
'One can escape from the *shinrui* but not from the neighbours';
'One cannot live without a neighbour, but one can do without cousins';
'The neighbour cannot be exchanged for thousands in money';
'One should not forget a present for one's neighbour when one comes back from a trip'; etc.

---

[1] Throughout Japan, including urban areas, the neighbourhood has a significant value in one's local life, as symbolically expressed in terms of *mukō-sangen-ryō-donari* (three households at front and two neighbouring households on both sides).

The permanence of the group composition is indeed important: it not only maintains friendship among the members, but it binds the households closely together through the long term give-and-take relationship. Hence a relationship of *tonari* does not necessarily arise from mere neighbourliness alone. The households of *tonari* must have a common history combined with joint activities. For example, the following distribution of the households of a *tonari* is often seen in a village: of five *tonari* households of X household, four are found in direct neighbouring households, but one household Y, is found three or four households away; on the other hand, household Z, though it is situated next to X, is excluded from the *tonari* of X. In such a case we find that Z is a comparatively new settler, while Y is as old as X, and Y and X have developed a particularly close friendship with each other. Thus the number and distribution of the households of a *tonari* depend upon the location of the household and upon a close relationship cultivated from generation to generation.

Function of kumi

The function and the idea of a *tonari* are extended to that of *kumi* in its larger context. (In some villages, for example in Koh, the *tonari* itself forms a *kumi*.) The *kumi* tends to have more organized group functions than *tonari*, e.g. as a local ceremonial unit, a labour exchange unit and a welfare operating unit. The description given above of the performance of a funeral is one of the best examples of this.

The corporate activities of the *kumi* cover the greater part of the villagers' lives. Building or repairing the houses and thatching roofs are essential duties in which they co-operate. They provide emergency help in cases of serious or sudden illness, and organize fire-fighting. There are cases where a *kumi* possesses communal property, such as communal forests from where the members may collect fertilizer, reeds for thatched roofs, timber for house buildings and wood for fires. The corporate function is shown in the case of a local festivity: every household of a *kumi* offers its house in turn for the festivity, and each household sends a woman and a man to help the household in charge to prepare for the party. The party is enjoyed by all members of households of the *kumi*; its core lies in drinking *sake* and eating the grand meals they have prepared. The expense incurred by the party may be met either by the household in which the party was held, or it may be shared alike by every household according to the number of its members. The manner of carrying out such local festivities varies according to local custom, but their function and basic operation are standard. They afford a great source of recreation for the peasants, and friendships are stimulated through them.

As can be seen from these activities, a *kumi* is not merely a neighbourhood group, but has importance as an exclusive economic body, in which labour, capital and credit circulate. In other words, it forms a common economic pool, upon which the groups' economic life depends closely. This form of economic exchange within a permanent set of households is very useful to the villagers since they themselves consume the greater part of their farm output and are thus left with little cash income. Hence, a *kumi* is most effective as a means of strengthening peasant household economy, and at the same time it helps in the maintenance of stock and capital of the community in the face of any shortage of net resources. In this way the households of a *kumi* are linked together by limitless, long-term obligations and duties which bind its members together, both economically and socially, into an exclusive group, so that it is difficult for a household to leave or a stranger to join.

Process of acquisition of membership in a kumi

As described in Chapter 2, most villages in Japan, on account of their particular economic history, have developed tightly organized, exclusive local corporate groups, and it would be a lengthy and costly matter, though not impossible, for a stranger to become a member of such a group. There are two stages in acquiring membership: the first is to become a *resident* (to be allowed to establish a household), and the second is to become a *full member*. In many villages a clear distinction is made between the two. For example, in Tsushima new settlers are termed *kiryūko*, while full members who have been resident over several generations are *honko*. *Kiryūko* are regarded as residents, but not being recognized as full members, do not enjoy the full membership rights. In Shino mura of Yamanashi prefecture, those who have arrived since the Meiji period are called *kitarimono*, and are completely excluded from the chance of becoming village officials.

A widely prevailing custom is that a newcomer, to become a resident, should offer the members a ceremonial gift. For example, a new settler should greet the members at the *kumi* meeting, presenting *sake* of one or two *shō*. Or he should prepare feasts and invite members of the *kumi* on various occasions, such as assemblies in celebration of the *kumi* shrine, the first gathering of the New Year, and other *kumi* meetings.

It always has been difficult in many villages for a stranger to obtain the rights of a resident. One of the more traditional and usual procedures adopted towards this end is for a stranger to establish a relationship with one of the households of the group —usually a wealthy and powerful one—who stands as his patron or guarantor. Such a household is called *oyabun*, *yoriya*, *wara-jinugi*, or *warajioya*, etc. Or a stranger can become a resident by marrying a woman of the group. In Kokuni district of Yamagata prefecture, it is reported, a newcomer should adopt the surname of his father-in-law with whom he has established a patron/client relationship at his entry (marriage) into the village. As already described, similar instances occurred during the formation of *dōzoku* and *oyako-kankei*. Hence, a *kumi* also may involve similar elements of *dōzoku* and *oyako-kankei*.

A newcomer, whether wealthy or not, would be placed at the bottom of the status ranking of the households of the group, and although he might be given the right of a resident, is not normally given full membership rights, such as using a communal forest, participating in group (or village) festivities, or becoming a village official. It costs a great deal and takes quite a long time to acquire *full membership* with all rights. For example, it might cost *sake* of one *da* (seventy *shō*), whereas it might cost *sake* of only one *shō* to become simply a resident; or it might take two years or even ten to twenty years residence before one gained full membership. The following are examples of extreme difficulty in acquiring full membership.

In Sueyoshi *mura* in Hachijo Islands, where the villagers live by the collection of seaweeds such as *tengusa* (*Gelidium amansii*), and *kobushi* (*Magnolia kobus*), a new settler is not allowed to collect *tengusa* and *kobushi* during the first three years. But if the newcomer married a woman of this village, and owned his own land and house, he obtained full rights in one year. In Shirahama in Shizuoka prefecture, where a share of the sale interests of *tengusa* is valuable, it takes thirty

5. An old-style village in a remote area. Urushi Buraku (Kagoshima Prefecture).

6. A gathering of a *tanokami-kō* at Urushi Buraku (*see* p. 148).

Above: The man second from the right is holding the *tanokami* (a god of the rice field); the next man is holding a bottle of *sake*; at the left a man is holding a *tsuto* (a straw container of rice cakes offered to the god); the seated women in the front are holding musical instruments, a *shamisen* (stringed instrument) and a *taiko* (drum).

Each local group possesses its own stone *tanokami*. The one on the right belongs to another local group of the same village.

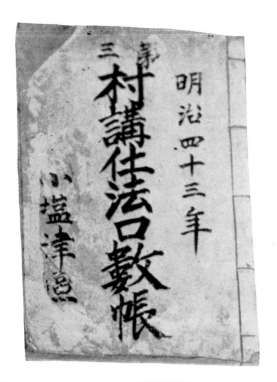

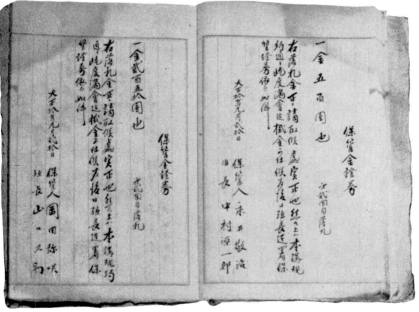

7. The book of rules and membership register of a *kō* association of *Koshiozu* (*see* pp. 146–7). The cover (dated 1910) at the top and typical entries below.

8*a*. *Hiyoshi-Jinja*, the village shrine of Koshiozu.

8*b*. Wedding Ceremony at Hii Buraku (*see* p. 157). The bride is wearing an elaborate headdress; the bridegroom is separated from her by a representative of the bridegroom's relatives. A friend of the bridegroom and one of his relatives are offering *sake* to each of the relatives of the bride in turn. Beside the bride is her elder sister.

years to get a half share of the sale interests of *tengusa*, which are collected by the whole group. It takes fifty years of being a resident to get an equal share as a full member.

Above all, the most difficult right to acquire is that of participation in local festivities. In Nishikatsuragi *mura* in Osaka prefecture, the first generation of new settlers is not allowed to participate in festivals of the *kumi* shrine; the second generation can however join in by paying the participation fee. Further, it is said that in Konugi *mura* in Shiga prefecture it took three generations of residence to obtain the right to participate in local ceremonies. In Mitsuka of Kasuga *mura* in Gifu prefecture, there was no strict rule for obtaining membership, but new settlers were treated as new members for as long as three to five generations.[1]

Such discrimination among village households was applied not only to these new settlers, but also, to some extent and in certain localities, to newly created branch households (even though they were those of sons of 'full members' of the village). For example in Shinokusa *buraku* in Yamanashi prefecture, the members of comparatively new branch households (with only two to three generations having passed since their establishment) were not allowed to become officials of the village. Though less extreme in nature, the normal usage in many villages has been that a new branch household ranks low in the village hierarchy, even though its parental household may have stood very high. Thus in Japanese villages, prestige and various other kinds of social recognition are always vested in the household, rather than the kin group. Here it can be seen again that the function of descent elements is limited.

The following example also reveals this aspect of *kumi* rules. It concerns a man (household head) who had once been a full member, and who had returned to his village after some years' absence. (This example comes from my own field work in Urushi *mura* in Kagoshima prefecture in March 1962.) The rule applied to him was basically the same as that applied to a stranger (resident), even though he knew everybody, had *shinrui* among them and, more important still, had once had full rights as a member of the group. When he left the village he had to cancel

---

[1] These customs are those collected by folklorists before the war. (For the best introduction to these data with bibliography, see Mogami, 1958.) Most such strict customs are now dying away. However, discrimination between older and new settlers is still found in many villages.

all his rights including that to the communal land, and these were not given back to him on his return to the group. The explanation was that he had not contributed his labour during his absence. He had failed in his duty as a member of the group, and was accordingly cut out of the group organization.[1] There were two ways by which he could have continued his membership in spite of his absence: either he could have left behind him a household member to fulfil the duties of his household to the group, or he could have sent money equivalent to his share of the labour in the collective activities of the *kumi* during his absence. Otherwise, even if he has close kin in the group, it is impossible to regain membership once his household has disappeared from the list of members of the *kumi*. He can join the group only by paying the necessary cost of his share of the communal land and an additional amount for entry into the group. Thus he is on the same footing as a stranger who comes to the village for the first time. This rule also applies to a new branch household, whose original household (his father's or elder brother's household) is a full member. In fact, in this village, a branch household has rarely been established.

The above examples of *kumi* rules reveal two important characteristics of the *kumi*. The first is that the *kumi* is a distinct economic unit, the essence of which lies in the actual functioning of its labour pool, rather than in communal rights of ownership to certain capital. The second is that the organization of a *kumi* is founded entirely on a household, not on an individual basis. Rights of access are the important variables in terms of household, and this does not depend upon kinship ties, but upon a long residence, by which labour contributions to the group automatically accrue. Actual residence for a consecutive period is regarded as the essential factor in group formation. The household principle operates to such a marked degree that the establishment of a household of a stranger or of a branch household of existing members is not allowed, unless a vacant house is available (through the death of all the members of a house, or the departure

---

[1] The same action can be applied to a household of a resident who fails to perform his duty in the corporate group, or acts against the group rule. In such a case the members of the group (the village) would cut off all social and economic relations with the household—this action is expressed by a well known term *murahachibu* (outcast from the village)—and the household's life in the village becomes unbearable.

of all the members from a house). In Hisami of Oki Island, and in Tokuyama mura of Gifu prefecture, a newcomer who could obtain such a vacant house must retain the name of the house, by which means he could become a full member of the village. Thus the occupier of an existing household could, whether or not there were kinship ties with the former member of that household, enjoy full rights in place of the former occupier.

Degrees of corporate activity of a kumi

The degree of exclusiveness of the *kumi* (and village) is relative to the amount of economic activity in which the villagers as a group are involved. This varies greatly according to the local situation. The rules are more severe where a *kumi* is heavily involved in economic activity. According to reports of folklorists, most of whom practised more than thirty years ago, some *kumi* possessed not only a communal forest, but also a seed-bed, a paddy store in case of famine, or a communal store where utensils, sitting mattresses and other necessities for use on important occasions (such as funerals, weddings, etc.) were kept. Such exceptional communal activity of a *kumi* would mostly have been found in villages in the interior with a relatively low economic standing, where hardly any economic differentiation among the households existed; which is in direct contrast economically to a village where an effective *dōzoku* existed. Thus a greater degree of solidarity and co-operation is likely to be found in a *kumi* in a village where *dōzoku* hardly exist.

Though the internal economic situation of a village in which a strongly functioning *kumi* is found differs from that of the village where we find *dōzoku*, the functional role and historical development of the *kumi* are very similar to the *dōzoku*. The rigid nature and strong solidarity of the *kumi* seem to have developed mostly from the later period of the Tokugawa to the Meiji period, when the pressure of the population upon the net resources was great, coupled with the relative absence of any alternative economic solution for the peasants. This corresponds with the historic conditions in which *dōzoku* developed. As in the case of the *dōzoku* and *oyako-kankei*, the function of the *kumi* has greatly decreased since the beginning of this century, for the villagers have become less dependent upon their own resources with the advent of industrialization into rural areas, and with better communication between urban and rural districts. These factors have tended to decrease the utility of corporation among households, and have weakened the solidarity of the local group to a greater or lesser degree according to the economic and ecological situations in a given village. Even in my limited observation through my own field work, there were the following contrasting cases: in villages situated in the remote hills in Kumamoto and Kagoshima prefectures, as in the case of Urushi already cited, the function of a *kumi* is strongly maintained. There, the villagers are engaged in subsistence economy without the means of earning sufficient cash income; and neither the economic situation nor the number of households in the village has changed very much over the last fifty years.

On the other hand, in Koshiozu in Aichi prefecture, the economy of which has greatly changed over the last thirty years, particularly since the war (from fishing and the cultivation of rice and sweet potatoes to modern horticulture), the economic function of the *kumi* has much decreased. In this village there are five *kumi*, locally called *seko*, each consisting of about two dozen households, which include major households of one or two *itto* (*dōzoku*). Each *seko* was once a strongly organized corporate group based on fishing activities, but today they have become convenient administrative units of village organization, with such changes in composition as were necessary to accommodate a geographical arrangement of households rather than a functional corporate body. This great change in the function of the *kumi* was largely brought about by the cessation of fishing, and by the receipt of cash incomes derived from horticulture, which resulted in the greater independence of households and more frequent and easier communication with urban centres. Interhousehold corporation today, where necessary, is carried out by only two or three households of *tonari*, or of a close *shinrui* in the same village.

However the villagers of Koshiozu are not entirely free from the traditional cohesion of the *kumi* as a corporate unit. They still feel a moral obligation to help fellow members of the *kumi*, in, say, building or repairing a house, or thatching roofs (though the latter is very rare today, since most roofs are tiled), even though carpenters could now easily be employed and would be cheaper than dependence on fellow helpers, to whom a thanking feast must be given according to traditional usage, and also snacks and meals with *sake* while the work is on. In olden days, meals prepared for the helpers would have been cooked at home out of materials which they had harvested; but now that the standard of living has risen, elaborate meals are ordered from a nearby restaurant, costing more than the carpenter's fee. Yet people would not dare to employ only carpenters, without asking the help of their neighbours. It is said that if they did this, the neighbours would not like it, and would become unfriendly, which would cause them inconvenience in their village life. Thus the moral influence of traditional *kumi* behaviour patterns is still so strong that it can cause unreasonable economic expense. But friendship too still exists among the households of the same *seko*. For instance, it is the *seko* group that plans and makes the recreation trip of a few days which has become fashionable among the rural population of today. Here indeed is the picture of a village in transition.

The case of Koshiozu village is an illustration of the changing aspects of the *kumi* function as a result of internal economic changes in the village. But there are also external factors which have reduced the strength of the *kumi* as a corporate group: i.e. the rapid increase in the number of households of outsiders which is being experienced by many villagers whose economy is directly linked to, or who are situated near, urban centres. For example Haru village in Oyita prefecture, three miles from the developing city of Beppu, has increased from 27 households in 1920 to 120 in 1961. There, naturally, the function of the *kumi* has little importance, and the unit of *kumi* has gone through various stages of reorganization. The present local unit in this village is called *han* (ward), which divides all households of the village into fairly uniform groups according to the location of a household cluster. This unit is formed regardless of the traditional *kumi*, once so important to village life. The traditional *kumi*, however, still quietly continues (as *soshiki-gumi*) among the members of the old households which existed there around 1920, but excludes the new households which have settled in the village during the last forty years.

Even in a village where the traditional *kumi* still maintains a definite function in daily life, there are normally other forms of local groups, which suit the contemporary village composition and include all households, thus achieving an effective village administration. One example of this kind of local grouping is the *tonarigumi* system, established all over Japan during the last war as a local unit connecting every household to the central administrative system. This unit, like a ward, divides the households of a village into fairly equal numbers on a geographical basis, as in the case of *han* in Haru village. The traditional *kumi* may be reorganized into the *tonarigumi* system as in Koshiozu: or the *tonarigumi* system may be formed in a different way, co-existing with the unit of traditional *kumi*, as in Haru. This depends on the local situation of each village, and on the degree of active functioning of the traditional local corporate groups.

Other forms of co-operation

In connection with the discussion on *kumi*, I now mention the forms of credit, reciprocity and mutual aid termed *yui* and *kō*, found widely in rural Japan.

Exchange of labour—yui: Exchange of labour, such as at the time of transplantation in spring, was normally done with the co-operation of two or three households, though in some villages in certain periods it might be done with the entire *kumi*. A household makes an arrangement for an exchange of labour with other household(s)—the latter may or may not be of *tonari*, *kumi* or *shinrui*—in the same village. This form of exchange is known throughout rural areas as *yui*.[1] The term *yui* signifies literally 'co-operate' or 'unite'. Sociologically it indicates the exchange of labour between households. In contrast with exchange of labour in terms of *kumi*, which is a constant long-term unit, exchange of labour in terms of *yui* is done by a clear-cut contract each time, adjusting itself to the convenience of each household engaged in it.

The work team would be formed by more than two households by *yui*, though theoretically the *yui* contract is established on the basis of two households. The labour given to X household by Y household should be similarly reciprocated by X to Y. It is borrowing in the form of labour with the obligation of future repayment. One day of work should be repaid by one day of work, not by money or in kind. The labour itself is called *yui*, and the act of returning the labour is called *yui-modoshi*.

---

[1] According to locality, it is also called *ii, i, ei, yu, yoe, yoikō, yekō, yoeikkō,* etc.

This exchange of labour is always measured according to local values, so that a-man-one-day unit of labour is returned by a-woman-one-and-a-half-days; one-day's labour in the busy spring season should be repaid by two-days' labour in the short winter; one-horse-two-days is repaid by one-man-one-day, etc. (For further information, see *Yui* in Yanagita, 1956, p. 1661.) Further, the detailed form of the *yui* contract involves conforming to local as well as to group customs: for example the contributors take their own meals with them, and the household which receives labour offers them snacks between meals; or the contributor take meals at home, without having any hospitality from the household which receives the labour; or the household which requested the labour offers a meal and *sake* after the work at the house; etc.

Exchange of labour in terms of *yui*, like that of *kumi*, served a useful purpose for peasants with little cash income. Today the form of such an exchange has greatly changed, an example of which can be drawn from Ōyanagi *buraku* in Miyagi prefecture, which I myself studied. There, the unit for the exchange of labour is formed by several households who jointly bought a cultivating machine. This set of households does not correspond to that of *kumi*, *dōzoku* or *shinrui*, since, when purchase of the machine was suggested, the desire to employ it varied with individual households, and it was difficult to come to any agreement to buy it through the traditional local groups. Accordingly the households who wanted the machine voluntarily shared the expense of buying it, and the individual amounts paid were decided according to the area of the arable land of each household. Thus a new group of households has been created. And this same group tends to form the work team for transplantation in spring time, which is carried out after ploughing by the machine. The exchange of labour for this transplantation is also carried out in a new way: all members jointly engage in the transplantation of all fields cultivated by these households; and after the transplantation is finished the balance of the excess of work given by a household possessing a small area of land is paid back in cash by a household possessing a large area of land, according to their agreed calculation. This form of exchange of labour based on a modern financial co-operative unit certainly weakens the traditional unit of *kumi* or *dōzoku*: and the traditional form of exchange of labour in terms of *yui* has therefore greatly declined.

Credit association—kō: *Kō* or *kō-gumi*, as a credit association, had been widely developed in rural areas when banking facilities were not easily available to peasants. The members of a *kō* who form a credit association lend money to one another at low interest from a fund contributed by the members. This mutual financing association functioned differently from *kumi*, since the need and interest varied with each household. A *kō* may be formed by several households (or individuals) who may or may not be members of the same *kumi*; or it may be formed by the majority of the households in a village. However, this kind of association seldom extends beyond the scale of a village. Whatever the composition of the *kō* credit association, the basic scheme is strikingly common all over Japan; it was already well established during the Tokugawa period,[1] and was used right up to pre-war days.

I give here a good example of a *kō* association from the data I collected in Koshiozu. The biggest *kō* consisted of the majority of the households of the village, and covered a twelve-year term: in the thirteenth year it dissolved and was replaced by a new *kō*. Instalments were paid yearly (in August or October), and completed by the thirteenth year. The last instalment was meant for the village funds, or as a donation to the village shrine. Table 13 shows the basic scheme of the *kō* proceedings, stated as a rule at the beginning of the record book.

According to the *Record Book of the Third Village Kō* (Daisan-sonkō-shihō-kōsū-chō) of Koshiozu, 1910,[2] the *kō* consisted of 136 household heads of the village, and of 156 shares (a share for one person ranged between 3 shares to 0·1 share); and its total instalment amounted to 1,300 yen, which made the repayment of the bidder 10 yen for 1 share, and 100 yen could be bid for 1 share. It seems that this type of operation was well suited to the peasant economy: at least once during twelve years, a peasant household had to meet great expenses, such as for repairing or building a house, or for a wedding. The villagers, who well

[1] A detailed description of one *kō* of the Tokugawa period (in 1827), in Yawata village of Nagano prefecture, is given in Sakurai, 1962, pp. 396–402.

[2] For every *kō*, a book was made, in which the basic rules as mentioned above were stated; and it contained a list of the members, and documents of receipt signed by the bidder and the man in charge. (See Plate 7)

TABLE 13. The Basic Scheme of the *Kō* Proceedings in Koshiozu

Suppose there were twelve people taking part with 100 yen contributed in total at each annual gathering and one person receiving the whole of that 100 yen each year. Those who have received their 100 yen must repay 10% of that amount (i.e. 10 yen) in each subsequent year. The rest of the money is collected from the others in equal shares. Thus the longer one waits to receive one's 100 yen the less one has to pay in total.

Year	Total contribution by those who have already received payment (Yen)	Total contribution of the rest (Yen)	Number of persons who have not yet received payment	Contribution of each of these		
				Yen	Sen	Rin
1st	0	100	12	8.	75.	0
2nd	10	90	11	8.	18.	2
3rd	20	80	10	8.	0	0
4th	30	70	9	7.	57.	8
5th	40	60	8	7.	50.	0
6th	50	50	7	7.	14.	3
7th	60	40	6	6.	66.	7
8th	70	30	5	6.	0	0
9th	80	20	4	5.	0	0
10th	90	10	3	3.	33.	3
11th	100	0	2	0	0	0
12th	110	0	1	0	0	0
13th	120	0	0	0	0	0

The penultimate beneficiary pays nothing in the 11th year and gets 100 yen, the last beneficiary pays nothing in the 11th or 12th years and gets 110 yen in the 12th year. The total 120 yen collected in the 13th year is contributed to the public fund mentioned above.

remember those days when they depended heavily on the *kō*, say that the demand to receive the initial payment used to be keen, and normally they competed for the bid: of course only one could be the successful bidder, all the other members benefiting by the discount he had bid.

Originally *kō* was a religious association, derived from Buddhistic activities, and only later developed into a credit association within a village community. However, along with it, there was also a religious association under the same name, *kō*. Again the former function has been lost through the development of banking facilities and local professional money-lenders, and it now functions as a social and ceremonial group. Today this function of *kō* is predominantly found in social gatherings with religious implications: each member (or household) of the group contri-

RJ L

butes a small amount of money to meet the expense of the gathering (many are held monthly) and enjoys chatting, drinking and eating, which greatly contributes to relaxation and the promotion of friendship among the villagers. This kind of *kō* is practised under various names, with differing religious implications and meeting dates.

Kō or *kō-gumi*, whether it may be a credit or a social-ceremonial association, is formed by common interest in a particular purpose, and it is therefore of a voluntary nature. It may be also formed by individuals and not necessarily by households: by sex or age group, such as a *kō* formed by women, known widely as *koyasu-kō*; *kō* formed by young men; by young women; by married women; by old people; and there are also occupational *kō*, such as of carpenters, blacksmiths, plasterers, wood-cutters, etc.

On the other hand, *kō-gumi* may be formed by the same households as form a *kumi* or *dōzoku*. It seems that in a village where *kumi* (or *dōzoku*) maintain, or once had, strong function and cohesion, a *kō-gumi* is likely to be formed of the identical households as those of the *kumi* (or *dōzoku*). For instance, the socio-religious function described as one of the functions of *kumi* on pp. 136–37 may be practised under the name of *kō*, the members of which consist of households of a *kumi*. *Tanokami-kō* (*kō* of rice field god) in Urushi village, which I observed, is practised by the households of an entire *kumi*; another religious gathering, *kōshin-kō*, is held by the households of a *dōzoku* in Koshiozu village.

In other villages various kinds of local groups may overlap with one another, and the composition and function of each will differ: a single household may belong to several corporate groups—*dōzoku, sōshiki-gumi, kō-gumi, tonari, tonari-gumi*, and other various kinds of local associations.

The picture of the actual corporate groups existing in a village is very complicated, and varies from village to village according to the particular history of each. Normally many kinds of household groups co-exist, each having definite functions which will modify and change as the years go by. Changes in the function and composition of each corporate group reflect changes in the economic situation of the village community. Analysis of these reveals the perceived possibilities of alternative action within the existing institutional framework, the village community.

Local household relations are further complicated by inter-household relations in terms of *shinrui*. I would like to conclude the discussion with the next chapter, which throws light on the function of *shinrui* in terms of the relations between households linked by marriage, contrasted with that of local corporate groups.

4

The Function of Marriage Relations

Theoretically a household has two kinds of relationship with other households: an economic and residential relationship by which the local corporate group is formed, as has been fully discussed in the previous chapter; and a kin relationship, which was dealt with in terms of the *shinrui* in Chapter 1. Empirically these two kinds of relation frequently cut across each other. However, the function of *shinrui* clearly differs from that of the local corporate groups. If household X and its *shinrui* household Y are in the same local corporate group they play dual roles on certain occasions.

Such a dual role is particularly common in the case of *dōzoku*, since its households are normally linked by *shinrui*, except for those branch households of servants or tenants. For example, the range of *shinrui* of household X would include most of the *dōzoku* households[1] and a set of households which do not form *dōzoku*. Thus the *dōzoku* and *shinrui* centred on household X overlap and do not coincide. This does not imply that a household of the *dōzoku* would be considered more important or closer than other non-*dōzoku* households at the same kinship distance. For instance, the value of mortuary offerings from households of the same kinship distance is surprisingly uniform, whether or not the house is a member of the *dōzoku*, and value decreases according to the distance of kinship from the dead person (see pp. 32–3). This shows that in such a case the households of the *dōzoku* are perceived with reference to the category of *shinrui*. However, the households of *dōzoku* or *kumi* help in the funeral preparations, which is an important function of the local corporate group,

---

[1] If household X belongs to an effective *dōzoku*, it would include some of the *dōzoku* households of distant kin, which might be excluded from the *shinrui* if they did not form an effective *dōzoku*.

while *shinrui* other than members of the local corporate group remain as guests to offer condolences. Those households which are involved in two categories at the same time, act as *shinrui* on one hand and on the other as members of the local corporate group.

Such a differentiation of the roles of *shinrui* and *dōzoku* can also be seen at weddings. For instance, in the case of Saito *dōzoku* previously mentioned, which included many households of non-kin, the preparation for the wedding ceremony of a member of the main household is shared by all households of the *dōzoku*, each taking some specific role. But the main gathering at the wedding consists of its *shinrui* members alone (i.e. excluding some households of *dōzoku*, and including *shinrui* households of non-*dōzoku*). In the case of a wedding of a member of its *bekke*, this is held exclusively by its *shinrui* members alone, without the participation of non-kin households of the *dōzoku*. Thus the two kinds of relationship—of the local corporate group and the *shinrui*—function according to a defined role without ambiguity or clash, and form an indispensable network centred on each household.

These two kinds of relationship represent two distinct ideological principles: the local corporate group is seen as a relationship of incorporation (constant), and the *shinrui* as a relationship of alliance (changeable). Both relationships are essential for each household, for they determine and define its social and political position within the community. This chapter is concerned particularly with relations of alliance: the functional meaning of the household affiliations occasioned by marriage, including the specific aspects of marriage contracts in rural Japan which have a direct bearing on the actual social and political organization.

THE IMPLICATIONS OF MARRIAGE

Marriage affiliations between households may or may not overlap with the relationships of a local corporate group: a marriage may occur between households of the same corporate group, or with a household from outside the group. A local corporate group is always formed within the boundary of a village, but relationships through marriage may extend beyond the village. However, the marriage affiliation derives from the social, economic and political position of a household within a village structure that includes the local corporate groups. Whom one marries is largely determined by the position of one's household within the network of household relationships in a village community. At the same time the relations of alliance through marriage cement a household's social position, and contribute to its political power within the village.

The network of relations of alliance is expressed by the term *engumi*. *Engumi* signifies a marriage itself, and an affinal relationship between two households; it also applies to the network structured by various affinal relations among a set of households centred on each household. The term *shinrui* signifies a category or aggregate of kin, but *engumi* is a term implying a more structural binding of households to each other by the exchange of an individual, as on marriage.

The term *engumi* is also used in adoption, as *yōshi-engumi*, which signifies either to adopt a son (or daughter), or to adopt a son-in-law (uxorilocal marriage: a man by his marriage becomes an adopted son-in-law of his wife's father. See pp. 4–5.) In both cases a man shifts his residence and changes his membership from his natal household (X) to another (Y). By this act, the two households X and Y establish *shinrui* relationship. The adoption of a son (or daughter) sets up a relationship analogous to marriage; it establishes *shinrui* between two households, and falls into the same category of *engumi*.

The changes in which an individual is involved by marriage (and adoption) are of both *economic* and *social* significance. The discussion first deals with the economic implications which are specific to Japanese peasants. Among Japanese peasants it is the custom for a wife to work in the fields as does her husband. A woman forms part of an important labour force on the farm. Hence residential movement of an individual (whether man or woman) from one household to another by marriage entails gain in the labour force for the household receiving the spouse, and a loss by the other. Whether a marriage is virilocal or uxorilocal, the household receiving the spouse is more eager for the marriage arrangement. There seems to be an unconscious feeling of reluctance on the part of the household which is giving away a bride (or bridegroom) since it is losing labour.[1] Perhaps because of this, the proposal always comes from the party which is to

[1] However this feeling is relative, since parents are eager to let their nubile daughters marry.

take a spouse. The major wedding ceremony and dinner are held at the household where the couple are to live, and the expense of the party is met by this household. In virilocal marriage the expense of the clothes and furniture brought by the bride is met in various ways according to local custom: it may be shared by both families or met by either the bride's or bridegroom's family. In this connection, there is a widespread custom called *yuinōkin*, in which the bridegroom's family presents a ceremonial gift in cash to the bride's family before the wedding takes place. This is meant to meet partly or fully the preparation expenses of the bride, depending upon the individual case. This presentation of the *yuinōkin* signifies the establishment of the final contract of marriage, similar to an announcement of engagement in Western society. In general among the peasants it is rare for the expenditure of the bride's family to exceed that of the bridegroom's.[1] Villagers say that the expense should be heavier for the household which is to receive the spouse, which seems quite reasonable since to take a bride (or bridegroom) is considered, and in fact is, an important gain in labour strength. This is demonstrated in such a widespread expression as 'to get *tema* (labour)' instead of saying 'to get a bride'.

The economic implications of marriage are not confined to the shift of labour force, but extend to the inter-household relationships that are created by the marriage. A household linked by marriage to a member of one's own household is considered a very important and most reliable household, and this affinal relationship has a significant function. It is the most appropriate household to ask for labour (and even financial help): in fact in some areas, marriage is interpreted as a contract of exchange of labour. Therefore the ideal household with which to have a marriage relationship is the household with a balanced labour force and an economic standard equivalent to one's own. These factors are considered more important than the personality and capability of the prospective spouse (Yanagita, 1948, p. 138). This feeling links up with the social implications of marriage which are to be discussed later.

---

[1] In contrast to this rural custom, among the urban population the expense of the bride's family tends to be heavier than that of the bridegroom's. The dowry system, developed among the urban population, has been gradually penetrating to rural areas, particularly since the war.

The important *social* consequence of marriage is the creation (or reinforcement—in cases of a marriage between *shinrui* members) of personal ties between the members of the two households. One of the native terms for marriage which is used most commonly in rural Japan is *oyakonori*, which means 'an establishment of father-son relationship', as already mentioned.[1] This shows the significance attached to the establishment of kinship between the future father-in-law and son-in-law. The symbolic ceremony expressing the establishment of such kinship culminates in these two men drinking the same *sake* at the house of the future father-in-law. Their relatives also participate. This act normally precedes, and is considered more significant than, the ceremony of matrimonial union between the young man and woman, which is also symbolically established by drinking *sake* from the same cup.

The strong tie established by a marriage between two households extends further to *shinrui* alliances of each household. Thus a marriage is a contract which initiates two kinds of household alliances. The social significance of marriage is often more emphasized than the physical creation of a new family, or the spiritual union of a man and woman. This is reflected in the native form of the wedding ceremony which does not require the presence of a religious man or priest. There is no religious implication in Japanese marriage as there is with Christians and Hindus, though it may now include a religious ceremony to celebrate the union of the couple.[2]

[1] Another common term for marriage is *yomeiri*, which means 'a daughter-in-law to enter (her husband's house)'. This reflects the dominant pattern of virilocal marriage as compared with uxorilocal marriage, *mukoiri* (a son-in-law to enter). Among the urban population, particularly after the war, the term *kekkon* (marriage) has come into common use. This term implies a greater independence of the couple. The implications of marriage are growing closer to those of the West. However, it is still common practice for a wedding to be announced as 'Wedding ceremony of House X and House Y', which indicates a strong legacy of the traditional *ie* institution.

[2] *Shinzen-kekkon*, a wedding ceremony at which a *Shintō* priest officiates before the altar of the shrine (and the ceremonial dinner which is held in a public hall), is a relatively new form of wedding introduced in the last fifty years. It has become the prevailing pattern among the urban population and has begun to be introduced to the rural population since the war. Again in urban areas after the war, a wedding ceremony may be performed by a pastor at a church in Western style, regardless of whether the couple and those connected with them are Christians or not. However, this is not yet so common as *shinzen-kekkon*.

The most important part of the native wedding ceremony is the introduction of the *shinrui* of both bride and bridegroom, so that additional *shinrui* relationships are then formed. This act of introduction, which occupies the major part of the ceremony, is followed by the ceremonial drinking of *sake* and the grand dinner party which continues all night (and perhaps for two or three days). Traditionally it is considered important that a set of people should drink and eat together: it is believed that invisible links are created among the participants by such an act (Yanagita, 1948, p. 195). In fact, through this long enjoyable drinking party, both groups of *shinrui* get to know one another and establish friendly relationships as *shinrui*. It is interesting to observe that during this ceremony and the succeeding dinner party, the bride and bridegroom play a surprisingly small role. In some localities the bride and bridegroom are even placed at the lowest seats in the room. The bridegroom in particular, after the ceremonial introduction of both parties, retires from his seat and entertains the party by pouring the *sake* into the guests' cups. According to Yanagita, the wedding ceremony was meant to be above everything the entrance ceremony of the mistress (or the successor of the mistress) into a new household. The main purpose was to make the set of people centred upon her one social group. It served also for social (public) recognition of the union of the couple, which had to be previously established (Yanagita, 1948, p. 230).[1]

The full details of a wedding ceremony and party, which vary according to local custom, would be irrelevant to the present discussion. However, I do describe briefly their major aspects since some knowledge of a native Japanese wedding is useful in connection with the present issue. Throughout Japan the basic arrangements and procedure for weddings are similar, though there are variations in detail according to locality and status of the household. The major part of the ceremony is held in the

---

[1] Yanagita held the view that the traditional form of Japanese marriage consisted of two steps: first, the celebration of the union of the couple, and secondly, the entrance of the wife to her husband's house. Between the two there was a considerable lapse of time when the husband used to visit his wife (see p. 13, note 1). In the course of time, as the custom of the visiting marriage has declined, the second ceremony has been gradually elaborated as the major wedding ceremony. This pattern also used to be practised by the upper strata of Japanese society among whom a marriage often takes place between households situated far away from each other.

household where the couple are going to live. The ceremony and the dinner party that follows are presided over by a representative of *shinrui*, or by one of the most influential people among the acquaintances either of the bride or bridegroom's family. The go-between, who sits at a higher seat during the ceremony, is also found from among such persons. The following example is taken from the wedding performed at Hii village in Aichi prefecture which I observed in February 1962. The households of the bride and bridegroom both belong to the upper sector of the community in neighbouring villages. The bridegroom, being the eldest son, is the successor in the household.[1] A wedding of this type is certainly ideal from the villagers' point of view.[2]

It started about three o'clock in the afternoon at the bride's house in Koshiozu village, a neighbouring village of Hii, with the arrival of several members of the *shinrui* of the bridegroom, accompanied by the bridegroom himself. There *shinrui* members of both the bride and bridegroom met and celebrated the wedding by *sake* and ceremonial snacks offered by the bride's parents. The congratulations continued till dark. At about eight o'clock the bride left her house accompanied by her *shinrui* and the bridegroom's *shinrui* who had come to receive her. (The bridegroom had gone back earlier.)

Her parents and distant *shinrui* members did not accompany the bride, but continued the drinking party after her departure for the bridegroom's house. In other localities the parents or the father may accompany the bride to the ceremonial party held at the bridegroom's: it is said that some of the bride's family must remain at the house, because they have to entertain those *shinrui* who are not invited to the party at the bridegroom's house. How many *shinrui* from both parties should be invited to the main party held at the bridegroom's house has been mutually decided previously, according to the social and economic standing of both households, particularly of the bridegroom's. Normally, distant *shinrui* of the bride are excluded from it. The distant *shinrui* of the bridegroom, though they are invited, do not attend the main party, but help in its preparation and serve the more important

[1] A grand formal wedding is held in this case; the wedding of a non-successor is normally held in a more simplified form.

[2] In Hii village a modern form of wedding ceremony, held in a public hall with or without a *Shintō* priest, has been gradually introduced since the war, but this particular wedding was performed according to the traditional way which most villagers still appreciate. The main reason for the change to the modern form is that the traditional way is far more costly; but simplification of the wedding ceremony is in line with the general trend towards modernization in village life.

guests who sit in the main room; and during or after this party they are entertained in a less formal way.

At the arrival of the bride, the villagers crowded from around the gate to the inner compound of the bridegroom's house to see the bride and to watch the ceremony. It is a sort of display of household status: from where has the bride come, what kind of bride is she, who are invited, what sort of people are the *shinrui* of the household? After this the bride changed from the white dress worn at her departure from her house into a colourful ceremonial dress (see p. 29), and in the main room about two dozen people—the most important *shinrui* from each party—lined up facing each other as representatives, and everybody was introduced. This time the bride and bridegroom were placed at the bottom of the two lines—the lowest seats. Then the couple changed their seats to the highest, separated by the man who is the most respected *shinrui* of the bridegroom. Facing them at the bottom of the room near the entrance was seated the man who officiated at the ceremony (he was an influential man from bride's *shinrui*). The guests from both parties lined up on both sides in the order of closeness of kinship to the couple. The parents of the bridegroom retired. When everybody was seated, the first cup of *sake* was distributed to all. While this was going on, the relatively distant *shinrui* of the bridegroom and parents were busy with the preparation of *sake* (which should be warmed up) and meals in the kitchen and adjoining room.

After this ceremony, snacks and *sake* were continually served to the guests. Meanwhile the bridegroom left his seat and joined in the preparations in the kitchen, bringing warmed *sake* to the guests, and helped by his young friends who are his neighbours. Soon after the bride also left her seat to visit each household in the village, accompanied by her elder sister and a female relative of the bridegroom. Traditionally the bride should be introduced to them saying 'we have got a *tema*', as mentioned already. This time she was introduced as a newly arrived daughter-in-law of so-and-so house, since nowadays it is considered that '*tema*' (labour) is an insulting word for a bride. The bride took about two hours to go round all the households, starting at about ten o'clock. During her absence from the party everybody enjoyed themselves, eating and drinking, with pleasant conversation, singing and even improvised dances. When the bride came back the grand formal wedding meal started. About two o'clock in the morning the party ended with the last drinking of *sake* (cold) offered in a big bowl to each guest in turn. After this most of them were finished, heavy and happy with drink. Some went to sleep then and there; others retired to their homes with many presents in their hands.

The ceremony of taking the nuptial cups (*sansankudo-no-sakazuki*), which I missed, was performed just before the bride set off to greet the villagers in the newly prepared room where the couple were to stay, with only the go-between present.

Obviously the whole wedding ceremony and party is a happy occasion for the *shinrui* people. With weddings it is very desirable that both parties should come from households of similar standing: internally it makes for a more satisfactory union of both parties, and externally justifies and demonstrates the status of both households and the *shinrui* concerned. It is of great satisfaction to villagers if all the *shinrui* members who should be invited to wedding or funeral ceremonies are from equally prosperous and respectable households. The status of a household in the village community is measured by the relative quality of the *engumi* in which the household is involved. The network of household alliances is of great importance to household status, which in turn is closely linked to actual interests and power relations within the village structure. Hence every household endeavours to avoid having a *shinrui* of lower status than its own. *Marriage should take place between households of equal status* is the golden rule.

In order to raise the status of a household, outstanding economic achievement is not sufficient; increased status can only be recognized socially through *engumi*. For a rising household with great economic success to enter into marriage with a household of higher status signifies social recognition, and so confers the deserved increased status. On the other hand, to marry into a household of considerably lower status implies a lowering of one's own status, and this lowering embraces the other households of one's network. Hence one's *shinrui* has a considerable say in the marriage contracts of members of one's household. In the case of a household which has greatly declined in status, it is difficult to arrange a marriage with a household of erstwhile equal status: no household included in a *shinrui* is willing to give a spouse to a household which has declined, so that it finally drops out of the network of *engumi*. The following is said of it: 'Household X has greatly declined, and you know, it has also broken the *engumi*.' The fact that a household has been unable to maintain relations of alliance (to have marriage relationships) with a set of households with which it once used to have, or might have had, such relations, is a clear recognition of its social and economic decline. Thus marriage has an important bearing on the social, economic and political position of a household in the village community. Marriage relationships are the clearest guide to the actual status of a household within a community. The rise or fall in the relative status of a household in the community is clearly reflected in the network of marriage relations of that household.

The limited duration of, and the possibility for the creation of, *shinrui* relations clearly demonstrate the flexibility of the relative status of a household within the village community. This is in contrast with the structure of Hindu society, in which unchanging descent and affinal groups exist, forming a kind of closed kin universe, which allows structurally for status groups such as caste. In the traditional structure of the village community in Japan, all households stand basically equal: there are no permanent status differentiations. This structure theoretically does not entail the development of constant status groups within a village community, such as a closed kin group, or constant status groups of gentry and of peasants. In rural Japan there have theoretically been no status *groups*, but only status *rankings*, which are of a relative nature, changing to suit a given situation. Because of this absence of clear-cut status groups, I think the Japanese are very conscious of relative higher and lower status in every aspect of village life.

This picture of a Japanese rural community accords with the kinship structure as shown in the concept of *shinrui* in Chapter 1. Japanese kinship structure, characterized by the equation of cognates and affines, results in a comparatively shallow and narrow range of recognized cognatic kin, and in the absence of a defined kin group of cognates and affines. This structure naturally allows unrestricted marriage contracts in terms of descent. There are no prescribed or preferred marriage rules in terms of descent; the degree of prohibition of marriage within the recognized kin is minimal, such as avoidance of immediate family members of the household. Marriages between cousins (cross as well as parallel), and between uncle and niece are permissible—sometimes preferred—on account of the economic and status benefits accruing. There is a high frequency of marriage between near kin. This is not because they prefer to marry near kin, but is a result of the great influence of local and economic factors upon marriage arrangements, as I describe presently.

SCOPE OF THE MARRIAGEABLE FIELD

The scope of the marriageable field is determined largely by the economic and social status of a household within a village community, and the local economic situation in which a village is involved.

Marriage between households of similar standing is the widely prevailing ideal in almost every locality in Japan. Whether one household marries into another household inside or outside its own village largely depends on the economic and political situation of the other households in the village, rather than on the actual availability of girls and boys of marriageable age, or on any consideration of descent. For example, in a village where considerable economic differentiation exists, a household of very high status often has difficulty in finding a suitable spouse of equal status within the village, so that such a household tends to marry into a household of high status in another village. It should be noted that such a marriage also has the effect of stressing the recognition of the high status of the household in its own village community. Thus exogamous marriage at the village level tends to appear among households of higher status.

On the other hand, as the status of a household decreases, so the range of choice within as well as outside the village increases. Among households of this type it is rather difficult to understand why a marriage should have taken place with a household outside the village, when it could apparently have taken place within the village. If one asks for reasons, one may be told that they preferred to have marriage relationships with a household about which they do not know too much. Others may say it was because someone (either a relative or an intermediary) suggested that this particular household would suit them. Thus casual information given about strangers with whom one is not too familiar may result in marriage. In this connection, my field work reveals that exogamous marriages between prosperous households of two villages seem to result in the creation of an avenue of inter-village marriage relationships, thus extending the area of marriage for the villagers as a whole. Several equally prosperous villages in the same economic area often form a local network of marriage alliances, in which each individual household is carefully graded according to status. This network certainly appears more clearly demarcated among households of the upper strata of society.

Such a marriage circle will not normally extend beyond the range of people with a common way of life and a similar type of economy, and where the villages already have some kind of economic and social relations with each other. This is because households of 'a similar standing' not only implies similar social and economic backgrounds upon which the activities of the households are centred, but also the sharing of familiar knowledge. Hence the marriageable range is largely determined by economic and sociological familiarity within easy distance, such as between neighbouring villages situated along the bank of the same river, where the cultivated lands of each village meet. This range is normally restricted to a distance of one day's journey on foot. As previously described, at the wedding the bridegroom's people are sent to bring the bride to the bridegroom's house where the ceremony is to take place on the same day (it is only very recently that a car has been used on such an occasion). It is rare for the bride's journey to take more than one day, except in the case of an extremely wealthy household which cannot find spouses within the area. It is most unusual, therefore, for marriages to be arranged between neighbouring villages divided by hilly uncultivated areas or by a high mountain, regardless of the actual distance.

The economic standing of the village itself also has a bearing on individual marriage arrangements. Take for example Hashikura village in Nagano prefecture, situated on the bank of a river where fertile wet rice fields spread downstream towards the west, and there are hilly fields in the eastward upper reaches of the river. The villagers of Hashikura have hardly ever arranged a marriage with the people of the villages to the east, but always with the villages to the west. They regard the former as of poorer and lower status (and economic standing) than themselves. These hill villages in the east form a local endogamous area among themselves; and the villages situated further inland tend to have village endogamy. In general, the tendency for village endogamy seems more pronounced among isolated villages of the interior that lack easy communication with other villages, and where the economic standing of each household of the village is more or less similar.

According to Yanagita the traditional rule for selecting a spouse in Japan confined the search to members of the same village (Yanagita, 1948). This seems a plausible assumption. A marriage cannot be arranged between complete strangers. It must also (in general) take place between those who fall into the same social category, for otherwise there is little possibility of mutual communication. In the absence of a kinship framework, the locality, i.e. the village, can provide the sociological entity. As contacts between villages increase, or the range of economic activity of an individual household widens, the marriage circle grows. The distribution of the marriage circle of a village reflects the ecological setting of the area, which more or less determines the type of agriculture and the degree of production. I found through my field work in various villages that a map showing the distribution and frequency of marriages between villages gives a remarkably true picture of the economic characteristics of those villages.

Here is an example of local marriage alliances in a single village, Gorohei-shinden, showing geographical range with relevant economic and social factors. The distribution of villages from which spouses of Gorohei members came during the past fifty years reveals the following facts[1]:

The total number of spouses is 294; out of this, 252 came from 55 villages situated in the valley plain along the river Chikuma (where Gorohei is situated) and its branch streams, within a distance of 12 km. from Gorohei; 15 came from other villages in the same prefecture (Nagano); 22 from outside the prefecture; and 5 are from unknown places.

The distribution of the 252 spouses that belonged to 55 villages is as follows:

23 from the village itself (Gorohei);
153 from 15 neighbouring villages within a distance of 5 km. from Gorohei, the details of which are as follows:

Number of spouses from one village	Number of villages
29	1
15	2
13	1
10	2
9	1
8	3
6	3
5	2
Total 153	15

[1] According to the data collected by me in September 1961.

76 from 40 villages situated outside the 5 km. radius of the above 15 villages, but within a distance of 12 km. from Gorohei, as follows.

Number of spouses from one village	Number of villages
4	5
3	4
2	13
1	18
Total 76	40

The number of spouses per village practically corresponds to the relative distance of a village from Gorohei, but the economic and social relations between a village and Gorohei are also involved. For example, more spouses came from the village (Kasuga) situated at the pivotal point of the irrigation canal to Gorohei (see p. 74), than from a village situated nearer than this. This is because the Gorohei people have frequent social intercourse with Kasuga villagers on account of contact through the work on irrigation. On the other hand, marriage alliances are seldom found between Gorohei and a village (Yawata), situated on an old main highway which links Tokyo and Kyoto, though the village is only 2 km. from Gorohei. This is because the economic activities of the two villages are quite different: the households of Yawata village have traditionally been engaged in commerce and the inn and restaurant business, with a small amount of agriculture. The villages from which the largest number of spouses came are those situated nearby (within about 5 km.), with similar ecological and economic backgrounds (at an altitude of about 500 m. and engaged mostly in wet-rice cultivation with similar standards of yield and a comparable economic history) to those of Gorohei.

The orientation of marriage arrangements of a village can change through temporary economic decline. At a time when Koshiozu village became very poor and very short of village property by comparison with neighbouring villages, the villagers tended to take spouses from within the village. Neighbouring villages were reluctant to give their daughters to Koshiozu, because of its poverty. Now, however, the village has completely overcome this difficult situation, and the marriage circle again extends through the neighbourhood.

Whatever the conditions may be, it can be concluded that selection of spouses in rural Japan, where the majority of the people are engaged in agriculture, is confined to a specific locality, within the range of economic activities of a household as well as of a village.

MARRIAGE AMONG NEAR RELATIVES

It is interesting to note that throughout the tendencies described above for marriage contracts to follow social and economic strata in the differing local situations, one common feature stands out in the network of marriage relations: it is the high frequency of marriage with near relatives. Whether marriage is exogamous or endogamous to a village, the social and local situation tends to limit the number of marriageable households for each household: a kind of endogamous field of a set of households of equal standing is formed, though its demarcation is not always clear. With the comparatively small degree of social, economic and geographical mobility among the population of a rural area, marriage alliances have spread among local households in the course of time, so that marriageable households would be linked by kinship or affinal relations in one way or another, though they may not always be *shinrui* to each other.

This tendency is naturally more pronounced among the upper sector of a community where the number of marriageable households is more limited, and political power relations are more involved. It is common for such a household to have three or four particular households which stand as important affines, with each of which the household has had more than two marriage alliances within three or four generations, as shown in Figure 14.

The analysis of such genealogical relations among a set of households and centred on a particular household, usually accords very well with the political power relations of the local community at a given period of the village history within a wider local setting. The political power relations and the ranking statuses among the households of a local community, though capable of change, seem to be fairly stable for periods of at least three generations. So if we take a period of three generations in any actual community, we would normally find fairly stable alliances among a particular set of households. The stability of the alliance tends to enhance the affinal relations, thus resulting in more marriages with near kin.

Apart from such political involvement in the upper sector of the community, the general tendency for marriage with near kin can also be explained as follows. First, as households linked through *shinrui* relations are of similar standing, marriage within this existing network is felt to be safer. Secondly, such a marriage contributes to the reinforcement of the *shinrui* relationship. Thirdly, it is easier to choose a spouse from among those with whom one is already familiar. Fourthly, if a marriage should take

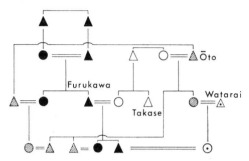

FIGURE 14. Marriage Relations among Four Households Centred
on Furukawa Household
(From the data collected by me in Koshiozu village in January 1962)

The four households, Furukawa (Koshiozu), Takase (Horikiri), Watarai (Horikiri) and Ōto (Kameyama), belong to the upper sector of their villages, which are situated within 3 km. of one another.

In the diagram, the present heads of the four households are indicated by the names of their households; and individual members are classified by the four household groups of which they are or were members.

place among members of a *shinrui*, the expense which would be incurred by the establishment of an additional *shinrui* relation is avoided.

A similar situation can be created by marriage among the members of any corporate group formed by households of relatively equal status. Such marriages also serve to strengthen the cohesion and solidarity of the group. Where a local group is formed by a *dōzoku*, these marriages (which occur between households without much status differentiation, see pp. 86, 87, 93) are normally between cousins (mostly parallel cousins), or uncle and niece. There are many examples of such cases from field research work.

There is little need to go into the case where a village itself forms an almost endogamous unit. There the limitation of choice of a spouse is set externally, as already described, and it naturally entails frequent opportunities for a spouse to come from among near relatives. This tendency to endogamy within such a village community is strengthened by the fact that since there is normally little economic differentiation, all households are more or less of similar standing and there is a greater range of spouses available within the community. So that, in this case too, marriages meet the rule that they should take place between households of equal standing.

As we can see from the various cases, it is a distinctive feature of rural Japan that the high frequency of marriages among close relatives springs from the habit of forming marriage ties between households of like economic and social standing.

Conclusion

The main purpose of this study has been the establishment of structural generalizations in terms of the kinship and economic organization of rural Japan. The analysis reveals distinctive and persistent characteristics of Japanese social structure in different periods and localities. In terms of current issues of social anthropology, the analysis offers an example of the organizational structure in a peasant society which lacks a unilineal descent system. The examination reveals that the primary elements which provide the frame of organization in rural Japan are *household, local corporate group* and *village*, not family, descent group or status group. It is primarily local circumstances that determine group organization. The significance of local circumstances in the analysis of non-unilineal societies has already been demonstrated by several important studies. However, by comparison with these studies, institutions found in rural Japan such as *ie* and *dōzoku* seem to be the products of economic and political development specific to Japanese society.

Fred Eggan, who remarked that 'bilateral societies, no less than others, must cope with the problems of transmission and continuity without too much confusion', presents from his study of Sagada Igorots a set of social institutions parallel with those of unilateral societies of the same general cultural level. They are the ward (*dap-ay*), the descent group and the personal kindreds (Eggan, 1960). Earlier Raymond Firth called attention to an ambilateral descent group, the Maori *hapu*, which was comparable to a lineage in a unilineal society (Firth, 1929, 2nd edn., 1959, pp. 112–15). Further, Edmund Leach analysed another peasant society which lacks a unilineal descent system. According to him, 'Pul Eliya is a society in which locality and not descent forms the basis of corporate grouping' (Leach, 1961a). But in spite of his emphasis on the locality, if this society is compared with that of rural Japan, descent in the former plays a significant role: for example admission to membership of a compound group and to a village is acquired through descent, though not by a charter of a particular type of descent principle. In Japan it is hard to find a descent group such as that of Sagada or of the Maori, or descent criteria as means of acquiring membership as in the case of Pul Eliya. In the absence of any specific function of descent, *residence* and *locality* become *primary* criteria for group formation in rural Japan. Though conditions appear very similar in many aspects to Pul Eliya as discussed by Leach, the crucial difference is that, for acquiring membership of a group, descent is not necessarily the primary requirement; instead it is the residential right and economic contributions which are important, though in fact descent links are often found among members of a group. Certainly kinship functions in various ways, but, without a positive rule, it is easily overruled by other factors.

The absence of a specific function of descent is manifested, for example, in the outstanding significance of the *ie*, the primary sociological group. An individual cannot belong to more than one household. He may have two kinds of kinship link, paternal and maternal, but such link do not give him any prescribed right to membership—this is the point of departure from the ambilateral descent group described by Firth. One's membership can be only acquired through residential right as a member of the household. Though such a system may appear unique, an embryonic form of *ie* is found in the *bilek* (household) of the Iban of Borneo described by J. D. Freeman (Freeman, 1958). He is right in differentiating the Iban system as *utrolateral* (one side or the other, but never both) against *ambilateral* (either of two: allowing two at a given time). However, a more important point is that this affiliation does not extend beyond the entity of the household. Hence I am a bit reluctant to use the term *utrolateral*, which tends to be mistaken for an indication of a system which includes a wider sociological entity than the household, such as ambilateral or unilineal descent groups, structurally free from common residence.

Terminology apart, the Iban system is similar to that of Japan in its basic structural working. 'Among the Iban, *at least one* of the children of a family, when he or she reaches maturity and marries, remains in the parents' *bilek*.' (*Op. cit.*, p. 24.) Here is the same structural concern with the succession of the household (*ie*). And the fact that adoption is widely prevalent in Iban society (occurring in about one-third of all apartments which form a long house), and that an adopted child has conferred upon him precisely the same rights within his new *bilek* family as those conferred on born members, shows that the structure here is similar to that of Japanese *ie*. Adoption cases may be more numerous since the death rate is higher among the Iban, and there would be more childless households. As for the rate of virilocal residence and uxorilocal residence, Freeman reports 49 per cent of cases against 51 per cent. This is certainly not parallel with that of Japan, where uxorilocal marriages occur only when a household has no son, or when a wealthy household establishes a branch household for its daughter (which is rather an exceptional case). The highest percentage of uxorilocal marriages (expressed in Japanese by the term 'marriage of an adopted-son-in-law') as far as my knowledge goes, is one-third of the total marriages (this includes marriages of couples who are both adopted) in a village.

I think such differences occur largely because of the highly developed farm-management system found in Japan: it is a decided advantage from the point of view of farm management to be succeeded by a son born in the household. Hence uxorilocal marriage tends to be undertaken only in the absence of a real son. Economic and cultural differences between Iban and Japanese societies are important here. The high degree of institutionalization resulting in a virilocal marriage pattern, the development of primogenitural succession, and the inclusion of non-kin such as servants in the household, etc.—which are not found in the Iban *bilek*—are products of an economic and historical development specific to Japanese society.

The majority of anthropologists (Japanese as well as Western) have approached their studies of social organization in rural Japan through kinship analysis, and have debated at length in terms of patrilineal lineage (referring to *dōzoku*) and personal kindred (referring to *shinrui*). The major developments of the discussion among Japanese scholars on this issue are summarized by Nakano (1958). Among Western scholars, Befu is one of the recent contributors (Befu, 1963); his discussion is even more oriented towards kinship than are the discussions of the Japanese scholars, and he also reviews briefly the earlier literature on this theme.

The crucial difference between my analysis and these kinship-dominated views lies in the application of the term *descent* which

I use in a strict sense: the frequent employment of fictive kinship in Japanese usage should be differentiated from the workings of the descent rules normally found in other societies. Membership of a descent group should be confined to that acquired by birth; under this rule individuals could not acquire it by marriage, nor by economic and/or residential arrangement. A descent group may allow in an adoptive or some other non-kin member, but this is considered very exceptional; but in Japan adoptions or the establishment of a fictive kinship relation is not considered 'exceptional', but rather as well-established practice. For the analysis of kinship, a distinction should be drawn between these operative norms, because they give rise to significant differences in the total structure, and they rest on quite different ideologies in the recognition of kinship relations.

From this point of view, as I have extensively discussed in Chapter 3, the *dōzoku* is not a patrilineal lineage. Moreover, Japanese do not have any ascribed descent membership as do the Chinese and Hindus. Such forms as *ie* and *dōzoku*, *in which a strongly male-centred principle operates, are institutions historically developed in the absence of a unilineal descent system*, and are not a survival from a unilineal descent system. These institutional systems are devices produced in the course of its political and economic development by a society which lacks a unilineal system. (This point becomes very clear if such institutions are compared with Chinese family and lineage systems particularly in view of their structure and function in the historical perspective.) This is the reason for the great variation in the formation and function of *dōzoku* and also in the degree of institutionalization of *ie*, to which local, economic and political factors within the wider context of the state organization contribute heavily.

Japanese society lacks not only a unilineal descent system but also lacks any kind of principle upon which to form a descent group with its own function that takes precedence over local economic factors. (*Shinrui* is not a descent group, as I discussed extensively in Chapter 1: many anthropologists carelessly equated *shinrui* with a descent group.) With a background of such a limited function for kinship, the units of household, local group and village have played significant roles in the formation of social organization in rural Japan.[1]

---

[1] The discussion in this book excludes Amai and the Okinawa Islands (south-

The distinctive features of this Japanese rural social organization can be described as follows. Given the household as the basis of social organization, the local corporate group has importance at the next level of organization after the household. A local corporate group comprises a set of neighbouring households among which kinship relations may or may not be found. According to the given situation of a community, it takes the form of *kumi* or *dōzoku* (or *oyako-kankei*). These forms represent somewhat analytical concepts: empirically a local group may involve two or three criteria which overlap each other; or a group may change its form from one to another according to a given situation. The *dōzoku* involves a charter of genealogy in terms of households, not of individual members. The genealogical pattern derives from a logical extension of the structural principle of the household, which differs from a descent group based on individuals. Further, the functional field of a *dōzoku* (and *oyako-kankei*) is always confined within a village community, unlike that of a descent group. The *kumi* is a more general form of local corporate group in which primary importance is not given to the genealogical relations of the households.

Whatever the internal organization may be, these local corporate groups play a role similar in some ways to a localized descent group in other societies. Likewise, the village, or a group of villages, may be compared with a clan or a caste in terms of sociological entity. The important analytical point here is that other societies with descent groups, whether unilineal or not, also have a local group which is not necessarily formed by the members of the descent group alone. Ample examples can be shown of this: for instance, the above mentioned Sagada Igorots described by Eggan belong to a descent group as well as a ward: and almost all unilineal people have a unilineal group on the one hand, and a hamlet or a village, differently composed, on the other. In such a society, theoretically, an individual belongs to

western Islands). These areas have normally been taken for granted by anthropologists in their discussions of rural Japan. But I hold strongly to the view that these areas form a social field independent of mainland Japan. Their native kinship concept reveals significant differences from that of mainland Japan: there descent plays a very important role in their social organization, and the concept of *ie* and *dōzoku* are almost non-existent, while the descent network has a greater function than the nominal existence of a local group like *kumi* (see Nakane, 1964a).

two constant groups of differing categories: local and descent. Hence, the network of social organization is more complicated, and involves a plurality of the basic systems.

On the other hand, in Japan a local (and economic) group is the sole group to which an individual belongs. (Even *shinrui* relations tend to be confined to a local group, such as a village or a set of several neighbouring villages.) Whatever duplication of group organizations there may be, one does not belong to two different constant groups, the systems of which are theoretically opposed to each other, being based on entirely different criteria, such as locality and descent. This social mechanism produces three distinct characteristics in social organization. First, personal relationships are confined to the *tangible* and *local* sphere, which limits the scope of the sociological body of individuals. Secondly, social organization tends to produce a one-sided structure, in which personal relationships and the system of organization usually function along a vertical line. Thirdly, groups become independent of each other with no elaborate or constant network cutting across the different groups, in the way that Hindu caste networks cut across various villages. I think these are indeed the distinctive characteristics of the structural principle underlying Japanese social organization. This type of social organization provides an excellent basis for development of an effective state administrative system able to extend down to the household level. Indeed, in Japan the state administrative system has played a significant role and greatly influenced the organization of the rural community, particularly since the Tokugawa period.

Many particular aspects of *ie, dōzoku, oyako-kankei* and *kumi* described in this essay are disappearing from rural life today, owing to the expansion of industrialization. However, the distinctive characteristics of Japanese social structure described in this analysis in their traditional rural milieu are, in my view, persisting in various modern communities such as factories, business firms, schools, intellectual groups, political parties, etc., with which I hope to deal in another essay.

BIBLIOGRAPHY

I. Bibliography of Works mentioned in the Discussion
II. Additional Bibliography Relating to the Subjects Discussed in this Book
III. Selected Works by Western Scholars

Abbreviations for Japanese publications:

KS   *Kōza-shakaigaku* (Handbooks of Sociology)
KZ   *Kazoku-seido-zenshū* (Handbooks of Family Systems)
MK   *Minzokugaku-kenkyū* (Japanese Journal of Ethnology)
MN   *Minzokugaku-nempō* (Annual Reports of Ethnology)
MZ   *Minzokugaku* (Journal of Folklore)
NK   *Nihon-minzokugaku-kaihō* (Bulletin of the Folklore Society of Japan)
NMT   *Nihon-minzokugaku-taikei* (Handbooks of Japanese Volkskunde)
SH   *Shakaigaku-hyōron* (Japanese Sociological Review)
SJ   *Shakaijinruigaku* (Social Anthropologist)
SN   *Sonraku-shakai-kenkyū-nempō* (Annual Reports of Village Community Studies)

Note: (1) Except where otherwise indicated, the place of publication of a book in Japanese is Tokyo.
(2) In accordance with Japanese practice, the surname is placed first in all Japanese names.

I. BIBLIOGRAPHY OF WORKS MENTIONED IN THE DISCUSSION

ARIGA KIZAEMON, 1938. *Nōson-shakai no kenkyū* (A study of agricultural village communities).

—— 1939. *Nambuninohe-gun Ishigami-mura ni okeru daikazokusei to nago-seido* (Large family system and tenant system in Ishigami village of Nambuninohe district): *Attic Museum Ihō*. **43**.

—— 1943. *Nihon kazoku-seido to kosaku-seido* (Japanese family system and tenant system).

—— 1947. Dōzoku to shinzoku (*Dōzoku* and *shinzoku*), *Nihon-Minzokugaku-no-tame ni*, vol. 2, pp. 1-70.

—— 1950. Nihon no ie (Japanese *ie*). *Nihon-minzoku*, pub. by the Japanese Anthropological Society, pp. 154-84.

—— 1958. Daikazoku no hōkai igo (After the disintegration of the large family). *Shinano*, vol. 10, no. 5, pp. 255-66.

—— 1959. Nihon ni okeru senzo no kannen (Idea of ancestors in Japan). In *Ie*, Ed. Kitano and Okada.

—— 1960. Kazoku to ie (Family and *ie*). *Tetsugaku*, no. 38, pp. 79-110.

BEFU, HARUMI, 1963. Patrilineal Descent and Personal Kindred in Japan. *American Anthropologist*, vol. 65, no. 6, pp. 1328-41.

DUMONT, LOUIS, 1957. Hierarchy and Marriage Alliance in South Indian Kinship. *Occasional Papers of the Royal Anthropological Institute of Great Britain and Ireland*, no. 12.

EGGAN, FRED, 1960. The Sagada Igorots of Northern Luzon. In *Social Structure in Southeast Asia*, Ed. by G. P. Murdock. Quadrangle Books, Chicago; London: Tavistock Publications.

FIRTH, RAYMOND, 1929. *Economics of the New Zealand Maori*. 2nd. edn. 1959. R. E. Owen, Government Printer, Wellington, New Zealand.

—— 1957. Note on Descent Groups in Polynesia. *Man*, vol. 57, pp. 4-8.

—— 1959. *Social Change in Tikopia*. Allen and Unwin, London.

FREEDMAN, MAURICE, 1963. 'Descent, Systems of' in *Encyclopaedia Britannica*, vol. 7.

FREEMAN, J. D., 1958. The Family System of the Iban of Borneo. *The Developmental Cycle in Domestic Groups*, Ed. Jack Goody. Cambridge Papers in Social Anthropology, no. 1.

—— 1961. On the Concept of the Kindred. *The Journal of the Royal Anthropological Institute of Great Britain and Ireland*, vol. 91, Part 2, pp. 192-220.

FUKUSHIMA MASAO, 1961. Zaibatsu-kaken to 'ie' seido (Family constitutions of *Zaibatsu* and the *ie* institution). In *Kazoku to hō: Hōshakaigaku*, no. 12, pp. 43-64.

FUKUTAKE TADASHI, 1949. *Nihon-nōson no shakaiteki-seikaku* (Social characteristics of Japanese agricultural villages).

—— 1954. *Nihon-nōson-shakai no kōzō-bunseki* (Structural analysis of Japanese agricultural villages).

FURUSHIMA TOSHIO, 1947. *Kazoku-keitai to nōgyō no hattatsu* (Family patterns and the development of agriculture).

FURUSHIMA TOSHIO (Ed.), 1952. *Sanson no kōzō* (Structure of the hill village).

—— 1953. *Warichi-seido to nōchi-kaikaku* (Village communal land and land reform).

ISODA SUSUMU, 1954. Nōson ni okeru gisei-teki-oyako-kankei ni tsuite (On fictive parent-child relations in an agricultural village. *Shakaikagaku-kenkyū*, vol. 5, no. 3, pp. 36-59.

JOHNSON, ERWIN H., 1964. The stem family and its extensions in modern Japan. *American Anthropologist*, vol. 66, no. 4, pp. 839-51.

KITANO SEIICHI, 1940. Kōshū-sanson no dōzoku-soshiki to oyakokata-kankō (*Dōzoku* system and *oyakokata* custom in a hill village in Yamanashi prefecture). *MN*, vol. 2, pp. 41-95.

—— 1941. Dōzoku-soshiki to oyakata-kokata shiryō (The data on *dōzoku* system and *oyakata-kokata*). *MN*, vol. 3, pp. 161-89.

LEACH, EDMUND, 1961a. *Pul Eliya, A village in Ceylon*—A Study of Land Tenure and Kinship. Cambridge, The University Press.

—— 1961b. *Rethinking Anthropology*. London School of Economics Monographs on Social Anthropology, no. 22.

MOGAMI KOKEI, 1958. Mura no soshiki to kaisō (Village systems and their stratifications). In *NMT*, **3**.

NAKAGAWA ZENNOSUKE, 1938. Ane-katoku-sōzoku (The elder daughter succession & inheritance system); Basshi-sōzoku (The youngest son succession & inheritance system). In *KZ: Shiron-hen*, V, *sōzoku* (Inheritance).

NAKANE CHIE, 1962. Nihon-dōzoku-kōzō no bunseki (Structural analysis of *dōzoku* in rural Japan). *Tōyōbunka-kenkyūjo-kiyō* (The Memoirs of the Institute for Oriental Culture), vol. 28, pp. 133–67.

—— 1964a. 'Hiki' no bunseki (Analysis of Hiki: Kinship System of Amami Bilateral Society). *Tōyōbunka-kenkyūjo-kiyō*, vol. 33, pp. 119–55.

—— 1964b. 'Ie' no kōzō-bunseki (Structural Analysis of *ie*). In *Ishida-Eiichirō-kyōju kanreki-kinen ronbunshū* (Essays presented to Professor Ishida Eiichiro on his 60th birthday).

NAKANO TAKASHI and MATSUSHIMA SHIZUO, 1958. *Nihon-shakai-yōron* (Principal discussion of Japanese society).

NAMIKI MASAYOSHI, 1959. Sangyō-rōdōsha no keisei to Nōka-jinkō (Development of industrial labourers and agricultural population). In *Nihon-shihonshugi to nōgyō* (Capitalism and agriculture in Japan), Ed. by S. Tōbata and K. Uno.

—— 1960. *Nōson wa kawaru* (Agricultural villages are changing).

NOJIRI SIGEO, 1942. *Nōmin-rison no jisshōteki-kenkyū* (Empirical study of migrations of peasants).

OISHI SHINZABURO, 1952. Kinsei-shotō ni okeru 'dogō' kaihatsu shinden ni tsuite (On a new village developed by a local powerful man in the early Tokugawa period). *Shigaku-zasshi*, vol. 63, no. 6, pp. 1-33.

—— 1955. Kinsei-teki sonraku-kyōdōtai to ie (Tokugawa village community and *ie*). *Tōyōbunka*, no. 18–19, pp. 1–28.

—— 1956. Edo-jidai ni okeru nōmin no ie to sono sōzoku-keitai ni tsuite (On *ie* and inheritance patterns of peasants and landowners in the Tokugawa period). In *Kazoku-seido no kenkyū* (The study of family systems) I, pp. 97–121.

—— 1962. Kyōho 19 nen no jomenhamenritsu kettei jijō ni tsuite (Documents on the fixing of revenue in A.D. 1734). *Shōkeihō-ronsō*, vol. 12, no. 4, pp. 187–96.

ŌMACHI TOKUZŌ, 1958. Kazoku (Family). In *NMT*, **3**.

OUCHI TSUTOMU, 1951. Nihon-nōson no hōkensei no honshitsu (The intrinsic nature of feudal characteristics of Japanese agricultural villages). In *Hoken-isei* (Remnants of feudal institutions).

—— 1960. *Nōgyōshi* (Modern history of agriculture).

SAKURAI TOKUTARŌ, 1962. *Kō-shūdan seiritsu-katei no kenkyū* (The study of the formation of *kō* associations).

SASAKI KIYOSHI, 1926. Hera-watashi no shiki (A ceremony of handing over the *hera*). *Minzoku*, vol. 1, no. 6, pp. 143–4.

SEKIYAMA NAOTARŌ, 1958. *Kinsei nihon no jinkō-kōzō* (The population structure of Tokugawa Japan).

—— 1959. *Nihon no jinkō* (The population of Japan).

SMITH, THOMAS C., 1959. *The Agrarian Origins of Modern Japan*. Stanford University Press, Stanford, California.

TAKAO KAZUHIKO, 1958. *Kinsei no nōson seikatsu* (Life of the Tokugawa agricultural villages).

YAMAZAKI HARUSHIGE, 1956. *Mura no rekishi* (History of Japanese villages).
YANAGITA KUNIO, 1943. *Zokusei-goi* (Meanings of folk vocabularies).
—— 1948. *Kon'in no hanashi* (Collection of essays on marriage customs in Japan).
YANAGITA KUNIO (Ed.), 1956. *Sōgō nihon minzoku goi* (Comprehensive dictionary of Japanese folk vocabularies), vol. 4.

II. ADDITIONAL BIBLIOGRAPHY RELATING TO THE SUBJECTS DISCUSSED IN THIS BOOK

There is an exceedingly large number of works relating to the issues discussed in this book. It is certainly not possible to list all of them here; rather, I present a Select Bibliography. Moreover, these works are scattered among the different trends and disciplines of the social sciences in Japan. Works by ethnologists and anthropologists are only part of the important writings on rural Japan. It was part of my original intention to bring together these writings from the several disciplines in order to achieve a more sophisticated interpretation in the field of social anthropology. In order to avoid complications, I do not refer directly to many of them in the text. Instead, I list here an *Additional Bibliography* arranged according to the discussion in each chapter.

In the following introductory note for the reader as a guide to the bibliography, I outline the major trends in these studies. The outline is arranged under four categories: Studies in Sociology, in Law, in Economics and Economic History, and in Folklore and Ethnology.

Studies in Sociology

Outstanding contributions by sociologists in the analysis of the *ie* and *dōzoku* institutions through actual fieldwork began to appear during the 1930's. Well-known scholars in this field are K. Ariga, H. Oikawa and S. Kitano. The reason for focusing their studies on the *ie* and the *dōzoku* was that in their view these represent the most important aspects of Japanese family structure, as well as being characteristic of Japanese society. The strength of their investigations lay in their fieldwork, which in those days represented quite a new method of approach.

K. Ariga stands out by reason of his extensive fieldwork in various villages in Japan. His study of Ishigami village, over a period of about thirty years, with its excellent analysis of village life, can be cited as the best sociological monograph that has ever been produced in Japan (see p. 96). Ariga was interested in the works of Durkheim, Mauss and Radcliffe-Brown, and was greatly stimulated by Malinowski's field method. Realizing the basic differences between the societies of the Trobriands and Japan, he developed his own method of dealing with the Japanese field. His originality is shown by his interpretation of the data in the wider economic, political and historical contexts. His contribution is important, particularly in showing the significant meanings of land tenure and farm management in his analysis of the *dōzoku* institutions. Not being a social anthropologist, he does not employ the methods and terms of social anthropology, but his field data are superb, and can easily be used for anthropological analysis, as I have shown in Chapter 3.

Almost at the same time as Ariga began to publish his works, the results of the fieldwork of Oikawa and of Kitano also appeared, and their studies stimulated each other. Though the number of Oikawa's publications is small, since he died at the age of thirty-five, they were of great value in establishing the concept of *ie* as an important sociological unit, differentiating it from that of the elementary family. He introduced the concept of *dōzoku* in his analysis of the inter-*ie* institutions found in a village community, and this influenced Ariga (1943 *op. cit.*). A most important work which demonstrates his outstanding skill in the analysis of the *dōzoku* system (Oikawa 1940), shows how he was influenced by, but was also critical of, the work of Ariga (1938 *op. cit.*).

The contribution of S. Kitano is in the analysis of *oyakata-kankei* and *dōzoku*. Indeed the concept of the *dōzoku*, which has produced important results in the study of Japanese sociology, was first presented by Kitano and Oikawa, based on their field surveys. Kitano's analysis has been directed to the degree of involvement of blood relations in these institutions, while that of Ariga was directed to economic factors. According to Kitano, the *oyako-kankei* is a basically different kind of institution from the *dōzoku*, while Ariga considers it an institution which is linked structurally to the *dōzoku*. I think Kitano's analysis of *oyako-kankei* itself is a unique contribution, but in his analysis of the *dōzoku* structure his weakness lies in a confusion between the descent of individual relations and the genealogy of inter-household relations.

The important issues raised by these scholars concerning *dōzoku* and its related institutions, together with the historical details of the development of their theories, are best described in the work of T. Nakano (1958, pp. 37–69). In it Nakano reviews these works and criticizes them pertinently. Though he is a sociologist, Nakano presents his important analysis in a way that is closely linked to issues of current social anthropology. A chronological review of the publications which belong to this field is also presented by Nakano under the title, 'The studies of *ie*—centred on the contribution of Dr. Ariga' in *Ie—its structural analysis*, edited by S. Kitano and Y. Okada, 1959. This book *Ie*, which is a presentation volume for the sixtieth birthday of Dr. Ariga, includes some interesting recent essays on *ie* and *dōzoku* by thirteen scholars who studied under, or who have had close contact with, Dr. Ariga, and also includes an essay by Ariga himself (1959, *op. cit.*). The majority of the scholars dealing with the *ie* and *dōzoku* institutions associate themselves with this trend represented by Ariga.

The main concern of the scholars described above is to look for the principle of *the* Japanese family system through the analysis of the *ie* and *dōzoku* institutions. They hold the view that from their analyses it should be possible to generalize for the whole of Japan. As against this attitude, there is another way of looking at the various social systems in Japan: some investigators take the view that the principle of the *dōzoku* organization represents one among several patterns of organization of Japanese social systems. They employ a typological approach, establishing another principle which opposes, or contrasts with, the principle found in the *dōzoku* organization. This kind of typological approach is represented by the work of the rural sociologist T. Fukutake, who established two different types of village structure.

According to T. Fukutake, the two types are called the 'dōzoku' type and the 'kogumi' type: the former was characterized by a hierarchical vertical organization, and the latter by a democratic horizontal organization. The *dōzoku* was organized on a 'feudal' (master-subject) status relationship between the main family, which was a powerful local landowner, and its related branch families, which were the tenants of the former. The 'kogumi' organization is found in those communities where the households are free of such a status relationship combined with land-ownership, or in communities where such a relationship has declined. Whereas the *dōzoku* is chiefly oriented along status lines, the interrelations between families under the 'kogumi' system are ordered primarily on the basis of economic conditions. For the establishment of this typology, Fukutake was stimulated by Ariga's works, in which Ariga presented two kinds of inter-household relations (*dōzoku* and *kumi*). Fukutake applied Ariga's analytical concepts in establishing the types of village communities. He stated that the difference between these two types arose from differences in the economic conditions of the village community, internally as well as externally; in such matters as types of land tenure and the degree of advent of a commercial economy. He further expounds his typology in terms of geographical distribution: for example, the former type is more prominent in the northeastern part of Japan, and the latter in the southwestern.

The typology advocated by Fukutake is shared by S. Isoda, who has made a considerable contribution to the analysis of political power-relations within the hierarchical village organization. Indeed many rural sociologists have been concentrating their interests on these hierarchical aspects of the community, and they have shown how land tenure systems are closely interrelated with the social position (ranking order) of the households in a village community. At this point they are met by rural economists, economic historians and legal sociologists. Thus village study in Japan has mobilized various kinds of experts and has become one of the most fashionable subjects for study, particularly after the war. This has encouraged a large number of field surveys.

While the studies of Ariga (and others) were concentrated mainly on the *ie* and *dōzoku* organizations, these later studies are more concerned with the village community as a whole. One major interest of these scholars has been the exploration of the 'feudal' elements of Japanese society, called *kyōdōtai* (a local corporate community of a pre-modern, i.e. feudal, type) to differentiate it from the modern community of the West and from the city communities of all industrialized countries including Japan. Their efforts have been directed towards visualizing Japan in comparison with the West, taking an evolutionary view as their theoretical basis: for example, the concept of *kyōdōtai* originated in *Gemeinde* in relation to *Grundeigentum*, a concept which was produced by Marx. They also carried out a number of field studies in which the period of survey in any one village was relatively short, most of them covering only a couple of weeks, but which included considerable numbers of villages scattered in many different areas. The reports of these studies, many of which dealt with changing social and economic aspects of village communities, are voluminous, but most of them are stamped with a single-minded approach which makes the discussion rather static. Partly because of such limitations in theory, this kind of study had its climax in the 1950's (*Sonraku-shakai kenkyū-kai*, or

Association for the Study of Village Communities, was established in 1953), and has become less fashionable these days. The contributions of these scholars are represented in a number of essays in *Sonraku-shakai-kenkyū-nempō* (I–IX) published by the above mentioned Association.

Studies in Law

I have said that legal sociologists shared a common interest with the sociologists just mentioned. Historically these legal sociologists come from another long tradition which has conducted study in terms of '*the* Japanese family system' in the field of law. These studies originated in an historical event known as 'the dispute on the family systems' at the time of the establishment of the first Civil Code at the beginning of the Meiji period. The proposed family system, tentatively produced by a visiting French lawyer, E. G. Boissondarde, was strongly opposed by leading Japanese statesmen and lawyers, who said that it would demoralize the beautiful Japanese tradition. The traditional *ie* system held by these leading people made it difficult for them to accept the Western model. As a result of this strong opposition, family law as constituting part of the old Civil Code followed the traditional pattern of the Bushi class. (In spite of enthusiasm for modernization in general at the beginning of the Meiji period, as far as family law was concerned, popular opinion tended to take the opposite view.) This event stimulated many legal sociologists to study the differences between the Western family and Japanese *ie*.

Hence these scholars have been mainly concerned with the legal analysis of the Japanese family institution, *ie*, compared with that of the West. According to them the Japanese family system is characterized by a strong patriarchal structure with the household head as apex, which was the predominant pattern among the upper and middle strata of Japanese society before the war, and was also the pattern set out by the old Civil Code. As many of them adopted the evolutionary view, the characteristics of the Japanese family were interpreted as deriving from a pre-modern (feudal) institutionalized pattern. This view was held particularly strongly just after the war, along with the establishment of the new Civil Code, under strong American influence.

Apart from the value of such opinions, these studies provide us with an excellent detailed analysis of the laws on Japanese family systems from the beginning of the Meiji period to the present, as well as of changes that have occurred since. Besides dealing with Civil Codes, they include research on local usage with special reference to legal analysis. Above all, the contributions of Z. Nakagawa stand out as a classic in the study of the family system focused on inheritance and succession. T. Kawashima, who classifies himself as a legal sociologist (or a sociologist of law) and who contributed much to the study of post-war legal and social change in Japan, also made, with the collaboration of his colleagues and students, village surveys, sharing the interests of those sociologists previously mentioned.

Voluminous publications come from this group. My Select Bibliography includes only their major works on the issues in which social anthropologists may be interested, and the majority will be found listed as references to Chapter 1.

RJ N

Studies in Economics and Economic History

Other important studies on agrarian society in Japan are to be found in two leading fields: agricultural economics and economic history. As already mentioned, some of these studies are closely related to those of sociologists. But there is also a multitude of works concerned with specific issues in these fields with which social anthropologists do not or cannot deal: land tenure systems, agricultural techniques and management, mobility of rural population, detailed analysis of archives, etc. These relate not only to the national level, but also to local communities. They supply extremely helpful references for the anthropologist. (The representative publications in this regard are listed as references to Chapter 2.) However, the use of such highly specialized works by an anthropologist requires some guidance from an expert.

Research by agricultural economists seems to be most advanced in studies of rural Japan. A great amount of reliable statistical data are also available. Some of these studies, particularly those after the war, are founded on field-work in villages. One of the most useful of the leading essays on the history of the economic situation of modern agrarian society in Japan is the *Modern History of Agriculture* by T. Ouchi (1959 *op. cit.*) the bibliography of which gives details of the major publications in this field (about 450 items are listed in all, but these are only the more important essays published in book form; essays in journals and works concerned with particular local communities are excluded).

Works by economic historians are principally concentrated on the Tokugawa period, while those of agricultural economists are devoted to the modern period. Recently among these scholars, regional studies analysing local records found in old village households have become very numerous. The Association for the Study of Local History (*Chihō-kenkyū-kyōgikai*) was established in 1950, and published *Kinsei-chihōshi-kenkyū-nyūmon* (Introduction to the Study of Local History of the Tokugawa Period) in 1955, which is a very helpful guide in dealing with local archives of the Tokugawa period. However, studies focused on the composition and structure of *ie* and village community, which are of most interest from the point of view of social anthropology, such as works by Oishi (*op. cit.*), are still on the threshold of the wealth of unexplored local records (see pp. 47–9n.).

The major and basic concern of these scholars has been the land tenure systems in relation to the national economic and political organization. Not only these rural economists and economic historians, but also the rural sociologists previously mentioned, have shown great interest in land-ownership and management of wet-paddy cultivation. I think that the strength of these Japanese researches lies in their economic analysis, and that the best of the rural studies in Japan is found among them.

Closely related with these works, there are important contributions by specialists of Japanese agriculture, such as works of T. Furushima and his colleagues and students. Though they are also called agricultural economists, their approach differs from that of those above mentioned economists. While the latter deal with the rural issues as part of the nation-wide economic structure, in relation to Japan's industrialization, the study of Furushima and his colleagues comes from their thorough knowledge of traditional Japanese agriculture. They are much interested in carrying out field surveys and in dealing with local archives, thus sharing a common interest with rural sociologists and economic historians. On the basis of their unique specialization, they present stimulating analyses of economic and social aspects of village communities, particularly of pre-modern elements. (T. Smith, in his work *The Agrarian Origin of Modern Japan*, depends considerably on Furushima's works.)

Studies in Folklore and Ethnology

In addition to the series of studies mentioned above, there are important contributions by folklorists and ethnologists. This group stands on quite distinctive ground. In Japan ethnology, including cultural anthropology, has had much closer relations with folklore than with sociology; ethnologists have not shown the same interests in the work of economists and economic historians as sociologists. Even today a majority of ethnologists have little communication with sociologists and other social scientists, even though some are dealing with the same subjects such as *ie*, *dōzoku* and the village. On the other hand, they have kept close contact with folklorists: many ethnologists who deal with Japan came from the field of folklore.

In the studies coming from this group, the greatest contribution has been made by that most eminent folklorist, the late K. Yanagita (1875-1962), who established the study of Japanese folklore. Yanagita himself made extensive field surveys collecting information on various local customs, stories and dialects, and he published extensively. Yanagita's voluminous works have recently been compiled under the name of *Teihon Yanagita-kunio-zenshū* (The comprehensive collection of the works of Yanagita Kunio), 28 volumes (1960–5). His influence has been felt by a wide range of scholars in various fields besides that of folklore; sociology, ethnology, anthropology and history, etc. The data collected from various parts of Japan by him and by his numerous collaborators were beautifully interpreted and presented in his unique literary style. His method of dealing with material was entirely inductive; he never became preoccupied with theory, nor did he ever develop a theory of his own. However, his interpretations and inferences were superb owing to his profound knowledge; no one else could compare with him in this field. I myself occasionally find that the results of my analysis in social anthropology coincide with some of his earlier inferences.

The wealth of material collected on his initiative, or under his influene, by many folklorists from various parts of Japan over the last half-century have been published in a number of articles and books. Though they are rather fragmentary from the point of view of current social anthropology, they contain a great deal of information which may help our interpretation of the data by supplying a wider ethnographic account. (There are a number of reports on customs which have already vanished.) One of the outstanding contributions of Yanagita and his followers was published in the form of the *Sōgō-nihon-minzoku-gaku-goi* (Comprehensive Dictionary of Japanese Folk Vocabularies) in five volumes (containing 35,000 items), published in 1955-6.

Another similar dictionary was published by the Japanese Society of Ethnology: *Nihon-shakai-minzoku-jiten* (Dictionary of Japanese folk-society and cul-

ture), four volumes, 1952–60. The results of the major studies in Japanese folklore were compiled as *Nihon-minzoku-gaku-taikei* (Handbooks of Japanese
Volkskunde), 13 volumes, edited by Omachi, Oka, Sakurada, Seki and
Mogami, in 1958–60. Among them the volume most relevant to the present
study is Volume III, 'Society and Folk', which includes the studies of village
community and kinship, referred to elsewhere. These dictionaries and handbooks are essential and very convenient for social anthropologists working in
rural Japan.

Many works of ethnologists dealing with Japan come close to the works of
folklorists. (In fact most of the ethnologists of the earlier generation had close
contact with Yanagita.) However, they have naturally been more concerned
with ethnological issues. They collected data on local customs and made
intensive field studies; their major interests are in making distribution maps
of various cultural items, or in discerning local cultural patterns. One of the
earlier and influential approaches is that of M. Oka, who was trained in Vienna
and who contributed much to the establishment of ethnology in Japan. According to Oka, there are at least two types of cultural complex in Japan,
represented by the 'dōzoku complex' and 'age-grade complex', an idea which
was expressed in *Nihon-minzoku no kigen* (The Origin of the Japanese People),
ed. E. Ishida *et al.* 1958. This view has influenced many ethnologists and anthropologists, and stimulated their fieldwork in various rural areas. The majority
of field reports since the war bear this typological concern. According to this
typological view, in the field of kinship systems in Japan there are two types:
the patrilineal type (*dōzoku*) and the bilateral type (*shinzoku*), each of which
represents the kinship principle of the northeastern part and the southwestern
part of Japan, respectively (for example, see Gamo, 1958).

Interestingly enough, the distribution of these different types of culture
complex in Japan roughly coincides with that of Fukutake's 'dōzoku' and
'kogumi', which are established on the basis of social status and economic
conditions. However, they differ in the following respect: in Fukutake's
typology, the two types are explained by different economic conditions—it is
in a way these varying conditions which have produced the different types—
but in the typology of the ethnologists, the two types are contrasted with
each other, as representing different cultural elements or principles existing
in Japan, so that it seems impossible to make a generalization about Japan as
a whole.

The typological approaches either of Fukutake or of Oka seem to have a particular attraction for many Japanese scholars; their influence is also frequently
noted in the works of western scholars who have dealt with rural Japan.
However, there are criticisms too: 'The tendency to deal with data in light
only of the researcher's typological preoccupation is regrettable. . . . I believe
that the study of the village community in Japan has not reached the stage
where the accumulating of basic field data can be neglected' (Takeuchi Toshimi,
1959, p. 122).

In general, studies of Japanese society by ethnologists (including those who
call themselves social anthropologists) are directed to look for regional differences within Japan, or to present detailed monographs of a small community,
rather than to look for generalizations. Furthermore, they deal with social

institutions as part of culture along with other cultural elements: they are primarily occupied with an ethnographic concern. Dominated by such an approach, the study of Japanese social organization in view of the structural comparison with that of other societies has been neglected. Apart from their methodological concern, richness of monographic information is the wealth of these Japanese works of scholarship, which are no doubt the important references for those who will deal with rural Japan.

The following are convenient references to glance at for ethnological works by Japanese scholars. (The majority of the works deal with Japan.) For the field-work: *Tokushū: Shakai-chōsa* (Special Number: Social Research—Symposium on the History and Prospects of Social Research in Japan), *Minzokugaku-kenkyū* (The Japanese Journal of Ethnology), vol. 17, no. 1, 1952. *Tokushū: Jittai-chōsa* (Classified List of Field Work by Members of the Japanese Society of Ethnology—in Ethnology, Sociology, Linguistics, Archaeology, Physical Anthropology and Related Sciences), *Minzokugaku-kenkyū*, vol. 28, no. 1, 1964. Both are published by *Nihon-minzokugaku-kyōkai* (The Japanese Society of Ethnology). For bibliography: *Minzokugaku-kankei zasshi ronbun sōmo-kuroku* (Bibliography of Japanese Articles in Ethnology) 1925–59, published by *Nihon-minzokugaku-kyōkai*, 1961. *Bunka-kei bunken-mokuroku XIII: Bunkajinrui* 1945–61 (Bibliography of Cultural Anthropology 1945–61), published by *Nihon-gakujutsu-kaigi* (Science Council of Japan), 1962.

These four trends represent the most influential approaches found among Japanese scholars, and they too have influenced more or less the interpetations of Western scholars who have dealt with Japanese kinship and village studies. Although they express different approaches, they nevertheless deal concretely with such entities as *ie* and village community, and as such they provide us with valuable material for anthropological study.

SELECT BIBLIOGRAPHY

Note: The Japanese romanized transcription of the titles of essays (but not of books) is omitted, and only the translation is given.

Chapter 1

AOYAMA MICHIO, 1948. *Nihon kazoku-seido no kenkyū* (A study of the Japanese family system).

BAI KŌICHI & WATANABE YŌZŌ, 1955, 1956. Inheritance patterns in agricultural villages (1), (2). *Hōritsu-jijō*, 26 (pp. 29–38), 27 (pp. 58–72).

EMA MIEKO, 1943. *Shirakawa-mura no daikazoku* (Large family institution in Shirakawa village).

FUKUSHIMA MASAO, 1945. *Ie* of a hill village and capitalism. *Tōyōbunka-kenkyūjo-kiyō*, vol. 6, pp. 1–97.

—— 1956. Formation of the *ie* institution in the first half of the Meiji period. In *Kazoku-seido no kenkyū* (The study of family system).

GAMŌ MASAO, 1958. Shinzoku. In *NMT*, **3**.

HASHIURA YASUO, 1941. *Nihon-minzokugaku-jō-yori mitaru kazoku-seido no kenkyū* (A study of family system viewed from Japanese folklore). 2 vols.

HIMEOKA, *et al.*, 1959. *Inkyo* system of Shima Koh village. *SH*, **36**, pp. 75–92.

HOZUMI SHIGETOH & NAKAGAWA ZENNOSUKE (Ed.), 1937–1938. *Kazoku-seido zenshū* (Handbooks of the family systems) 10 vols. (*Shiron-hen* I–V, *Horitsu-hen* I–V).

ISHIRYŌSUKE, 1950. The system of primogeniture. In *Hōritsugaku-taikei*, Part II.

ISONO SEIICHI & ISONO FUJIKO, 1958. *Kazoku-seido* (Family system).

KAWASHIMA TAKEYOSHI, 1948. *Nihon-shakai no kazoku-teki kōsei* (Family oriented composition of Japanese society).

—— 1959. *Ideologii toshite no kazoku-seido* (The family system as ideology).

KAWASHIMA TAKEYOSHI (Ed.), 1965. *Nōka-sōzoku to nōchi* (Inheritance of agricultural family and farm land), Zaidanhōjin-Nōsei-chōsakai.

KIHARA KENTARŌ, 1954. Formality and informality of *shinrui* relationships— A case from a hill village, Osawasato in Izu. *SH*, **15**, pp. 37–55.

KITANO & OKADA (Ed.), 1959. *Ie—sono kōzō-bunseki* (*Ie*—Its structural analysis).

KOYAMA TAKASHI, 1936. A hill village and its family composition. In *Nempō-shakaigaku*, vol. 4.

—— 1948a. An analysis of *shinzoku* relations. *Shakaikagaku-hyōron*, 3.

—— 1948b. A review of family studies. In *Shakaichōsa no riron to jissai*.

—— 1960. *Gendai Kazoku no kenkyū* (Research on the modern family).

MAEDA TAKASHI, 1960. Actual state of ancestor worship and inheritance in Japanese village communities. *SH*, **38**, pp. 87–105.

MASUYA TATSUNOSUKE, 1928. On the large family system in Aomori prefecture. *Shakaigaku-zasshi*, no. 54, pp. 77–86.

MIURA SHŪKŌ, 1924. Family system with particular reference to parent-child relations. In *Hōsei-shi no kenkyū*.

MIYAMOTO TSUNEICHI, 1949. Family and kinship. In *Kaison seikatsu no kenkyū* (Ed. Yanagita Kunio).

MORIOKA KIYOMI, 1957. Family. In *KS*, V.

—— 1963. Family and *Shinzoku*. In *Shakaigaku* (Ed. T. Fukutake).

MURATAKE SEIICHI, 1962. *Inkyo* family system of Hachijō-jima. *Jinmongakuhō*, no. 29, pp. 63–91.

NAKADA KAORU, 1926. *Hōsei-shi ronshū* (Collection of discussions on the history of legal systems) I: *Shinzoku-hō* (Code of relatives), *Sōzoku-hō* (Code of inheritance).

NAKAGAWA ZENNOSUKE, 1952. *Nihon no kazoku-seido* (Family system in Japan).

NAKAGAWA ZENNOSUKE, M. AOYAMA, H. TAMAKI, M. FUKUSHIMA, H. KANEKO & T. KAWASHIMA (Ed.), 1955. *Kazoku-mondai to kazoku-hō* (Discussions on family and family laws) I: *Kazoku* (Family); IV: *Oyako* (Parent and child); VI: *Sōzoku* (Inheritance), 1961.

NAKANE CHIE, 1962, Koh. *Asahi Journal*, vol. 4, no. 6, pp. 79–82.

NAKANO TAKASHI, 1957. Family and *shinzoku*. In *KS*, IV.

Nihon kazoku kenkyū bunken (Bibliography of Japanese family studies) 1 & 2, 1950. In *Kikan-shakaigaku*, 3 & 4.

Nihon-shakaigaku-kai (Japanese Sociological Association), (Ed.), 1956–7. *Kazoku-seido no kenkyū* (The study of family system), 2 vols.

ŌMACHI TOKUZŌ, 1938. On *inkyo*. In *Nempo-shakaigaku*, vol. 5.

—— 1950. On *inkyo* family institution. *Jinruikagaku*, vol. 2, pp. 114–19.
—— 1958. Family. In *NMT*, **3**.
—— 1959. Inheritance by selection and *inkyo*. *Shakai to denshō*, vol. 3, no. 2, pp. 51–60.

TAKAYANAGI NAOJI, 1959. *Kindai-nihon ni okeru kazoku-seido to hōritsu* (Family system and law of modern Japan).

TAKEDA AKIRA, 1953. On ultimogeniture in Japan. *Nippon-minzokugaku*, vol. 1, no. 1, pp. 41–65.

—— 1956a. On a special type of retirement, the father living with the eldest son and the mother with the second son. *Nippon-minzokugaku*, vol. 3, no. 4, pp. 1–23.

—— 1956b. A study on *inkyo* family system. *Shigaku-kenkyū*, no. 10, pp. 1–29.

—— 1960. Youngest son inheritance in a village of Kagoshima prefecture. *NK*, **14**, pp. 5–15.

—— 1963. Law and custom. *Shakai-to-denshō*, vol. 7, no. 1, pp. 1–21.

TAKEUCHI TOSHIMI, 1958. *Inkyo* and adopted son. In *Kadokawa-shoten kyōdo-kenkyū-kōza*, vol. 10, no. 1.

TAMAKI HAJIME, 1955. *Kindai-nihon ni okeru kazoku-kōzō* (Family structure in modern Japan).

—— 1957. *Nihon ni okeru daikazoku-sei no kenkyū* (A study of large family institutions in Japan).

TODA TEIZO, 1937. *Kazoku-kōsei* (Family composition).

—— 1944. *Ie to kazoku-seido* (*Ie* and family system).

TOSHITANI NOBUYOSHI, 1961. Structure and function of 'ie' institution—A study of the property and inheritance of 'ie'. *Shakaikagaku-kenkyū*, vol. 13, no. 1–2 (pp. 1–85) & no. 4 (pp. 12–102).

WAGATSUMA TŌSAKU, 1959. *Yome no tengoku* (Heaven of daughters-in-law: Koh village).

YAMAMOTO NOBORU & NAKAGAWA KIYOKO, 1960. Some considerations of the ways of the father family. *SH*, **37**, pp. 37–76.

YANAGITA KUNIO, 1929. *Ie-kandan* (Talks on *ie*).

Chapter 2

ANDŌ SEIICHI, 1950. The composition of the agricultural community in the early Tokugawa period. *Shien*, **43**, pp. 95–120.

—— 1959. *Edo-jidai no nōson* (Agricultural villages of the Tokugawa period).

AOKI SHIGERU, 1953. Family history of a local landlord. *Nihonshi-kenkyū*, **19**, pp. 29–37.

ENDŌ SHINNOSUKE, 1953. Formation of 'village community' in the Tokugawa period. *Shigaku-zasshi*, vol. 64, no. 2, pp. 49–66.

—— 1954. Establishment of *mura* through the study of the land registration in the early Tokugawa period. *Shakai-keizaishigaku*, vol. 20, no. 2, pp. 45–71.

FUJITA GORŌ, 1952. *Hōken-shakai no tenkai-kōzō* (Development structure of feudal society).

FURUSHIMA TOSHIO, 1948. *Kinsei nihon nōgyō no kōzō* (Structure of Japanese agriculture in the Tokugawa period).

—— 1949–50. *Nihon nōgyō gijutsushi* (History of Japanese agricultural techniques).

—— 1954. *Kinsei iriai-seido-ron* (Discussion on the village land system in the Tokugawa period).

—— 1956. *Nihon nōgyō-shi* (Japanese agricultural history).

—— 1963. *Kinsei nihon nōgyō no tenkai* (Development of Japanese agriculture in the Tokugawa era).

HARADA TOMOHIKO, 1964. A plan of *buraku* history of the latter Tokugawa period. *Keizaigakū-zasshi*, vol. 51, no. 4, pp. 50–67.

HAYASHI MOTOKI, 1955. *Hyakushō ikki no dentō* (Tradition of peasant revolts).

HIRASAWA KIYOTO, 1955. *Kinsei minami-shinano nōson kenkyū* (A study of Tokugawa agricultural villages in south Nagano prefecture).

HŌGETSU KEIGO, 1943. *Chūsei kangaishi no kenkyū* (A study of the history of medieval irrigation).

HOZUMI SIGETOH (Ed.), 1921. *Goningumi hōki-shū* (Regulations of *Goningumi*). Second volume in 1944.

IIZUKA KŌJI, 1957. Post-war land reform and Japanese agriculture. *Toyobunka* 24, pp. 1–12.

IKEDA KEISEI, 1955. Development of peasant family and Kinai villages in the early Tokugawa period. *Historia*, no. 12, pp. 61–71.

IMAI RINTARŌ & YAGI HIROTETSU, 1955. *Hōkenshakai no nōson-kōzō* (Structure of agricultural villages in Feudal society).

KANAZAWA NATSUKI, 1954. *Inasaku no keizai-kōzō* (Economic structure of paddy cultivation).

KAWAI ETSUZŌ (Ed.), 1954–5. *Nōgyō-nōmin-mondai kōza* (Lectures on the problems of agriculture and peasants). 3 vols.

KIKUCHI TOSHIO, 1963. *Shinden-kaihatsu* (Development of *shinden*).

KINOSHITA REIJI, 1949. *Nihon nōgyō kōzō ron* (Discussion on Japanese agricultural structure).

—— 1964. Formation and development of *kabu* of Tokugawa farmers. *Shakai-keizaishigaku*, vol. 29, no. 4–5, pp. 88–112.

KITAJIMA MASAMOTO, 1954. Review of Tokugawa village studies since the war. (1) & (2). *Shigaku-zasshi*, vol. 63, no. 10 (pp. 49–68) & 11 (pp. 58–83).

—— 1956. Peasant family in the Tokugawa period. In *Kazoku-seido no kenkyū*, 1, pp. 53–77.

KITAMURA TOSHIO, 1950. *Nihon kangai-suiri kankō no shiteki kenkyū* (A historical study of Japanese irrigation systems).

KOBAYASHI SHIGERU, 1963. *Kinsei nōson keizai-shi no kenkyū* (A study of economic history of Tokugawa agricultural villages).

KODAMA KŌTA, 1949. Large family institution of the Tokugawa village. *Shisō*, **302**, pp. 56–66.

—— 1951. *Kinsei nōmin seikatsu shi* (History of Tokugawa peasant life).

—— 1953. *Kinsei nōson-shakai no kenkyū* (A study of Tokugawa agricultural villages).

—— 1964. Status and family. In *Iwanami-koza Nihon-rekishi*. **10**: *Kinsei 2.*

KONDŌ YASUO & ŌTANI SHŌZŌ (Ed.), 1954. *Nōson mondai kōza* (Lectures on the issues of agricultural villages), 3 vols.

KUROMASA IWAO, 1928. *Hyakushō-ikki no kenkyū* (A study of peasant revolts).

—— 1959. *Hyakushō-ikki no kenkyū*: Additional edition.

MAEDA MASAHARU, 1950. *Nihon kinsei sonhō no kenkyū* (A study of Tokugawa village rules).

MATSUMOTO MASAAKI, 1964. A study on establishment and development of a Tokugawa village—Jōnan-chō, Masushiro-gun in Kumamoto prefecture. *MK*, vol. 27, no. 2, pp. 13–29.

MATSUO KOTOBUKI, 1963. *Shinden* village in Kinai district in the early Tokugawa period. In *Bakuhan-taisei kakuritsu-ki no shomondai*.

MATSUURA K. & HAMASHIMA H. (Ed.), 1963. *Nihon-shihonshugi to sonraku-kōzō* (Japan's capitalism and village structure).

MIYAKAWA MITSURU, 1953. The village administration system and land registration in the Tokugawa period. *Nihonshi-kenkyū*, **19**, pp. 2–28.

MIYAMOTO MATAJI (Ed.), 1955. *Nōson-kōzō no shiteki-bunseki* (Historical analysis of the agricultural village structure).

—— 1960. *Han-shakai no kenkyū* (A study of local communities of Tokugawa fiefs).

MORI TAKESHI (Ed.). 1963. *Kinsei sonraku no kenkyū* (A study of a Tokugawa village).

MORITA SHIRŌ, 1963. *Jinushi-keizai to chihō-shihon* (Landlord economy and local capital).

NAKAMURA KICHIJI, 1938. *Kinsei shoki nōseishi kenkyū* (A study of the early Tokugawa agricultural policies).

—— 1956. *Sonraku-kōzō no shiteki-bunseki* (A historical analysis of village structure)—*Kemuriyama mura*.

—— 1957. *Nihon no sonraku kyōdōtai* (Village community in Japan).

—— 1960. The system of *koku* registration and feudal characteristics. *Shigaku-zasshi*, vol. 69, no. 7 (pp. 1–47) & no. 8 (pp. 26–40).

—— 1962. *Kaitaiki hōken-nōson no kenkyū* (A study of the feudal agricultural village at its disintegrating stage)—*Imai mura*.

Nakamura Kichiji kyōju Kanreki kinen ronshū Kankōkai (The Association for publishing the presentation volume for the sixtieth birthday of Professor Nakamura Kichiji), 1965. *Kyōdōtai no shiteki-kōsatsu* (Historical study of *kyōdōtai*).

OGURA TAKEICHI, 1963. *Kindai ni okeru nihon-nōgyō no hatten* (The development of Japanese agriculture in Modern era).

OISHI SHINZABURŌ, 1953. Land tenure system and village structure. *Shakai-keizaishi-gaku*, vol. 19, no. 1, pp. 87–105.

—— 1958. *Hōkenteki-tochi-shoyū no kaitai-katei* (Disintegrating process of the feudal land tenure system).

OKA MITSUO, 1963. *Hōken-sonraku no kenkyū* (A study of feudal villages).

ŌNO TAKEO, 1936. *Nihon-sonrakushi gaisetsu* (Outline of Japanese village history).

ŌSHIMA KIYOSHI, 1958. *Nōchi-kaikaku to nōgyo-mondai* (Land reform and agriculture problems).

ŌTAKE HIDEO, 1962. *Hōken-shakai no nōmin kazoku* (Peasant family of feudal society).

—— 1955. Kinship system of Tokugawa peasant society. *Kōbe hōgaku zasshi*, vol. 4, no. 4.

OUCHI TSUTOMU, 1955. Village structure and peasant movements. In *SN*, II, pp. 1–27.

—— 1957. *Nōka keizai* (Economy of agricultural households). Nihon-tōkei-kenkyūjo keizai-bunseki shiriizu 6.

SAHEKI NAOMI, 1963. *Nihon nōgyō kinyū-shi ron* (On the history of Japanese agriculture finance).

SAKAMOTO KEIICHI, 1953. Characteristics of wet-paddy cultivation society. *Jinmon-gakuhō*, **3**, pp. 143–64.

SASAKI JUNNOSUKE, 1958. Agricultural structure and local landlords under the Tokugawa system. In *Nihon-jinushi-sei-shi-kenkyū*.

—— 1963. Formation of the Tokugawa village. In *Iwanami-kōza Nihonrekishi*, **10**: *Kinsei II.*

SHIMADA TAKESHI, 1951. Disintegration of a village in the Tokugawa. period. *Keizaigaku*, **21**, pp, 94–139.

SHIMAZAKI MINORU, 1958. On the analysis of stratification in postwar agricultural villages. *Keizai-hyōron*, vol. 7, no. 4, pp. 62–77.

SHIMIZU MORIMITSU & MAEDA SEIJI, 1961. *Kinsei-kōshin-chiiki no nōson-kōzo* (The structure of an agricultural village in a backward area in the Tokugawa period). Tatsunoguchi mura. Kyoto.

SHIONO YOSHIO, 1953. Leaders of peasant revolts in the later Tokugawa period. *Nihonshi-kenkyū*, **19**, pp. 38–58.

SONODA KYŌICHI, 1960. Land reform and village structure. *SH*, **41**, pp. 35–47.

TAKEYASU SHIGEHARU, 1963. The maintenance of land and agricultural management in Kawachi district in the early Tokugawa period. In *Bakuhan-taisei kakuritsu-ki no shomondai.*

TŌBATA S. & KAMIYA K., 1964. *Gendai nihon no nōgyō to nōmin* (Agriculture and farmer in Contemporary Japan): *Nihon-nōgyō no zenbō*, vol. 5. Nōgyō-sōgō-kenkyūjo.

TŌBATA S. & UNO K., 1959. *Nihon shihonshugi to nōgyō* (Capitalism and agriculture in Japan).

Tōdai nōson shiryō chōsa kai (Association of survey of village archives, University of Tokyo), 1953. *Kinsei nōson no kōzō* (Structure of the Tokugawa agricultural villages).

TŌHOKU-KEIZAI-SHIRYŌ-SHITSU, 1963. Commentary on records of peasant revolts in the early Tokugawa period. *Tōhoku-keizai*, **39.**

TOTANI TOSHIYUKI, 1949. *Kinsei nōgyō keiei shi ron* (On agricultural management in the Tokugawa period).

TSUCHIYA TAKAO (Ed.), 1950. *Hōken-shakai no kōzō-bunseki* (Structural analysis of feudal society).

UNO KŌZO (Ed.), 1961. *Nihon-nōson-keizai no jittai* (Actual state of agricultural economy in Japan).

WAKITA OSAMU, 1963. *Kinsei-hōken-shakai no keizai-kōzo* (Economic structure of Tokugawa feudal society).

WASHIMI TŌYŌ, 1958. A study of village structure in Kinai district in the early Tokugawa period. *Shakai-keizaishigaku*, vol. 23, no. 5 & 6, pp. 84–130.

YAGI AKIO, 1952. On a study of agricultural village structure in the Tokugawa period. *Keizaigaku*, **26**, pp. 146–56.

YAMAOKA EIICHI, 1954. Family and social structure of hill villages through the Tokugawa records. *SH*, **13** & **14**, pp. 150–65.

YAMAZAKI RYŪZO, 1963. Development of village economy and differentiation in peasant community of later Tokugawa period. In *Iwanami-kōza Nihonrekishi: Kinsei 4.*

Chapter 3

ANDŌ KIICHIRŌ, 1960. Disintegration of *dōzoku* cohesion and festivity of a household god. *SH*, **37**, pp. 59–76.

AOYAGI KIYOTAKA, 1961. On the customs of *oyabun*, *nakōdo* and *nazuke-oya* Kamiyamabe, Nishinose-cho in Yamanashi prefecture. *NK*, **20**, pp. 1–7.

ARIGA KIZAEMON, 1928. On *yosomono* (Strangers). *Minzoku*, vol. 3, no. 2, pp. 178–84.

—— 1933. Tenants, *yui* and *yosomono*. *MZ*, vol. 5, no. 4, pp. 73–75.

—— 1935. Transplantation and the system of village life. *MK*, vol. 1, no. 3, pp. 31–50.

—— 1938. *Sanaburi*: Transplantation and the system of village life. *MK*, vol. 4, no. 1 (pp. 23–48), & no. 2 (pp. 1–34).

—— 1948. *Sonraku-seikatsu* (Village Life).

—— 1949b. Problems of social stratification in Japanese social structure. *MK*, vol. 14, no. 4, pp. 13–22.

—— 1956. Village community and *ie*. In *SN* III.

—— 1962. *Dōzoku* and its change. *SH*, **46**, pp. 2–7.

—— 1965. *Nihon no kazoku* (Family of Japan).

FUKUTAKE TADASHI, 1962. Village community ('Buraku') in Japan and its democratization. In *Japanese Culture—Its development and Characteristics.* Ed. by R. J. Smith & R. K. Beardsley. Viking Fund Publications in Anthropology, no. 34.

FUKUTAKE, HIDAKA & TAKAHASHI (Ed.), 1957. *Kōza-shakaigaku* (Handbooks of sociology) IV: *Family, village, city.*

FUSE TETSUJI, 1962. A study on analytical method of structure of village community. *SH*, **50**, pp. 2–26.

GAMŌ MASAO, 1960. *Nihonjin no seikatsu-kōzō josetsu* (Introductory discussion on life structure of the Japanese people).

GAMŌ MASAO, TSUBOI HIROFUMI & MURATAKE SEIICHI, 1963. Society and folklore of Aogashima. In *Minzokugaku nōto* (Collection of essays presented to Professor Oka Masao on his sixtieth birthday).

HASHIURA YASUO, 1937. Co-operative labour and mutual assistance. In *Sanson-seikatsu no kenkyū* (Ed. Yanagita Kunio).

HASUMI OTOHIKO, 1959. Village community and rural sociology. In *SN*, VI.

HATTORI HARUNORI, 1952. One type of *oyabun-kobun-kankei* in Yamanashi prefecture. In *Yamanashi-daigaku gakugeibu kenkyūhōkoku*, **3**.

HAYAKAWA KŌTARŌ, 1937. Social character of individual labour force in agricultural custom, *yui*. *MK*, vol. 3, no. 2, pp. 29–88.

HIMEOKA SUSUMU, *et al.*, 1953. *Tokushū: San-son no jittai-chōsa* (Special number: Field survey of a hill village—Higashi-kusano-mura in Shiga prefecture). *Sociology*, no. 5.

HORI ICHIRŌ, 1951. *Minkan-shinkō* (Folk-beliefs in Japan).
—— 1959. Japanese folk-beliefs. *American Anthropologist*, vol. 61, pp. 405–24. (This is an English translation of part of the *Minkan-shinkō*.)
IKAWA FUMIKO, 1964. Comments on Befu's 'Patrilineal descent and personal kindred in Japan. (Brief Communications) *American Anthropologist*, vol. 66, pp. 1159–62.
IMANISHI KINJI, 1952. *Mura to ningen* (Village and people). Kyoto.
ISODA SUSUMU, 1947. Family systems and social structure of Japanese villages. *Daigaku*, no. 2, pp. 14–21.
—— 1951a. Two types of agricultural village structures. *Hōshakaigaku*, no. 1, pp. 50–64.
—— 1951b. On the 'type' of village structures. *Shakaikagaku-kenkyū*, vol. 3, no. 2, pp. 1–23.
—— 1954–5. On fictive *oyako-kankei* in agricultural villages (1), (2) & (3). *Shakaikagaku-kenkyū*, vol. 5, no. 3 (pp. 36–59), no. 4 (pp. 33–51), & vol. 6, no. 1 (pp. 73–93).
ISODA SUSUMU (Ed.), 1955. *Sonraku-kōzō no kenkyū* (A study of village structure)—Kiyahira mura in Tokushima prefecture. Tokyo daigaku shakaikagaku-kenkyūjo kenkyū-hōkoku, 8.
IZUMI SEIICHI & GAMO MASAO, 1952. Regional characteristics in Japanese society. In *Nihon chiri shin-taikei*, **2**.
KAWAMURA NOZOMI, 1957. *Dōzoku* organization and village community. *Tōyōdaigaku-kiyō*, 11, pp. 73–84.
—— 1958. Problems of 'genealogy' in the study of village structure. *SH*, 8, no. 3, pp. 109–22.
—— 1959. Some problems in the sociological study of a village community. *SJ*, vol. 2, no. 2, pp. 17–36.
KAWASHIMA TAKEGOSHI, 1954. Status and class distinction in an agricultural village. In *Nihon-shihonshugi kōza*.
KAWASHIMA TAKEYOSHI & SHIOMI TOSHITAKA, 1947. On *kane-oya*. *MK*, vol. 12, no. 1, pp. 33–40.
Keiōgijuku-daigaku sonraku-chōsakai (Association of village surveys, Keiō University), 1962. The system of village festivities and politico-economic structure in a village community. *Keiō-daigaku shakaigaku-kenkyūka-kiyō*, no. 1, pp. 38–125.
KIHARA KENTARŌ, 1953. An observation on status consciousness in a hill village community. *SH*, **12**, pp. 52–80.
KITANO SEIICHI, 1937. *Dōzoku* groups in Wakamiya of Sarashina village in Nagano prefecture. *MK*, vol. 3, no. 3, pp. 1–36.
—— 1939. On the inheritance of a branch household in Yamasangō in Fukushima prefecture. *MK*, vol. 5, no. 2, pp. 44–54.
—— 1946. The data on *dōzoku* groups. In *Kazoku-mondai to kazoku-hō*, V.
—— 1953. Problems of social structure of Tsushima villages. *Jinmonkagaku*, vol. 4, pp. 138–45.
—— 1960. *Oyabun-kobun* in hill villages in Yamanashi prefecture. In *Osaka-daigaku bungakubu kiyō*, vol. 7, pp. 207–26.
—— 1962. '*Dōzoku*' and '*ie*' in Japan: the meaning of family genealogical relationships. In *Japanese Culture*, pp. 42–46.

KONDŌ YASUO, 1955. *Mura no kōzō* (Structure of the village).

MAKITA SHIGERU, 1948. *Sonraku-shakai* (Village community): Shakaigaku-sōsho, 2.

MATSUBARA JIRŌ, 1957. Structure of agricultural village community. In *Kōza-shakaigaku* IV.

MIYAKOMARU TOKUICHI, 1958. Basis of *dōzoku* corporate group: cohesion of *make* in Gunma prefecture. *NK*, **1**, pp. 17–23.

MIYATA NOBORU, 1961. Village and *kō* association. *NK*, 20, pp. 7–16.

MOGAMI KŌKEI, 1938. *Dōzoku* organization. *KZ: Shrionhen* IV.

MORIOKA KIYOMI, 1957. Hokkaido Shinotsuhei mura and village structure. *Shakaikagaku-ronshū*, **4**, pp. 1–197.

MURATAKE SEIICHI, 1959. Recent studies on Japanese village communities in the fields of ethnology and cultural anthropology. In *SN*, VI.

MURATAKE SEIICHI, *et al.*, 1959. Social organization of a fishing village: Niijima Island, Izu province. *MK*, vol. 22, no. 3–4, pp. 48–88.

NAGAI MICHIO, 1953. *Dōzoku*, a preliminary study of the Japanese 'extended family' group and its social and economic functions (based on the researches of K. Ariga). Ohio State University Research Foundation Interim Report no. 7.

NAGATA SHŪICHI, 1959. Some questions regarding the *dōzoku* organization in Japan. *SJ*, vol. 2, no. 1, pp. 1–15.

NAKAGAWA ZENNOSUKE, 1938. Large family and branch household. In *KZ: Shiron-hen* IV, *Ie*.

NAKAMURA CHIHYŌE, 1952. Branch households in a post-war agricultural village. In *Nōgyō-sōgō-kenkyū*, vol. 6, no. 3, pp. 147–87.

NAKAMURA MASAO, 1959. Data on *dōzoku* and *oyakata-kokata-kankei* in Tsushima villages. In *Ie*.

NAKANO TAKASHI, 1956. Starting point and theme of *dōzoku-dan* study. In *Nihon-shakaigaku no kadai*.

—— 1958. Main household and branch households. In *Kadokawashoten kyōdo-kenkyū-kōza*.

NINOMIYA TETSUO, 1958. The formation, development and disintegration of a *dōzoku* organization. *SH*, **32**, pp. 37–58.

OGAWA TŌRU, 1947. *Magi* and *oyagu* in Ojika-hanto Wakimoto village. *MK*, vol. 12, no. 2, pp. 57–65.

—— 1951. Form of a village community and *ie*: a case of a hill village in Yamanashi prefecture. *Jinmonkagaku*, vol. 3, pp. 110–20.

ŌHASHI KAORU, 1953. Restudy of *dōzoku* and its related concepts (On the theories of Ariga and Kitano). *Sociology*, **4**, pp. 1–21.

OIKAWA HIROSHI, 1938a. On the branch household in Tsukahara village in Nagano prefecture. *MK*, vol. 4, no. 3, pp. 49–72.

—— 1938b. A branch household and the division of cultivated land. *MK*, vol. 1, pp. 163–206.

—— 1940. The *dōzoku* system associated with marriages and funeral rites and ceremonies. *MN*, vol. 2, pp. 1–40.

OKA MASAO, M. GAMŌ, S. MURATAKE, & Y. GODA, 1959. Society and folk customs in Hachijo Island. In Tokyo board of Education, *Izushotō bunkazai sōgō-chōsahōkokusho*, no. 4.

OKADA YUZURU, 1952. Kinship organization in Japan. *Journal of Educational Sociology*, **26**, pp. 27–31.
—— 1959. Meaning of the *dōzoku* study in Japan. In *Ie*.
—— 1959. *Shakai jinruigaku no kihon mondai* (Basic problems of Japanese social anthropology).
SAITŌ YOSHIO & TANOZAKI AKIO, 1958. Social custom of agricultural household in Sōma district. *Bunka*, vol. 22, no. 4, pp. 109–28.
SATŌ AKATSUKI & SATO SETSU, 1961. *Dōzoku* corporation in Ide *buraku* in Oita prefecture. *NK*, **20**, pp. 16–27.
SEKI KEIGO, 1947. A type of *dōzoku* cohesion: the concept of *maki*. *MK*, vol. 11, no. 2, pp. 132–46.
—— 1963. *Minzoku-gaku* (Folklore).
SHIMAZAKI MINORU, 1959. Review of researches on village communities. In *SN*, VI.
SHIOMI TOSHIO, Y. WATANABE, Y. ISHIMURA, T. OSHIMA & H. NAKAO (Ed.). 1957. *Nihon no nōson* (Agricultural villages of Japan).
SOGA TAKESHI, 1965. Status hierarchy in a rural community and its dissolution. *SH*, **60**, pp. 49–66.
Sonraku-shakai-kenkyūkai (Association for the Study of Village Communities), 1954. *SN I: Sonraku kenkyū no seika to kadai* (Results and problems of village study).
—— 1955. *SN II: Nōchi-kaikaku to nōmin-undō* (Land reform and peasant movements).
—— 1956. *SN III: Sonraku-kyōdōtai no kōzō-bunseki* (Structural analysis of village communities).
—— 1957. *SN IV: Nōson kajō-jinkō no sonzai-keitai* (The state of surplus population in agricultural villages).
—— 1958. *SN V: Sengo-nōson no henbō* (Changes in postwar agricultural villages).
—— 1959. *SN VI: Sonraku-kyōdōtai-ron no tenkai* (Development of theories on the village community).
—— 1960. *SN VII: Seiji-taisei to sonraku* (The political system and villages).
—— 1961. *SN VIII: Nōsei no hōkō to sonraku-shakai* (The orientation of agricultural administration and village community).
—— 1963. *SN IX: Nōmin-sō bunkai to nōmin-soshiki* (Differentiation in the agricultural community and peasant organization).
SUMIYA KAZUHIKO, 1953. Village corporation and demands of irrigation water. *SH*, **12**, pp. 39–60.
—— 1963. *Kyōdōtai no shiteki kōzō-ron* (Historical structure of kyōdōtai). Chapters V & VI (pp. 303–81).
SUMIYA, et al., 1955. Village structure of Izu Ihama *buraku*. *Jinmon-gakuhō*, 12.
SUMIYA, et al., 1958. Community structure of Ōgōchi village. In Tokyo Board of Education, *Ōgōchi bunkazai hōkoku*.
SUZUKI EITARO, 1953. *Nihon nōson shakaigaku genri* (Principles of Japanese rural sociology).
SUZUKI EITARO & KITANO SEIICHI, 1952. *Nōson shakai chōsa* (Survey of agricultural village communities).

SUZUKI JIRO, 1956. *Toshi to sonraku no shakaigaku-teki kenkyū* (Sociological study of the city and the village).

TAKAHASHI TŌICHI, 1957. A study of village structure. *Hōshakaigaku*, no. 10, pp. 132–52.

TAKEUCHI TOSHIMI, 1941. *Ujiko* system and its changes. *MK*, vol. 7, no. 1, pp. 39–79.

—— 1942a. Funeral corporation in a village. In *Kazoku to sonraku* (Family and village community), II.

—— 1942b. A system of *kō* groups. *MK*, vol. 8, no. 3, pp. 34–84.

—— 1957. Agriculture and the village community. In *SN*, II.

—— 1959. Neighbourhood relations and *ie*. In *Ie*.

—— 1962. Dōzoku and its change. *SH*, **46**, pp. 8–22.

TAKEUCHI, EMA & FUJIKI, 1959. The village structure and the age-grading system in Tohoku district. *Tōhoku-daigaku kyōikugaku-bu kenkyū nempō*, VII.

TANOZAKI AKIO & SUZUKI HIROSHI, 1959. The social structure and land-owner system in a rice single-crop area. *Shakaigaku-kenkyū*, **16**, pp. 1–40.

TODA TEIZO & SUZUKI EITARO (Ed.). *Kazoku to sonraku* (Family and village), I (1939), II (1942).

TSUKAMOTO TETSUNDO, 1951. A study of *dōzoku* organization. *SH*, **5**, pp. 136–62.

TSUKAMOTO TETSUNDO & MATSUBARA JIRŌ, 1955. Control of the *dōzoku* by the main household, and the village structure. *SH*, **18** (pp. 47–72) and **19** (pp. 23–44).

UEDA KAZUO, 1955. The basic structure of an agricultural village in a backward area. *SH*, **17**, pp. 80–88.

USHIJIMA MORIMITSU, 1962a. *Katari* in Sue mura—Its social function and process of change. *MK*, vol. 26, no. 3, pp. 14–22.

—— 1962b. *Nushidori* and *kō* in Sue mura—Social role in the process of change. *SH*, **51**, pp. 64–86.

YAMAGUCHI ASATARŌ, 1947. On social elements of *oya*. *Nihon-minzokugaku no-tameni*, vol. 2, pp. 71–112.

YAMAGUCHI YAICHIRŌ, 1959. Life of *kyōdōtai* village—The organization of life of kyōdōtai in Shirio buraku in the northest edge of Honshu. *Nippon-minzokugaku*, vol. 4, no. 4, pp. 1–17.

YAMAMOTO EIJI, 1959. Structure of a fictive *oyako* group. *Toyama-daigaku-keizai-ronshū*. **3**.

YANAGITA KUNIO, 1938. *Oyakata, kokata*. In *KZ: Shiron-hen* III, *Oyako* (Parent-child).

YANAGITA KUNIO (Ed.), 1937. *Sanson-seikatsu no kenkyū* (Studies of hill village life).

—— 1949. *Kaison-seikatsu no kenkyū* (Studies of fishing village life).

YODA MORIMICHI, 1956. An irrigation association and a village association. *Jinmon-ronkyu*, vol. 7, no. 2.

YOSHIDA TEIGO, 1963. Cultural integration and change in Japanese villages. *American Anthropologist*, vol. 65, no. 1, pp. 102–16.

—— 1964. Social conflict and cohesion in a Japanese rural community. *Ethnology*, vol. 3, no. 3, pp. 219–31.

Chapter 4

ARIGA KIZAEMON, 1935–6. Young men's associations and marriages (1), (2). *Shakai-keizaishigaku*, vol. 4, pp. 1183–225, 1311–40.

—— 1937. *Yuinō* and labour system (1), (2) & (3). *Shakai-keizaishigaku*, vol. 6, pp. 253–89, 408–28, 543–65.

—— 1948. *Nihon-kon'in-shi-ron* (Historical discussion on Japanese marriages).

EMA MIEKO, 1958. Marriages of Shirakawa village and its vicinity. *NK*, 4, pp. 23–26.

EMORI ITSUO, 1957. A social structural study on the origin of 'temporary visiting marriages' in Japan. *Shakaikagaku-kenkyū*, vol. 8, no. 5–6, pp. 103–99.

GAMŌ MASAO, 1958. Types of marriages in Japan; indices for typological classification. *SJ*, 4, pp. 1–11.

GŌDA HIROFUMI, 1958. Field report on duo-patrilocal residence in a fishing village—Madomari buraku of Kagoshima prefecture, southern part of Kyūshū. *SJ*, 4, pp. 55–64.

HIROHAMA YOSHIO, 1938. *Yuinō*, In *KZ: Horitsu-hen* I, *Yuinō*.

KAWASHIMA TAKEYOSHI, 1953. *Kekkon* (Marriage).

KOBAYASHI KAZUO, 1956. Ritual consolidation of affinal relations involved in the marriage ceremony. *Nippon-minzokugaku*, vol. 3, no. 4, pp. 59–65.

KOYAMA TAKASHI, 1954. Significant meaning of marriage circles. In *Shakai-gaku no shomondai*.

MATSUMOTO YOSHIO, 1955. Marriages among near kin in the ancient period. *Shigaku*, vol. 28, no. 1, pp. 1–14.

Minzoku 2–3: Comparison of local marriage customs, 1927. (Twenty-eight reports from different localities.)

MURATAKE SEIICHI & ŌKO KIN'ICHI, 1964. Family, *shinrui* and marriage in Kosado-Okawa. In *Sado*, Kyūgakukai-rengō-sado-chōsa-iinkai.

NAKAGAWA ZENNOSUKE et al., 1955. *Kazoku-mondai to kazoku-hō* II: *Kekkon* (Marriage).

NAKAKUBO HISAO, 1956. Marriage customs of upland villages in Nara prefecture. *Nippon-minzokugaku*, vol. 3, no. 4, pp. 66–69.

NAKAYAMA TARŌ, 1956. *Nippon-Kon'in shih* (History of Japanese marriages).

Nōrin-shō (The Department of Agriculture and Forestry), 1954. *Nōson no konrei to sōgi* (Wedding and funeral ceremonies in agricultural villages).

OGYU CHIKASATO & TASHIRO A., 1956. Marriage and kinship systems in Sado Island. *Jinruigaku-shūhō*, 18, pp. 73–108.

ŌMACHI TOKUZŌ, 1937. History of marriage customs in Japan. In *KZ: Shiron-hen I, Kon'in* (marriages).

—— 1949. *Ashi-ire* marriage of Izu-toshima. *MK*, vol. 14, no. 3, pp. 76–81.

——1950. Women of Hachijō-jima Island—Marriage in the peripheral islands of Japan. *MK* vol. 15, no. 1, pp. 11–21.

—— 1960. Marriages and women of Izu-toshima. *Minkan-denshō*, vol. 24, no. 1, pp. 6–18.

SAKURADA KATSUNORI, 1932a. Young men's associations and the wedding ceremony. *MZ*, vol. 4, no. 9, pp. 19–28.

—— 1932b. An additional note of young men's associations and the wedding ceremony. *MZ*, vol. 4, no. 12, pp. 23–27.

SATO MITSUTAMI, 1956. Marriage institution in the borderland of Echigo and Dewa provinces. *Nippon-minzokugaku*, vol. 3, no. 4, pp. 44–55.

SEGAWA KIYOKO, 1936. Marriage area and age difference between husband and wife in small villages in Kanto district. In *Nempo-Shakaigaku*, vol. 4.

—— 1953. *Satogaeri* (a visit to parental house on leave) of wife. *Nippon-minzokugaku*, vol. 1, no. 1, pp. 6–38.

—— 1954. Young men's associations and marriage. *Jinruikagaku*, VI, pp. 52–56.

—— 1956. On cottages of newly married couples. *Tōyōbunka*, **21**, pp. 1–40.

TAKAMURE ITSUE, 1953. *Shōsei-kon no kenkyū* (The study of uxorilocal marriages in Japan).

TAKEUCHI TOSHIMI, 1953. The mobility of families in an agricultural village. *Tōhoku-daigaku-kyōikugaku-bu kenkyū nempō*, II.

—— 1960. A study on marriage areas. In *Shakaigaku no mondai to hōhō* (Subjects and methods of sociology), pp. 258–72.

TODA TEIZO, 1934. *Kazoku to kon'in* (Family and marriage).

WATANABE KŌICHI, 1956. Some trends in marriage of highlanders with emphasis on the taking of brides from adjacent lowland villages. *Nippon-minzokugaku*, vol. 3, no. 4, pp. 55–58.

WATANABE MASUTARŌ, 1942. Wedding and *maki*. MK, vol. 8, no. 4, pp. 58–69.

YAMAJI KŌSEN, 1928. Transplantation and marriage. MZ, vol. 3, no. 4, pp. 167–8.

YAMAMOTO NOBORU, 1950. Exclusiveness and egalitarianism of a hill village community, viewed through marriage relations. SH, **3**, pp. 123–51.

YANAGITA KUNIO & ŌMACHI TOKYOZO, 1937. *Kon'in-shūzoku-goi* (Vocabularies on marriage customs).

YOKOTA TADAO, 1954. On marriage relations in a hill village. *Jinruikagaku*, vol. 6, pp. 46–52.

III. SELECTED WORKS BY WESTERN SCHOLARS

The majority of the works are by American anthropologists since the war.

Abbreviations:

AA   *American Anthropologist*
OPCJS *Occasional Papers, Center for Japanese Studies, University of Michigan*
SWJA *Southwestern Journal of Anthropology*

BEARDSLEY, R. K., 1951. The household in the status system of Japanese villages. *OPCJS*, no. 1.

BEARDSLEY, R. K., J. W. HALL & R. E. WARD, 1959, *Village Japan*. Chicago, University of Chicago Press.

BEFU, HARUMI, 1962a. Corporate emphasis and patterns of descent in the Japanese family. In *Japanese culture: Its development and characteristics*, eds., Robert J. Smith and Richard K. Beardsley. Viking Fund Publications in Anthropology, no. 34.

—— 1962b. Hamlet in a nation, the place of three Japanese rural communities in their broader social context. Doctoral dissertation, University of Wisconsin.

—— 1963b. Classification of unilineal-bilateral societies. *SWJA*, **19**, pp. 335–55.

—— 1964. Befu's Rejoinder. *AA*, vol. 66, no. 5, pp. 1162–4. (Brief Communications.)

BEFU, HARUMI & EDWARD NORBECK, 1958. Japanese usages of terms of relationship. *Southwestern Journal of Anthropology*, 14, pp. 66–86.

BELLAH, ROBERT N., 1957. *Tokugawa Religion: the values of pre-industrial Japan*. Glencoe, Free Press.

BENNETT, J. W. & I. ISHINO, 1955. Futomi: A case study of the socio-economic adjustment of a marginal community in Japan. *Rural Sociology*, **20**, pp. 41–50.

CORNELL, J. B., 1956. Matsunagi: A Japanese mountain community. *OPCJS*, no. 5.

—— 1961. Outcaste relations in a Japanese village. *AA*, vol. 63, pp. 282–96.

—— 1964. Dōzoku: An example of evolution and transition in Japanese village society. *Comparative Studies in Society and History*, vol. VI, no. 4, pp. 449–80.

DE VOS, GEORGE & H. WAGATSUMA, 1961. Value attitudes toward role behavior of women in two Japanese villages. *AA*, vol. 63, pp. 1204–30.

DONOGHUE, J. D., 1957. An *eta* community of Japan: the social persistence of outcaste groups. *AA*, vol. 59.

DORE, RONALD P., 1958. *City life in Japan: life in a Tokyo ward*. London, Routledge and Kegan Paul.

—— 1959. *Land reform in Japan*. London, Oxford University Press.

EMBREE, JOHN F., 1939. *Suye Mura: A Japanese village*. Chicago, University of Chicago Press.

—— 1941. Some social functions of religion in rural Japan. *American Journal of Sociology*, **47**, pp. 184–9.

—— 1944. Japanese administration at the local level. *Applied Anthropology*, **3**. pp. 11–18.

EYRE, JOHN D., 1955. The changing role of the former Japanese landlord. *Land Economics*, **31**, pp. 34–46.

ISHINO, IWAO. 1953. Oyabun-kobun: A Japanese ritual kinship institution. *AA*, vol. 55, pp. 695–707.

—— 1962. Social and technological change in rural Japan: continuities and discontinuities. In *Japanese Culture*, pp. 100–12.

ISHINO, IWAO & JOHN W. BENNETT, 1953. Types of Japanese rural community. Columbus, Ohio State University Research Foundation, Interim Technical Report, no. 6.

JOHNSON, ERWIN, 1962. The emergence of a self-conscious entrepreneurial class in rural Japan. In *Japanese Culture*, pp. 91–99.

LOCKWOOD, W. W., 1955. *The economic development of Japan; Growth and structural change 1868–1938*. London.

MATSUMOTO Y. SCOTT, 1962. Notes on primogeniture in postwar Japan. In *Japanese Culture*, pp. 55–72.

NORBECK, EDWARD, 1951. Westernization as evident on the *buraku* level. *MK*, vol. 16, no. 1, pp. 38–45 (in Japanese).

—— 1953. Age-grading in Japan. *AA*, **55**, pp. 373–84.

—— 1954. *Takashima: A Japanese fishing community*. Salt Lake City, University of Utah Press.

—— 1960. Economic change and Japanese social organization. In *Essays in the Science of Culture*, eds. G. Dole and R. Carnerio. New York, Thos. Y. Crowell.

—— 1961. Postwar cultural change and continuity in Northeastern Japan. *AA*, vol. 63, pp. 297–321.

—— 1962. Common-interest associations in rural Japan. In *Japanese Culture*, pp. 73–85.

NORBECK, EDWARD & H. BEFU, 1958a. Informal fictive kinship in Japan. *AA*, vol. 60, pp. 102–17.

—— 1958b. Japanese usages of terms of relationship. *SWJA*, **14**.

PELZEL, J. & F. KLUCKHOHN, 1957. A theory of variation in values applied to aspects of Japanese social structure. *Bulletin of the Research Institute of Comparative Education and Culture, Kyūshū University*.

PLATH, DAVID W., 1964. Where the family of god is the family: the role of the dead in Japanese households. *AA*, vol. 66, pp. 300–17.

REDFIELD, R., M. H. FRIED & R. K. BEARDSLEY, 1954. Community studies in Japan and China: A symposium. *The Far Eastern Quarterly*, **14**, pp. 3–10, 37–53.

SMITH, ROBERT J., 1952. Co-operative forms in a Japanese agricultural community. *OPCJS*, no. 3.

—— 1961. The Japanese rural community: norms, sanction, and ostracism. *AA*, vol. 63, pp. 522–33.

—— 1962a. Stability in Japanese kinship terminology: the historical evidence. In *Japanese Culture*, pp. 25–33.

—— 1962b. Japanese kinship terminology: the history of a nomenclature. *Ethnology*, vol. 1, no. 3, pp. 349–59.

SMITH, ROBERT J. & JOHN B. CORNELL, 1956. Two Japanese villages. *OPCJS*, no. 5.

SMITH, ROBERT J. & E. P. REYES, 1957. Community interrelations with the outside world: the case of a Japanese agricultural community. *AA*, 59, pp. 463–72.

SMITH, THOMAS C. (Ed.), 1960. *City and village in Japan: Economic development and cultural change*, vol. IX, no. 1, Part II.

STEINER, KURT, 1956. The Japanese village and its government. *Far Eastern Quarterly*, **15**, pp. 185–99.

SUTTON, J. L., 1953. Rural politics in Japan. *OPCJS*, no. 4.

TITIEV, M., 1953. Changing patterns of *kumiai* structure in rural Okayama. *OPCJS*, no. 4.

WARD, ROBERT E., 1951a. Patterns of stability and change in rural Japanese politics. *OPCJS*, no. 1.

—— 1951b. The socio-political role of the *buraku* (hamlet) in Japan. *American Political Science Review*, **45**, pp. 1025–40.

INDEX

Adoption, adopted-son, adopted-son-in-law, 4–5, 9, 23, 24, 63, 67, 83, 86, 88, 91, 92, 94, 99, 110, 112, 123, 152, 168–9, 170
Agriculture Association, 129
Aichi Prefecture, 9
Aiji, 129–32
Ainoshima buraku (Nagano Pref.), 125
Akita Prefecture, 8
Amami and Okinawa Islands, 170n.-1n.
Ancestor, 17, 90, 96n., 105–7; cult, 6, 105, 106; festival, 125; ancestral household, 37; ancestral altar, shrine, 3, 11
Ariga Kizaemon, 27, 96–112, 115–19, 126, 128
Asao buraku (Yamanashi Pref.), 124, 129–32, 133, 135

Befu, Harumi, 85, 169
Bon (annual ancestor festival), 125
Branch household, 14, 15, 81, 83–4, 86, 89, 90, 91, 92, 93, 94–123, 139, 140, 151; *see also Dōzoku*
Buddhistic activities, 147
Bunke, bekke, see Branch household
Bushi, 44, 45, 46, 49n., 50, 51, 96, 106n

Civil Code, 6, 8, 9, 10, 11, 17, 19, 21, 22, 26, 30, 39, 40, 84
Communal, forest, 136, 138, 141; land, 140; property, 136; seed-bed, 141; store, 141
Comparison with (contrast to), Chinese (system), v, vii–viii, 5, 20–1, 30n., 39, 40, 85, 107, 170; Hindu (system), v, 5, 85, 159, 170, 172; South Indian kinship, 30–1
Cousins, 26n.–27n., 31, 32, 33, 34, 35, 37, 70, 86, 92, 135, 159, 165
Credit association, 146–8

Daimyō (feudal lords), 44, 45, 50
Descent, 21, 28, 30, 31, 83, 84, 85, 105, 106, 107, 139, 159, 160, 167, 169–70, 172; group, vii, 2, 86–7, 89, 95, 106, 159, 167, 170, 171; principle, 25, 34, 86, 94, 167
Divorce, 22, 23
Dowry, 153n
Dōzoku, vii–viii, 33, 82–123, 125, 126, 127, 128, 129, 130, 131, 133, 138, 141, 145, 148, 150, 165, 167, 169, 170, 171, 172; composition and structure, 82–94; definition, 90–1; development and decline, 113–23; shrine, 93, 105, 107, 117, 118, 119
Dumont, Louis, 30

Economic differentiation, 49, 53, 64, 71–2, 91, 93, 102, 112, 120, 128, 141, 160, 166
Eggan, Fred, 167, 171
Embree, J. F., v
Endogamy, at the village level, 35, 160, 161, 164–6
Engumi, 152, 158
Enka, 28

Father's status, 16–21
Festivity, 36, 106, 136–7, 138, 139
Firth, R., 86, 107–8, 167, 168
Freedman, M., 85
Freedman, J. D., 27, 168–9
Fukushima Masao, 123, 125
Fukutake Tadashi, 92, 93, 124, 125, 129–32
Funeral, 27, 31, 32, 33n., 36, 93, 101, 121, 125, 126, 134–5, 136, 141, 150, 158; association (*sōshiki-gumi, shini-gumi*), 134, 136, 143, 148
Furushima Toshio, 66, 124, 125, 127

Genealogical relation (genealogy in terms of household), 7, 83, 88–91, 94, 98–9, 106, 121, 128, 171

Gift, exchange, 29, 36–7; ceremonial, 138; wedding, 36, 135

Go-between, 127, 156, 158

Goningumi, 69n.–71n.

Gorohei-shinden village (Nagano Pref.), vi, 61–71, 73–9, 120–2, 162–3

Grave, 29, 107, 134, 135; graveyard, 99–100, 1–7

Hachite mura (Nagano Pref.), 66

Haru village (Oita Pref.), 143, 144

Hashikura village (Nagano Pref.), 161

Hera-watashi, 24

Hii village (Aichi Pref.), 156

Hisami of Oki Island, 141

Hokkaido and Okinawa, 56, 57

Honbyakushō and *kakaebyakushō*, 62–71, 80, 121n.–2n.

Horikiri (Aichi Pref.), 165

Horticulture, 121, 122n., 142

House-name, 2

House-site land (residential site), 14, 16, 41, 83, 94, 100–4, 114, 118, 120, 121, 122, 126, 129–31

Hyakushō-ikki (peasant revolts), 51

Iban, 168–9

Ibaragi Prefecture, 8

Ie, concept, 1–2; principles of succession, 2–7

Ietsuki-musume, 24

Industrialization, viii, 51–7, 82, 115, 123, 141, 172; modernization, 30n., 112, 129, 156n.

Inheritance, 1, 4, 6–7, 49n., 63, 64, 71

Inkyo, 11, 16, 17, 103

Inkyo-bunke, 11, 14–15

Inkyo-sei (system), 11–16, 23

Inseki, 30

Ishigami buraku, 96–108

Isoda Susumu, 124

Itoko, 26n.–7n., 34; *see also* Cousins

Ittō, 93, 121, 142

Iwate Prefecture, 8

Izu-Oshima, Izu-Toshima, 12

Jibikiami, 122n.

Johnson, E. H., 85n.

Kabu, 63, 64, 71

Kagoshima Prefecture, 142

Kameyama (Aichi Pref.), 165

Kasuga (Nagano Pref.), 163

Kindred, 27, 169

Kinship terminology, 30, 33–5

Kitano Seiichi, 128

Kochi Prefecture, 9

Koh village (Mie Pref.), 11–12, 14, 32–3, 34–5, 136

Kojiki, 22n.

Kokuni district (Yamagata Pref.), 138

Konugi mura (Shiga Pref.), 139

Koshiki-jima (Kagoshima Pref.), 12

Koshiozu village (Aichi Pref.), vi, 12, 35, 93n., 114, 121–2, 122n., 127, 142–3, 144, 146–7, 156–8, 163, 165

Koshuken, 17, 19, 84n.

Koyasu-kō, 148

Kō, Kōgumi, 144, 146–8

Kōden, see mortuary offerings

Kōshin-kō, 148

Kumamoto Prefecture, 28n., 37, 142

Kumi, characteristics of, 140; corporate activity, 141–4; function 136–7; rules, 139–40; shrine, 138, 139

Kuruwa, 121

Kyushu, 19

Labour, co-operation, 77, 113; exchange, 88, 113n., 136, 144–6, 153; pool, 113, 137, 140; replacement, 108; service, 101, 102, 113, 140; unpaid (free) labourers, 109, 112, 113

Lakher, 22

Land, apportion, 10, 13, 83, 86, 88, 91, 95, 100, 109, 110, 113, 126; fragmentation, subdivision, 48, 65, 66, 67, 74, 109; lease, 64, 95, 96, 100–3, 109, 113, 126

Land holding situation (1872–1955), 51–8

Landowner (landlord) and tenant, 49–50, 53–8, 59–61, 62, 64, 67, 74, 75–6, 94–104, 109, 111, 112, 114, 117, 118, 121, 123, 124, 126, 131, 150
Leach, E., 22, 167, 168
Lineage, vii–viii, 7, 84, 85, 86, 89, 91, 107, 169, 170

Mabiki, 51
Main line (direct line) and branch lines (side lines), 92–3
Maki, 129–32
Maori *hapu*, 167, 168
Marriage, 5, 9, 11, 13n., 23, 24, 27, 28, 29, 31, 32, 37, 38, 86, 88, 93, 95, 97, 101, 110, 121, 127, 131, 138; Chapter 4 (150–66), 169; contract, 154, 158, 159; rule, 158, 159; Japanese terms for marriage: *yomeiri* (virilocal), *mukoiri* (uxorilocal), *kekkon*, 154; see also *Oyako-nari*
Measurement, quantity of rice: *shō*, 32n., *koku*, 42n.; acreage: *tan*, *chō*, 42n.; field areas: *hitsu*, *maki*, 73–4
Meiji period (1868–1912), 4n., 8n., 22n., 43, 51, 52, 94, 97, 111, 112, 118, 119, 137, 141
Mie buraku (Kyoto Pref.), 128
Minji-kanrei ruishu and *Zenkoku-minji-kanrei ruishū*, 8, 8n.
Mistress of the household, 13, 24–6, 36
Mitsuka of Kasuga mura (Gifu Pref.), 139
Miyagi Prefecture, 8, 37, 83
Miyazaki Prefecture, 9
Mogami Kōkei, 139n.
Mortuary offerings, 32–3, 36, 134, 150
Mother-in-law, 13n., 23
Mura (village), 41–3
Murahachibu, 140

Nagahama *dōzoku*, 127–8
Nagano Prefecture, 9
Nagasaki Prefecture, 9

Nakagawa Zennosuke, 8n.
Nakane, C., 85, 171n.
Nakano Takashi, 40, 169
Nakasai (Iwate Pref.), 97
Namiki Masayoshi, 52n., 53n.
Nayosechō, 62n.
New comers (household), 80, 108, 116, 126, 137–9, 140–1; see also *Nurewaraji*
Ninbetsu-aratame and *shūmon-aratame* (Tokugawa censuses), 48n.–9n.
Nishikatsuragi mura (Osaka Pref.), 139
Nojiri Shigeo, 53
Nosa *dōzoku*, 110–11
Nuptial cup (*Sansankudo-no-sakazuki*), 157–8
Nurewaraji, 116, 126; *warajiniūgi*, 138; *warajioya*, 126

Obligations, 32, 36, 90, 100, 101, 114, 126, 134, 137, 142, 144
Oishi Shinzabro, 42n., 48, 61–70, 75–7, 80, 123
Okinawa, 170n.–1n., 56, 57
Omachi Tokuzo, 8n.
Ouchi Tsutomu, 52, 56, 57
Oyabun-kobun, 123–32
Oyakatadori, 128
Oyako, 26n.–27n., 35, 123
Oyako-kankei (patron and client relationship), 68, 71, 82, 95, 123–32, 133, 138, 141, 171, 172
Oyako-nari, 28, 153
Oyanagi Buraku (Miyagi Pref.), 145

Patron and client relationship, see *Oyako-kankei*
Population flow, village to urban area, 51, 52–3
Prestige, 6, 25, 80, 91, 92, 93, 106n., 139
Primogeniture (eldest son succession), 8–11, 169
Pul Eliya, 167–8

Ramage, 7, 86

Ranking, 59, 72, 80, 81, 124, 138, 139, 159, 164
Registration, 41, 45, 62, 66, 67
Religions, association, 147; foundation, 108; institutions, 105n.; unity, 105
Revenue Association, 147
Ritual conduct, 93

Sagada Igrots, 167, 168, 171
Saito dōzoku, 96–111, 114, 151
Sake, drinking, 127, 136, 143, 145, 148, 154, 155, 156, 157; presentation, 138
Sakurai Tokutarō, 146n.
Saraike village (Osaka Pref.), 71–2
Sasaki Kiyoshi, 24n.
Sawada buraku (Okayama Pref.), 115–17
Sekiyama Naotarō, 49n.
Seko, 121, 142
Shimodaiichi mura (Hyogo Pref.), 71, 73
Shinokusa buraku (Yamanashi Pref.), 139
Shinomura (Yamanashi Pref.), 137
Shinrui, 26–40, 84, 88, 135, 139, 142, 145, 149, 150, 151, 152, 154, 155, 156, 157, 158, 159, 164–5, 169, 170, 172
Shinseki, 27n.; see also Shinrui
Shinzoku (Goshintō), 38–40, 84
Shirahama (Shizuoka Pref.), 138–9
Shizuoka Prefecture, 9
Shrine, 3, 105, 107, 115, 117, 138, 139, 146
Smith, T. C., 85n.
Sōshiki-gumi, see Funeral association
Status differentiation, among brothers, 6–7, 64; households of a dōzoku, 91–3, 99, 165; households of a village, 47, 49, 61–9, 72, 80–1, 117, 159, 122n.
Status group, 71, 159, 167
Status of Japanese woman, 25–6
Sueyoshi mura (Hachijo Islands), 138
Suijin-roku, 42

Surname, 4, 30, 42, 83, 84, 93, 123, 129, 130, 138

Takao Kazuhiko, 58–61, 71–3
Tanokami-kō, 148
Taxation, Tokugawa period (1603–1868), 50; change to the modern system (1872), 54
Tema (labour), 153, 157
Temple affiliation, 67–9, 105n.
Tenant, see Landowner
Titled farmers, 49, 54; see also honbyakushō
Tokugawa Bakufu, 44, 45
Tokugawa peasantry, 41–51, 58–81
Tokugawa population, 46, 47–9
Tokugawa state administration, 43–7
Tokuyama mura (Gifu Pref.), 141
Tonari, 135–6, 142, 144, 148
Tonari-gumi, 144, 148
Transplantation, 76–7, 113n., 144, 145
Tsushima Island, 137

Ultimogeniture (youngest son succession), 9, 10
Urushi mura (Kagoshima Pref.), 139–40, 142
Ushio buraku (Shimane Pref.), 124

Variation, residential pattern, 11–16
Village council, 79, 129
Village officials, 45, 62, 66, 137, 138, 139

Wakae village (Osaka Pref.), 58–61, 64
Water network (irrigation system), 73–80
Wedding, 13n., 27, 36, 93, 125, 126, 127, 141, 146, 151; feast, 135; gift, 135; ceremony, 127, 153, 154, 155–8

Yamagata Prefecture, 8
Yamanashi Prefecture, 125
Yamazaki Harushige, 55

Yanagita Kunio, 13n., 27n., 127n., 145, 153, 155, 161
Yashiki, 41; *see also* House-site land
Yawata village (Nagano Pref.), 146, 163
Yokoza, 18, 19

Yoriya, 138
Yōshi-engumi, see Engumi
Yui, 144-6
Yuinōkin, 153

Zaibatsu, 123

LONDON SCHOOL OF ECONOMICS
MONOGRAPHS ON SOCIAL ANTHROPOLOGY

Titles marked with an asterisk are now out of print. Those marked with a dagger have been reprinted in paperback editions and are only available in this form.

1, 2. RAYMOND FIRTH
   The Work of the Gods in Tikopia, 2 vols., 1940. Second edition, 1 vol., 1967.

3. E. R. LEACH
   Social and Economic Organization of the Rowanduz Kurds, 1940. Available from University Microfilms Ltd.

*4. E. E. EVANS-PRITCHARD
   The Political System of the Anuak of the Anglo-Egyptian Sudan, 1940. (Revised edition in preparation.)

5. DARYLL FORDE
   Marriage and the Family among the Yakö in South-Eastern Nigeria, 1941. Available from University Microfilms Ltd.

*6. M. M. GREEN
   Land Tenure of an Ibo Village in South-Eastern Nigeria, 1941.

7. ROSEMARY FIRTH
   Housekeeping among Malay Peasants, 1943. Second edition, 1966.

*8. A. M. AMMAR
   A Demographic Study of an Egyptian Province (Sharquiya), 1943.

*9. I. SCHAPERA
   Tribal Legislation among the Tswana of the Bechuanaland Protectorate, 1943. (Revised edition in preparation.)

*10. W. H. BECKETT
   Akokoaso: A Survey of a Gold Coast Village, 1944.

11. I. SCHAPERA
   The Ethnic Composition of Tswana Tribes, 1952.

*12. JU-K'ANG T'IEN
   The Chinese of Sarawak: A Study of Social Structure, 1953. (Revised edition in preparation.)

*13. GUTORM GJESSING
   Changing Lapps, 1954.

14. ALAN J. A. ELLIOTT
   Chinese Spirit-Medium Cults in Singapore, 1955.

*15. RAYMOND FIRTH
   Two Studies of Kinship in London, 1956.

16. LUCY MAIR
   Studies in Applied Anthropology, 1957.

†17. J. M. GULLICK
   Indigenous Political Systems of Western Malaya, 1958.

†18. MAURICE FREEDMAN
Lineage Organization in Southeastern China, 1958.

†19. FREDRIK BARTH
Political Leadership among Swat Pathans, 1959.

★20. L. H. PALMIER
Social Status and Power in Java, 1960.

†21. JUDITH DJAMOUR
Malay Kinship and Marriage in Singapore, 1959.

†22. E. R. LEACH
Rethinking Anthropology, 1961.

23. S. M. SALIM
Marsh Dwellers of the Euphrates Delta, 1962.

†24. S. VAN DER SPRENKEL
Legal Institutions in Manchu China, 1962.

25. CHANDRA JAYAWARDENA
Conflict and Solidarity in a Guianese Plantation. 1963.

26. H. IAN HOGBIN
Kinship and Marriage in a New Guinea Village, 1963.

27. JOAN METGE
A New Maori Migration: Rural and Urban Relations in Northern New Zealand, 1964.

28. RAYMOND FIRTH
Essays on Social Organization and Values, 1964.

29. M. G. SWIFT
Malay Peasant Society in Jelebu, 1965.

30. JEREMY BOISSEVAIN
Saints and Fireworks: Religion and Politics in Rural Malta, 1965.

31. JUDITH DJAMOUR
The Muslim Matrimonial Court in Singapore, 1966.

32. CHIE NAKANE
Kinship and Economic Organization in Rural Japan, 1967.

33. MAURICE FREEDMAN
Chinese Lineage and Society: Fukien and Kwangtung, 1966.

34. W. H. R. RIVERS
Kinship and Social Organization, Second edition with commentaries by R. Firth and D. M. Schneider. In press.

35. ROBIN FOX
The Keresan Bridge: A Problem in Pueblo Ethnology. In press.